BUSINESS ISSUES, COMPETITION AND ENTREPRENEURSHIP

THE FOREIGN CORRUPT PRACTICES ACT

A RESOURCE GUIDE FOR BUSINESSES AND INDIVIDUALS

BUSINESS ISSUES, COMPETITION AND ENTREPRENEURSHIP

Additional books in this series can be found on Nova's website under the Series tab.

Additional E-books in this series can be found on Nova's website under the E-book tab.

LAW, CRIME AND LAW ENFORCEMENT

Additional books in this series can be found on Nova's website under the Series tab.

Additional E-books in this series can be found on Nova's website under the E-book tab.

BUSINESS ISSUES, COMPETITION AND ENTREPRENEURSHIP

THE FOREIGN CORRUPT PRACTICES ACT

A RESOURCE GUIDE FOR BUSINESSES AND INDIVIDUALS

RANDELL HOUPT
EDITOR

nova publishers
New York

For permission to use material from this book please contact us:
Telephone 631-231-7269; Fax 631-231-8175
Web Site: http://www.novapublishers.com

Additional color graphics may be available in the e-book version of this book.

Library of Congress Cataloging-in-Publication Data

ISBN: 978-1-62417-845-0

Published by Nova Science Publishers, Inc. † New York

CONTENTS

PREFACE

The Foreign Corrupt Practices Act (FCPA) is a critically important statute for combating corruption around the globe. Corruption has corrosive effects on democratic institutions, undermining public accountability and diverting public resources from important priorities such as health, education, and infrastructure. When business is won or lost based on how much a company is willing to pay in bribes rather than on the quality of its products and services, law-abiding companies are placed at a competitive disadvantage, and consumers lose. This book addresses a wide variety of topics, including who and what is covered by the FCPA's anti-bribery and accounting provisions; the definition of a "foreign official", what constitutes proper and improper gifts; travel and entertainment expenses; the nature of facilitating payments; how successor liability applies in the mergers and acquisitions context; the hallmarks of an effective corporate compliance program; and the different types of civil and criminal resolutions available in the FCPA context.

Chapter 1 - This guide is intended to provide information for businesses and individuals regarding the U.S. Foreign Corrupt Practices Act (FCPA). The guide has been prepared by the staff of the Criminal Division of the U.S. Department of Justice and the Enforcement Division of the U.S. Securities and Exchange Commission. It is non-binding, informal, and summary in nature, and the information contained herein does not constitute rules or regulations. As such, it is not intended to, does not, and may not be relied upon to create any rights, substantive or procedural, that are enforceable at law by any party, in any criminal, civil, or administrative matter. It is not intended to substitute for the advice of legal counsel on specific issues related to the FCPA. It does not in any way limit the enforcement intentions or litigating positions of the

U.S. Department of Justice, the U.S. Securities and Exchange Commission, or any other U.S. government agency.

Companies or individuals seeking an opinion concerning specific prospective conduct are encouraged to use the U.S. Department of Justice's opinion procedure discussed in Chapter 9 of this guide.

Chapter 2 - The Foreign Corrupt Practices Act of 1977 (FCPA) was enacted principally to prevent corporate bribery of foreign officials. This act had three major parts: (1) it required the keeping by corporations of accurate books, records, and accounts; (2) it required issuers registered with the Securities and Exchange Commission to maintain a responsible internal accounting control system; and (3) it prohibited bribery by American corporations of foreign officials.

For a number of years after passage of the act, Congress debated amending it in response to numerous criticisms. On August 23, 1988, the President signed into law the Omnibus Trade and Competitiveness Act of 1988, of which Title V is known as the Foreign Corrupt Practices Act Amendments of 1988.

The amendments maintained the three major parts of the 1977 Act, but significant changes were made. One of these changes enacted a "knowing" standard in order to find violations of the act. This standard was intended to encompass "conscious disregard" and "willful blindness." The amendments provided certain defenses against finding violations of the act, such as that the gift is lawful under the laws of the foreign country and that the gift is a bona fide and reasonable expenditure or for the performance or execution of a contract with the foreign government.

In 1998 the act was further amended in order to implement the Organization of Economic Cooperation and Development Convention on Combating Bribery of Foreign Public Officials in International Business Transactions. These amendments expanded the scope of coverage to include some foreign persons and extended jurisdiction beyond the borders of the United States. Criticisms of the act have continued. Especially prominent recently have been suggestions that businesses convicted of violating the Foreign Corrupt Practices Act should be debarred from receiving federal government contracts. Bills were introduced in the 111th Congress to address this issue. In addition to congressional scrutiny of the act, the executive branch appears to have increased oversight of suspected American businesses for alleged violations. There have been a number of settlements and indictments concerning violations of the act. In early 2012 the federal government had both successes and losses resulting from its FCPA charges.

In: The Foreign Corrupt Practices Act
Editor: Randell Houpt

ISBN: 978-1-62417-845-0

Chapter 1

A RESOURCE GUIDE TO THE U.S. FOREIGN CORRUPT PRACTICES ACT*

U.S. Department of Justice and the Enforcement Division of the U.S. Securities and Exchange Commission

This guide is intended to provide information for businesses and individuals regarding the U.S. Foreign Corrupt Practices Act (FCPA). The guide has been prepared by the staff of the Criminal Division of the U.S. Department of Justice and the Enforcement Division of the U.S. Securities and Exchange Commission. It is non-binding, informal, and summary in nature, and the information contained herein does not constitute rules or regulations. As such, it is not intended to, does not, and may not be relied upon to create any rights, substantive or procedural, that are enforceable at law by any party, in any criminal, civil, or administrative matter. It is not intended to substitute for the advice of legal counsel on specific issues related to the FCPA. It does not in any way limit the enforcement intentions or litigating positions of the U.S. Department of Justice, the U.S. Securities and Exchange Commission, or any other U.S. government agency.

---

* This is an edited, reformatted and augmented version of Criminal Division of the U.S. Department of Justice and the Enforcement Division of the U.S. Securities and Exchange Commission Publication, dated November 14, 2012.

Companies or individuals seeking an opinion concerning specific prospective conduct are encouraged to use the U.S. Department of Justice's opinion procedure discussed in Chapter 9 of this guide.

FOREWORD

We are pleased to announce the publication of *A Resource Guide to the U.S. Foreign Corrupt Practices Act.* The Foreign Corrupt Practices Act (FCPA) is a critically important statute for combating corruption around the globe. Corruption has corrosive effects on democratic institutions, undermining public accountability and diverting public resources from important priorities such as health, education, and infrastructure. When business is won or lost based on how much a company is willing to pay in bribes rather than on the quality of its products and services, law-abiding companies are placed at a competitive disadvantage—and consumers lose. For these and other reasons, enforcing the FCPA is a continuing priority at the Department of Justice (DOJ) and the Securities and Exchange Commission (SEC).

The *Guide* is the product of extensive efforts by experts at DOJ and SEC, and has benefited from valuable input from the Departments of Commerce and State. It endeavors to provide helpful information to enterprises of all shapes and sizes— from small businesses doing their first transactions abroad to multi-national corporations with subsidiaries around the world. The *Guide* addresses a wide variety of topics, including who and what is covered by the FCPA's anti-bribery and accounting provisions; the definition of a "foreign official"; what constitute proper and improper gifts, travel and entertainment expenses; the nature of facilitating payments; how successor liability applies in the mergers and acquisitions context; the hallmarks of an effective corporate compliance program; and the different types of civil and criminal resolutions available in the FCPA context. On these and other topics, the *Guide* takes a multi-faceted approach, setting forth in detail the statutory requirements while also providing insight into DOJ and SEC enforcement practices through hypotheticals, examples of enforcement actions and anonymized declinations, and summaries of applicable case law and DOJ opinion releases.

The *Guide* is an unprecedented undertaking by DOJ and SEC to provide the public with detailed information about our FCPA enforcement approach and priorities. We are proud of the many lawyers and staff who worked on this project, and hope that it will be a useful reference for companies, individuals, and others interested in our enforcement of the Act.

Lanny A. Breuer
Assistant Attorney General
Criminal Division
Department of Justice

Robert S. Khuzami
Director of Enforcement
Securities and Exchange Commission

Corporate bribery is bad business. In our free market system it is basic that the sale of products should take place on the basis of price, quality, and service. Corporate bribery is fundamentally destructive of this basic tenet. Corporate bribery of foreign officials takes place primarily to assist corporations in gaining business. Thus foreign corporate bribery affects the very stability of overseas business. Foreign corporate bribes also affect our domestic competitive climate when domestic firms engage in such practices as a substitute for healthy competition for foreign business.[1]

—United States Senate, 1977

INTRODUCTION

Congress enacted the U.S. Foreign Corrupt Practices Act (FCPA or the Act) in 1977 in response to revelations of widespread bribery of foreign officials by U.S. companies. The Act was intended to halt those corrupt practices, create a level playing field for honest businesses, and restore public confidence in the integrity of the marketplace.[2]

The FCPA contains both anti-bribery and accounting provisions. The anti-bribery provisions prohibit U.S. persons and businesses (domestic concerns), U.S. and foreign public companies listed on stock exchanges in the United States or which are required to file periodic reports with the Securities and Exchange Commission (issuers), and certain foreign persons and businesses acting while in the territory of the United States (territorial jurisdiction) from making corrupt payments to foreign officials to obtain or retain business. The accounting provisions require issuers to make and keep accurate books and records and to devise and maintain an adequate system of internal accounting controls. The accounting provisions also prohibit individuals and businesses from knowingly falsifying books and records or knowingly circumventing or failing to implement a system of internal controls.

The Department of Justice (DOJ) and the Securities and Exchange Commission (SEC) share FCPA enforcement authority and are committed to fighting foreign bribery through robust enforcement. An important component of this effort is education, and this resource guide, prepared by DOJ and SEC staff, aims to provide businesses and individuals with information to help them abide by the law, detect and prevent FCPA violations, and implement effective compliance programs.

The Costs of Corruption

Corruption is a global problem. In the three decades since Congress enacted the FCPA, the extent of corporate bribery has become clearer and its ramifications in a trans-national economy starker. Corruption impedes economic growth by diverting public resources from important priorities such as health, education, and infrastructure. It undermines democratic values and public accountability and weakens the rule of law.[3] And it threatens stability and security by facilitating criminal activity within and across borders, such as the illegal trafficking of people, weapons, and drugs.[4] International corruption also undercuts good governance and impedes U.S. efforts to promote freedom and democracy, end poverty, and combat crime and terrorism across the globe.[5]

Corruption is also bad for business. Corruption is anti-competitive, leading to distorted prices and disadvantaging honest businesses that do not pay bribes. It increases the cost of doing business globally and inflates the cost of government contracts in developing countries.[6] Corruption also introduces significant uncertainty into business transactions: Contracts secured through bribery may be legally unenforceable, and paying bribes on one contract often results in corrupt officials making ever-increasing demands.[7] Bribery has destructive effects within a business as well, undermining employee confidence in a company's management and fostering a permissive atmosphere for other kinds of corporate misconduct, such as employee self-dealing, embezzlement,[8] financial fraud,[9] and anti-competitive behavior.[10] Bribery thus raises the risks of doing business, putting a company's bottom line and reputation in jeopardy. Companies that pay bribes to win business ultimately undermine their own long-term interests and the best interests of their investors.

Historical Background

Congress enacted the FCPA in 1977 after revelations of widespread global corruption in the wake of the Watergate political scandal. SEC discovered that more than 400 U.S. companies had paid hundreds of millions of dollars in bribes to foreign government officials to secure business overseas.[11] SEC reported that companies were using secret "slush funds" to make illegal campaign contributions in the United States and corrupt payments to foreign officials abroad and were falsifying their corporate financial records to conceal the payments.[12]

Congress viewed passage of the FCPA as critical to stopping corporate bribery, which had tarnished the image of U.S. businesses, impaired public confidence in the financial integrity of U.S. companies, and hampered the efficient functioning of the markets.[13] As Congress recognized when it passed the FCPA, corruption imposes enormous costs both at home and abroad, leading to market inefficiencies and instability, sub-standard products, and an unfair playing field for honest businesses.[14] By enacting a strong foreign bribery statute, Congress sought to minimize these destructive effects and help companies resist corrupt demands, while addressing the destructive foreign policy ramifications of transnational bribery.[15] The Act also prohibited off-the-books accounting through provisions designed to "strengthen the accuracy of the corporate books and records and the reliability of the audit process which constitute the foundations of our system of corporate disclosure."[16]

> No problem does more to alienate citizens from their political leaders and institutions, and to undermine political stability and economic development, than endemic corruption among the government, political party leaders, judges, and bureaucrats.
>
> — USAID Anti-Corruption Strategy

In 1988, Congress amended the FCPA to add two affirmative defenses: (1) the local law defense; and (2) the reasonable and bona fide promotional expense defense.[17] Congress also requested that the President negotiate an international treaty with members of the Organisation for Economic Co-operation and Development (OECD) to prohibit bribery in international business transactions by many of the United States' major trading partners.[18] Subsequent negotiations at the OECD culminated in the Convention on Combating Bribery of Foreign Officials in International Business Transactions

(Anti-Bribery Convention), which, among other things, required parties to make it a crime to bribe foreign officials.[19]

DOJ Contact Information
Deputy Chief (FCPA Unit)
Fraud Section, Criminal Division
Bond Building
1400 New York Ave, N.W.
Washington, DC 20005
Telephone: (202) 514-7023
Facsimile: (202) 514-7021
Email: FCPA .Fraud@usdoj.gov

In 1998, the FCPA was amended to conform to the requirements of the Anti-Bribery Convention. These amendments expanded the FCPA's scope to: (1) include payments made to secure "any improper advantage"; (2) reach certain foreign persons who commit an act in furtherance of a foreign bribe while in the United States; (3) cover public international organizations in the definition of "foreign official"; (4) add an alternative basis for jurisdiction based on nationality; and (5) apply criminal penalties to foreign nationals employed by or acting as agents of U.S. companies.[20] The Anti-Bribery Convention came into force on February 15, 1999, with the United States as a founding party.

National Landscape: Interagency Efforts

DOJ and SEC share enforcement authority for the FCPA's anti-bribery and accounting provisions.[21] They also work with many other federal agencies and law enforcement partners to investigate and prosecute FCPA violations, reduce bribery demands through good governance programs and other measures, and promote a fair playing field for U.S. companies doing business abroad.

Department of Justice

DOJ has criminal FCPA enforcement authority over "issuers" (i.e., public companies) and their officers, directors, employees, agents, or stockholders acting on the issuer's behalf. DOJ also has both criminal and civil enforcement responsibility for the FCPA's anti-bribery provisions over "domestic concerns"—which include (a) U.S. citizens, nationals, and residents and (b) U.S. businesses and their officers, directors, employees, agents, or stockholders acting on the domestic concern's behalf—and certain foreign persons and businesses that act in furtherance of an FCPA violation while in the territory of the United States. Within DOJ, the Fraud Section of the Criminal Division has primary responsibility for all FCPA matters.[22] FCPA matters are handled primarily by the FCPA Unit within the Fraud Section, regularly working jointly with U.S. Attorneys' Offices around the country.

DOJ maintains a website dedicated to the FCPA and its enforcement at http://www.justice.gov/criminal/fraud/ fcpa/. The website provides translations of the FCPA in numerous languages, relevant legislative history, and selected documents from FCPA-related prosecutions and resolutions since 1977, including charging documents, plea agreements, deferred prosecution agreements, non-prosecution agreements, press releases, and other relevant pleadings and court decisions. The website also provides copies of opinions issued in response to requests by companies and individuals under DOJ's FCPA opinion procedure. The procedures for submitting a request for an opinion can be found at http://www. justice.gov/criminal/fraud /fcpa/docs /frgncrpt.pdf and are discussed further in Chapter 9. Individuals and companies wishing to disclose information about potential FCPA violations are encouraged to contact the FCPA Unit at the telephone number or email address above.

Securities and Exchange Commission

SEC is responsible for civil enforcement of the FCPA over issuers and their officers, directors, employees, agents, or stockholders acting on the issuer's behalf. SEC's Division of Enforcement has responsibility for investigating and prosecuting FCPA violations. In 2010, SEC's Enforcement Division created a specialized FCPA Unit, with attorneys in Washington, D.C. and in regional offices around the country, to focus specifically on FCPA enforcement.

The Unit investigates potential FCPA violations; facilitates coordination with DOJ's FCPA program and with other federal and international law enforcement partners; uses its expert knowledge of the law to promote consistent enforcement of the FCPA; analyzes tips, complaints, and referrals regarding allegations of foreign bribery; and conducts public outreach to raise awareness of anti-corruption efforts and good corporate governance programs.

SEC Contact Information
FCPA Unit Chief
Division of Enforcement
U .S . Securities and Exchange Commission
100 F Street, N.E.
Washington, DC 20549
Online: Tips, Complaints, and
Referrals website
http://www .sec .gov/complaint/tipscomplaint .shtml
Office of Investor Education and Advocacy:
(800) SEC-0330

The FCPA Unit maintains a "Spotlight on FCPA" section on SEC's website at http://www.sec.gov/spotlight/ fcpa.shtml. The website, which is updated regularly, provides general information about the Act, links to all SEC enforcement actions involving the FCPA, including both federal court actions and administrative proceedings, and contains other useful information.

Individuals and companies with information about possible FCPA violations by issuers may report them to the Enforcement Division via SEC's online Tips, Complaints and Referral system, http://www.sec.gov/complaint /tipscomplaint.shtml. They may also submit information to SEC's Office of the Whistleblower through the same online system or by contacting the Office of the Whistleblower at (202) 551-4790. Additionally, investors with questions about the FCPA can call the Office of Investor Education and Advocacy at (800) SEC-0330.

For more information about SEC's Whistleblower Program, under which certain eligible whistleblowers may be entitled to a monetary award if their information leads to certain SEC actions, see Chapter 8.

Law Enforcement Partners

DOJ's FCPA Unit regularly works with the Federal Bureau of Investigation (FBI) to investigate potential FCPA violations. The FBI's International Corruption Unit has primary responsibility for international corruption and fraud investigations and coordinates the FBI's national FCPA enforcement program. The FBI also has a dedicated FCPA squad of FBI special agents (located in the Washington Field Office) that is responsible for investigating many, and providing support for all, of the FBI's FCPA investigations. In addition, the Department of Homeland Security and the Internal Revenue Service-Criminal Investigation regularly investigate potential

FCPA violations. A number of other agencies are also involved in the fight against international corruption, including the Department of Treasury's Office of Foreign Assets Control, which has helped lead a number of FCPA investigations.

Departments of Commerce and State

Besides enforcement efforts by DOJ and SEC, the U.S. government is also working to address corruption abroad and level the playing field for U.S. businesses through the efforts of the Departments of Commerce and State. Both Commerce and State advance anti-corruption and good governance initiatives globally and regularly assist U.S. companies doing business overseas in several important ways. Both agencies encourage U.S. businesses to seek the assistance of U.S embassies when they are confronted with bribe solicitations or other corruption-related issues overseas.[23]

The Department of Commerce offers a number of important resources for businesses, including the International Trade Administration's United States and Foreign Commercial Service (Commercial Service). The Commercial Service has export and industry specialists located in over 100 U.S. cities and 70 countries who are available to provide counseling and other assistance to U.S. businesses, particularly small and medium-sized companies, regarding exporting their products and services. Among other things, these specialists can help a U.S. company conduct due diligence when choosing business partners or agents overseas. The International Company Profile Program, for instance, can be part of a U.S. business' evaluation of potential overseas business partners.[24] Businesses may contact the Commercial Service through its website, http://export.gov/ eac/, or directly at its domestic and foreign offices.[25]

Additionally, the Department of Commerce's Office of the General Counsel maintains a website, http://www. commerce.gov/os/ogc/transparency-and-anti-briberyinitiatives, that contains recent articles and speeches, links to translations of the FCPA, a catalogue of anti-corruption resources, and a list of international conventions and initiatives. The Trade Compliance Center in the Department of Commerce's International Trade Administration hosts a website with anti-bribery resources, http://tcc.export. gov/Bribery. This website contains an online form through which U.S. companies can report allegations of foreign bribery by foreign competitors in international business transactions.[26] The Department of Commerce also provides information to companies through a number of U.S. and international publications designed to assist firms in complying with anti-corruption laws. For example, the

Department of Commerce has included a new anti-corruption section in its Country Commercial Guides, prepared by market experts at U.S. embassies worldwide, that contains information on market conditions for more than 100 countries, including information on the FCPA for exporters.[27]

The Department of Commerce has also published a guide, *Business Ethics: A Manual for Managing a Responsible Business Enterprise in Emerging Market Economies*, which contains information about corporate compliance programs for businesses involved in international trade.[28]

The Departments of Commerce and State also provide advocacy support, when determined to be in the national interest, for U.S. companies bidding for foreign government contracts. The Department of Commerce's Advocacy Center, for example, supports U.S. businesses competing against foreign companies for international contracts, such as by arranging for the delivery of an advocacy message by U.S. government officials or assisting with unanticipated problems such as suspected bribery by a competitor.[29] The Department of State's Bureau of Economic and Business Affairs (specifically, its Office of Commercial and Business Affairs) similarly assists U.S. firms doing business overseas by providing advocacy on behalf of U.S. businesses and identifying risk areas for U.S. businesses; more information is available on its website, http://www.state.gov/e/ eb/cba/. Also, the Department of State's economic officers serving overseas provide commercial advocacy and support for U.S. companies at the many overseas diplomatic posts where the Commercial Service is not represented.

The Department of State promotes U.S. government interests in addressing corruption internationally through country-to-country diplomatic engagement; development of and follow-through on international commitments relating to corruption; promotion of high-level political engagement (e.g., the G20 Anticorruption Action Plan); public outreach in foreign countries; and support for building the capacity of foreign partners to combat corruption. In fiscal year 2009, the U.S. government provided more than $1 billion for anti-corruption and related good governance assistance abroad.

The Department of State's Bureau of International Narcotics and Law Enforcement Affairs (INL) manages U.S. participation in many multilateral anti-corruption political and legal initiatives at the global and regional level. INL also funds and coordinates significant efforts to assist countries with combating corruption through legal reform, training, and other capacity-building efforts. Inquiries about the U.S. government's general anti-corruption efforts and implementation of global and regional anti-corruption initiatives may be directed to INL on its website, http://www. state.gov/j/inl/c

/crime/corr/index.htm, or by email to: anticorruption@state.gov. In addition, the U.S. Agency for International Development (USAID) has developed several anti-corruption programs and publications, information about which can be found at http://www.usaid.gov/what-we-do/democracy-human-rights-and-governance/promot-ing-accountability-transparency.

Finally, the Department of State's brochure "Fighting Global Corruption: Business Risk Management," available at http://www.ogc.doc.gov/pdfs/Fighting_Global_ Corruption.pdf, provides guidance about corporate compliance programs as well as international anticorruption initiatives.

International Landscape: Global Anti-Corruption Efforts

In recent years, there has been a growing international consensus that corruption must be combated, and the United States and other countries are parties to a number of international anti-corruption conventions. Under these conventions, countries that are parties undertake commitments to adopt a range of preventive and criminal law measures to combat corruption. The conventions incorporate review processes that allow the United States to monitor other countries to ensure that they are meeting their international obligations. Likewise, these processes in turn permit other parties to monitor the United States' anti-corruption laws and enforcement to ensure that such enforcement and legal frameworks are consistent with the United States' treaty obligations.[30] U.S. officials regularly address the subject of corruption with our foreign counterparts to raise awareness of the importance of fighting corruption and urge stronger enforcement of anti-corruption laws and policies.

OECD Working Group on Bribery and the Anti-Bribery Convention

The OECD was founded in 1961 to stimulate economic progress and world trade. As noted, the Anti-Bribery Convention requires its parties to criminalize the bribery of foreign public officials in international business transactions.[31] As of November 1, 2012, there were 39 parties to the Anti-Bribery Convention: 34 OECD member countries (including the United States) and five non-OECD member countries (Argentina, Brazil, Bulgaria, the Russian Federation, and South Africa). All of these parties are also members of the OECD Working Group on Bribery (Working Group).[32]

The Working Group is responsible for monitoring the implementation of the Anti-Bribery Convention, the 2009 Recommendation of the Council for Further Combating Bribery of Foreign Public Officials in International

Business Transactions, and related instruments. Its members meet quarterly to review and monitor implementation of the Anti-Bribery Convention by member states around the world. Each party undergoes periodic peer review.[33] This peer-review monitoring system is conducted in three phases. The Phase 1 review includes an in-depth assessment of each country's domestic laws implementing the Convention. The Phase 2 review examines the effectiveness of each country's laws and anti-bribery efforts. The final phase is a permanent cycle of peer review (the first cycle of which is referred to as the Phase 3 review) that evaluates a country's enforcement actions and results, as well as the country's efforts to address weaknesses identified during the Phase 2 review.[34] All of the monitoring reports for the parties to the Convention can be found on the OECD website and can be a useful resource about the foreign bribery laws of the OECD Working Group member countries.[35]

The United States was one of the first countries to undergo all three phases of review. The reports and appendices can be found on DOJ's and SEC's websites.[36] In its Phase 3 review of the United States, which was completed in October 2010, the Working Group commended U.S. efforts to fight transnational bribery and highlighted a number of best practices developed by the United States. The report also noted areas where the United States' anti-bribery efforts could be improved, including consolidating publicly available information on the application of the FCPA and enhancing awareness among small- and medium-sized companies about the prevention and detection of foreign bribery. This guide is, in part, a response to these Phase 3 recommendations and is intended to help businesses and individuals better understand the FCPA.[37]

U.N. Convention against Corruption

The United States is a state party to the United Nations Convention Against Corruption (UNCAC), which was adopted by the U.N. General Assembly on October 31, 2003, and entered into force on December 14, 2005.[38] The United States ratified the UNCAC on October 30, 2006. The UNCAC requires parties to criminalize a wide range of corrupt acts, including domestic and foreign bribery and related offenses such as money laundering and obstruction of justice. The UNCAC also establishes guidelines for the creation of anti-corruption bodies, codes of conduct for public officials, transparent and objective systems of procurement, and enhanced accounting and auditing standards for the private sector. A peer review mechanism assesses the implementation of the UNCAC by parties to the Convention, with a focus in the first round on criminalization and law enforcement as well as international legal cooperation.[39] The United States has been reviewed under the Pilot Review Programme, the report of which is available on DOJ's website. As of November 1, 2012, 163 countries were parties to the UNCAC.[40]

Other Anti-Corruption Conventions

The Inter-American Convention Against Corruption (IACAC) was the first international anti-corruption convention, adopted in March 1996 in Caracas, Venezuela, by members of the Organization of American States.[41]

The IACAC requires parties (of which the United States is one) to criminalize both foreign and domestic bribery. A body known as the Mechanism for Follow-Up on the Implementation of the Inter-American Convention Against Corruption (MESICIC) monitors parties' compliance with the IACAC. As of November 1, 2012, 31 countries were parties to MESICIC.

The Council of Europe established the Group of States Against Corruption (GRECO) in 1999 to monitor countries' compliance with the Council of Europe's anticorruption standards, including the Council of Europe's Criminal Law Convention on Corruption.[42] These standards include prohibitions on the solicitation and receipt of bribes, as well as foreign bribery. As of November 1, 2012, GRECO member states, which need not be members of the Council of Europe, include more than 45 European countries and the United States.[43]

The United States has been reviewed under both MESICIC and GRECO, and the reports generated by those reviews are available on DOJ's website.

THE FCPA: ANTI-BRIBERY PROVISIONS

The FCPA addresses the problem of international corruption in two ways: (1) the anti-bribery provisions, which are discussed below, prohibit individuals and businesses from bribing foreign government officials in order to obtain or retain business and (2) the accounting provisions, which are discussed in Chapter 3, impose certain record keeping and internal control requirements on issuers, and prohibit individuals and companies from knowingly falsifying an issuer's books and records or circumventing or failing to implement an issuer's system of internal controls. Violations of the FCPA can lead to civil and criminal penalties, sanctions, and remedies, including fines, disgorgement, and/or imprisonment.

In general, the FCPA prohibits offering to pay, paying, promising to pay, or authorizing the payment of money or anything of value to a foreign official in order to influence any act or decision of the foreign official in his or her official capacity or to secure any other improper advantage in order to obtain or retain business.[44]

Who Is Covered by the Anti-Bribery Provisions?

The FCPA's anti-bribery provisions apply broadly to three categories of persons and entities: (1) "issuers" and their officers, directors, employees, agents, and shareholders; (2) "domestic concerns" and their officers, directors, employees, agents, and shareholders; and (3) certain persons and entities, other than issuers and domestic concerns, acting while in the territory of the United States.

Issuers—15 U.S.C. § 78dd-1

Section 30A of the Securities Exchange Act of 1934 (the Exchange Act), which can be found at 15 U.S.C. § 78dd-1, contains the anti-bribery provision governing issuers.[45] A company is an "issuer" under the FCPA if it has a class of securities registered under Section 12 of the Exchange Act[46] or is required to file periodic and other reports with SEC under Section 15(d) of the Exchange Act.[47] In practice, this means that any company with a class of securities listed on a national securities exchange in the United States, or any company with a class of securities quoted in the over-the-counter market in the United States and required to file periodic reports with SEC, is an issuer. A company thus need not be a U.S. company to be an issuer. Foreign companies with American Depository Receipts that are listed on a U.S. exchange are also issuers.[48] As of December 31, 2011, 965 foreign companies were registered with SEC.[49] Officers, directors, employees, agents, or stockholders acting on behalf of an issuer (whether U.S. or foreign nationals), and any co-conspirators, also can be prosecuted under the FCPA.[50]

How Can I Tell If My Company Is an "Issuer"?

- It is listed on a national securities exchange in the United States (either stock or American Depository Receipts); or
- The company's stock trades in the over-the-counter market in the United States and the company is required to file SEC reports.
- To see if your company files SEC reports, go to SEC's website at http://www.sec.gov/edgar/searchedgar/webusers.htm.

Domestic Concerns—15 U.S.C. § 78dd-2

The FCPA also applies to "domestic concerns." [51] A domestic concern is any individual who is a citizen, national, or resident of the United States, or any corporation, partnership, association, joint-stock company, business trust, unincorporated organization, or sole proprietorship that is organized under the laws of the United States or its states, territories, possessions, or commonwealths or that has its principal place of business in the United States.[52] Officers, directors, employees, agents, or stockholders acting on behalf of a domestic concern, including foreign nationals or companies, are also covered.[53]

Territorial Jurisdiction—15 U.S.C. § 78dd-3

The FCPA also applies to certain foreign nationals or entities that are not issuers or domestic concerns.[54] Since 1998, the FCPA's anti-bribery provisions have applied to foreign persons and foreign non-issuer entities that, either directly or through an agent, engage in *any* act in furtherance of a corrupt payment (or an offer, promise, or authorization to pay) while in the territory of the United States.[55] Also, officers, directors, employees, agents, or stockholders acting on behalf of such persons or entities may be subject to the FCPA's anti-bribery prohibitions.[56]

What Jurisdictional Conduct Triggers the Anti-Bribery Provisions?

The FCPA's anti-bribery provisions can apply to conduct both inside and outside the United States. Issuers and domestic concerns—as well as their officers, directors, employees, agents, or stockholders—may be prosecuted for using the U.S. mails or any means or instrumentality of interstate commerce in furtherance of a corrupt payment to a foreign official. The Act defines "interstate commerce" as "trade, commerce, transportation, or communication among the several States, or between any foreign country and any State or between any State and any place or ship outside thereof ...."[57] The term also includes the *intrastate* use of any interstate means of communication, or any other interstate instrumentality.[58] Thus, placing a telephone call or sending an e-mail, text message, or fax from, to, or through the United States involves interstate commerce—as does sending a wire transfer from or to a U.S. bank or otherwise using the U.S. banking system, or traveling across state borders or internationally to or from the United States.

Those who are not issuers or domestic concerns may be prosecuted under the FCPA if they directly, or through an agent, engage in *any* act in furtherance of a corrupt payment while in the territory of the United States, regardless of whether they utilize the U.S. mails or a means or instrumentality of interstate commerce.[59] Thus, for example, a foreign national who attends a meeting in the United States that furthers a foreign bribery scheme may be subject to prosecution, as may any co-conspirators, even if they did not themselves attend the meeting. A foreign national or company may also be liable under the FCPA if it aids and abets, conspires with, or acts as an agent of an issuer or domestic concern, regardless of whether the foreign national or company itself takes any action in the United States.[60]

In addition, under the "alternative jurisdiction" provision of the FCPA enacted in 1998, U.S. companies or persons may be subject to the anti-bribery provisions even if they act outside the United States.[61] The 1998 amendments to the FCPA expanded the jurisdictional coverage of the Act by establishing an alternative basis for jurisdiction, that is, jurisdiction based on the nationality principle.[62] In particular, the 1998 amendments removed the requirement that there be a use of interstate commerce (e.g., wire, email, telephone call) for acts in furtherance of a corrupt payment to a foreign official by U.S. companies and persons occurring wholly outside of the United States.[63]

What Is Covered?—The Business Purpose Test

The FCPA applies only to payments intended to induce or influence a foreign official to use his or her position "in order to assist ... in obtaining or retaining business for or with, or directing business to, any person."[64] This requirement is known as the "business purpose test" and is broadly interpreted.[65]

Not surprisingly, many enforcement actions involve bribes to obtain or retain government contracts.[66] The FCPA also prohibits bribes in the conduct of business or to gain a business advantage.[67] For example, bribe payments made to secure favorable tax treatment, to reduce or eliminate customs duties, to obtain government action to prevent competitors from entering a market, or to circumvent a licensing or permit requirement, all satisfy the business purpose test.[68]

Hypothetical: FCPA Jurisdiction

Company A, a Delaware company with its principal place of business in New York, is a large energy company that operates globally, including in a number of countries that have a high risk of corruption, such as Foreign Country. Company A's shares are listed on a national U S stock exchange.

Company A enters into an agreement with a European company (EuroCo) to submit a joint bid to the Oil Ministry to build a refinery in Foreign Country EuroCo is not an issuer. Executives of Company A and EuroCo meet in New York to discuss how to win the bid and decide to hire a purported third-party consultant (Intermediary) and have him use part of his "commission" to bribe high-ranking officials within the Oil Ministry. Intermediary meets with executives at Company A and EuroCo in New York to finalize the scheme. Eventually, millions of dollars in bribes are funneled from the United States and Europe through Intermediary to high-ranking officials at the Oil Ministry, and Company A and EuroCo win the contract. A few years later, a front page article alleging that the contract was procured through bribery appears in Foreign Country, and DOJ and SEC begin investigating whether the FCPA was violated.

Based on these facts, which entities fall within the FCPA's jurisdiction?

All of the entities easily fall within the FCPA's jurisdiction Company A is both an "issuer" and a "domestic concern" under the FCPA, and Intermediary is an "agent" of Company A. EuroCo and Intermediary are also subject to the FCPA's territorial jurisdiction provision based on their conduct while in the United States. Moreover, even if EuroCo and Intermediary had never taken any actions in the territory of the United States, they can still be subject to jurisdiction under a traditional application of conspiracy law and may be subject to substantive FCPA charges under *Pinkerton* liability, namely, being liable for the reasonably foreseeable substantive FCPA crimes committed by a co-conspirator in furtherance of the conspiracy.

Examples of Actions Taken to Obtain or Retain Business

- Winning a contract
- Influencing the procurement process
- Circumventing the rules for importation of products
- Gaining access to non-public bid tender information
- Evading taxes or penalties
- Influencing the adjudication of lawsuits or enforcement actions
- Obtaining exceptions to regulations - Avoiding contract termination

In 2004, the U.S. Court of Appeals for the Fifth Circuit addressed the business purpose test in *United States v. Kay* and held that bribes paid to obtain favorable tax treatment— which reduced a company's customs duties and sales taxes on imports—could constitute payments made to "obtain or retain" business within the meaning of the FCPA.[69] The court explained that in enacting the FCPA, "Congress meant to prohibit a range of payments wider than only those that directly influence the acquisition or retention of government contracts or similar commercial or industrial arrangements."[70] The *Kay* court found that "[t]he congressional target was bribery paid to engender assistance in improving the business opportunities of the payor or his beneficiary, irrespective of whether that assistance be direct or indirect, and irrespective of whether it be related to administering the law, awarding, extending, or renewing a contract, or executing or preserving an agreement."[71] Accordingly, *Kay* held that payments to obtain favorable tax treatment can, under appropriate circumstances, violate the FCPA:

> Avoiding or lowering taxes reduces operating costs and thus increases profit margins, thereby freeing up funds that the business is otherwise legally obligated to expend. And this, in turn, enables it to take any number of actions to the disadvantage of competitors. Bribing foreign officials to lower taxes and customs duties certainly *can* provide an unfair advantage over competitors and thereby be of assistance to the payor in obtaining or retaining business.
>
> * * *
>
> [W]e hold that Congress intended for the FCPA to apply broadly to payments intended to assist the payor, either directly or indirectly, in obtaining or retaining business for some person, and that bribes paid to foreign tax officials to secure illegally reduced customs and tax liability constitute a type of payment that can fall within this broad coverage.[72]

Paying Bribes to Customs Officials

In 2010, a global freight forwarding company and six of its corporate customers in the oil and gas industry resolved charges that they paid bribes to customs officials. The companies bribed customs officials in more than ten countries in exchange for such benefits as:

- evading customs duties on imported goods
- improperly expediting the importation of goods and equipment

- extending drilling contracts and lowering tax assessments
- obtaining false documentation related to temporary import permits for drilling rigs
- enabling the release of drilling rigs and other equipment from customs officials

In many instances, the improper payments at issue allowed the company to carry out its existing business, which fell within the FCPA's prohibition on corrupt payments made for the purpose of "retaining" business. The seven companies paid a total of more than $235 million in civil and criminal sanctions and disgorgement.

In short, while the FCPA does not cover every type of bribe paid around the world for every purpose, it does apply broadly to bribes paid to help obtain or retain business, which can include payments made to secure a wide variety of unfair business advantages.[73]

What Does "Corruptly" Mean?

To violate the FCPA, an offer, promise, or authorization of a payment, or a payment, to a government official must be made "corruptly."[74] As Congress noted when adopting the FCPA, the word "corruptly" means an intent or desire to wrongfully influence the recipient:

> The word "corruptly" is used in order to make clear that the offer, payment, promise, or gift, must be intended to induce the recipient to misuse his official position; for example, wrongfully to direct business to the payor or his client, to obtain preferential legislation or regulations, or to induce a foreign official to fail to perform an official function.[75]

Where corrupt intent is present, the FCPA prohibits paying, offering, or promising to pay money or anything of value (or authorizing the payment or offer).[76] By focusing on intent, the FCPA does not require that a corrupt act succeed in its purpose.[77] Nor must the foreign official actually solicit, accept, or receive the corrupt payment for the bribe payor to be liable.[78] For example, in one case, a specialty chemical company promised Iraqi government officials approximately $850,000 in bribes for an upcoming contract. Although the company did not, in the end, make the payment (the scheme was thwarted by the U.S. government's investigation), the company still violated the FCPA and was held accountable.[79]

Also, as long as the offer, promise, authorization, or payment is made corruptly, the actor need not know the identity of the recipient; the attempt is sufficient.[80] Thus, an executive who authorizes others to pay "whoever you need to" in a foreign government to obtain a contract has violated the FCPA—even if no bribe is ultimately offered or paid.

What Does "Willfully" Mean and When Does It Apply?

In order for an individual defendant to be criminally liable under the FCPA, he or she must act "willfully."[81] Proof of willfulness is not required to establish corporate criminal or civil liability,[82] though proof of corrupt intent is.

The term "willfully" is not defined in the FCPA, but it has generally been construed by courts to connote an act committed voluntarily and purposefully, and with a bad purpose, i.e., with "knowledge that [a defendant] was doing a 'bad' act under the general rules of law."[83] As the Supreme Court explained in *Bryan v. United States*, "[a]s a general matter, when used in the criminal context, a 'willful' act is one undertaken with a 'bad purpose.' In other words, in order to establish a 'willful' violation of a statute, 'the Government must prove that the defendant acted with knowledge that his conduct was unlawful.'"[84]

Notably, as both the Second Circuit and Fifth Circuit Courts of Appeals have found, the FCPA does not require the government to prove that a defendant was specifically aware of the FCPA or knew that his conduct violated the FCPA.[85] To be guilty, a defendant must act with a bad purpose, i.e., know generally that his conduct is unlawful.

What Does "Anything of Value" Mean?

In enacting the FCPA, Congress recognized that bribes can come in many shapes and sizes—a broad range of unfair benefits[86]—and so the statute prohibits the corrupt "offer, payment, promise to pay, or authorization of the payment of any money, or offer, gift, promise to give, or authorization of the giving of *anything of value* to" a foreign official.[87]

An improper benefit can take many forms. While cases often involve payments of cash (sometimes in the guise of "consulting fees" or "commissions" given through intermediaries), others have involved travel expenses and expensive gifts. Like the domestic bribery statute, the FCPA does not contain a minimum threshold amount for corrupt gifts or payments.[88] Indeed, what might be considered a modest payment in the United States could be a larger and much more significant amount in a foreign country.

Regardless of size, for a gift or other payment to violate the statute, the payor must have corrupt intent—that is, the intent to improperly influence the government official. The corrupt intent requirement protects companies that engage in the ordinary and legitimate promotion of their businesses while targeting conduct that seeks to improperly induce officials into misusing their positions. Thus, it is difficult to envision any scenario in which the provision of cups of coffee, taxi fare, or company promotional items of nominal value would ever evidence corrupt intent, and neither DOJ nor SEC has ever pursued an investigation on the basis of such conduct. Moreover, as in all areas of federal law enforcement, DOJ and SEC exercise discretion in deciding which cases promote law enforcement priorities and justify investigation. Certain patterns, however, have emerged: DOJ's and SEC's anti-bribery enforcement actions have focused on small payments and gifts only when they comprise part of a systemic or long-standing course of conduct that evidences a scheme to corruptly pay foreign officials to obtain or retain business. These assessments are necessarily fact specific.

Cash

The most obvious form of corrupt payment is large amounts of cash. In some instances, companies have maintained cash funds specifically earmarked for use as bribes. One U.S. issuer headquartered in Germany disbursed corrupt payments from a corporate "cash desk" and used offshore bank accounts to bribe government officials to win contracts.[89] In another instance, a four-company joint venture used its agent to pay $5 million in bribes to a Nigerian political party.[90] The payments were made to the agent in suitcases of cash (typically in $1 million installments), and, in one instance, the trunk of a car when the cash did not fit into a suitcase.[91]

Gifts, Travel, Entertainment, and Other Things of Value

A small gift or token of esteem or gratitude is often an appropriate way for business people to display respect for each other. Some hallmarks of appropriate gift-giving are when the gift is given openly and transparently, properly recorded in the giver's books and records, provided only to reflect esteem or gratitude, and permitted under local law.

Items of nominal value, such as cab fare, reasonable meals and entertainment expenses, or company promotional items, are unlikely to improperly influence an official, and, as a result, are not, without more, items that have resulted in enforcement action by DOJ or SEC. The larger or more extravagant the gift, however, the more likely it was given with an improper purpose. DOJ and SEC enforcement cases thus have involved single instances of large, extravagant gift-giving (such as sports cars, fur coats, and other luxury items) as well as widespread gifts of smaller items as part of a pattern of bribes.[92] For example, in one case brought by DOJ and SEC, a defendant gave a government official a country club membership fee and a generator, as well as household maintenance expenses, payment of cell phone bills, an automobile worth $20,000, and limousine services. The same official also received $250,000 through a third-party agent.[93]

In addition, a number of FCPA enforcement actions have involved the corrupt payment of travel and entertainment expenses. Both DOJ and SEC have brought cases where these types of expenditures occurred in conjunction with other conduct reflecting systemic bribery or other clear indicia of corrupt intent. A case involving a California-based telecommunications company illustrates the types of improper travel and entertainment expenses that may violate the FCPA.[94] Between 2002 and 2007, the company spent nearly $7 million on approximately 225 trips for its customers in order to obtain systems contracts in China, including for employees of Chinese state-owned companies to travel to popular tourist destinations in the United States.[95] Although the trips were purportedly for the individuals to conduct training at the company's facilities, in reality, no training occurred on many of these trips and the company had no facilities at those locations. Approximately $670,000 of the $7 million was falsely recorded as "training" expenses.[96]

Examples of Improper Travel and Entertainment

- a $12,000 birthday trip for a government decision-maker from Mexico that included visits to wineries and dinners
- $10,000 spent on dinners, drinks, and entertainment for a government official
- a trip to Italy for eight Iraqi government officials that consisted primarily of sightseeing and included $1,000 in "pocket money" for each official

- a trip to Paris for a government official and his wife that consisted primarily of touring activities via a chauffeur-driven vehicle

Likewise, a New Jersey-based telecommunications company spent millions of dollars on approximately 315 trips for Chinese government officials, ostensibly to inspect factories and train the officials in using the company's equipment.[97] In reality, during many of these trips, the officials spent little or no time visiting the company's facilities, but instead visited tourist destinations such as Hawaii, Las Vegas, the Grand Canyon, Niagara Falls, Disney World, Universal Studios, and New York City.[98] Some of the trips were characterized as "factory inspections" or "training" with government customers but consisted primarily or entirely of sightseeing to locations chosen by the officials, typically lasting two weeks and costing between $25,000 and $55,000 per trip. In some instances, the company gave the government officials $500 to $1,000 per day in spending money and paid all lodging, transportation, food, and entertainment expenses. The company either failed to record these expenses or improperly recorded them as "consulting fees" in its corporate books and records. The company also failed to implement appropriate internal controls to monitor the provision of travel and other things of value to Chinese government officials.[99]

Companies also may violate the FCPA if they give payments or gifts to third parties, like an official's family members, as an indirect way of corruptly influencing a foreign official. For example, one defendant paid personal bills and provided airline tickets to a cousin and close friend of the foreign official whose influence the defendant sought in obtaining contracts.[100] The defendant was convicted at trial and received a prison sentence.[101]

As part of an effective compliance program, a company should have clear and easily accessible guidelines and processes in place for gift-giving by the company's directors, officers, employees, and agents. Though not necessarily appropriate for every business, many larger companies have automated gift-giving clearance processes and have set clear monetary thresholds for gifts along with annual limitations, with limited exceptions for gifts approved by appropriate management. Clear guidelines and processes can be an effective and efficient means for controlling gift-giving, deterring improper gifts, and protecting corporate assets.

The FCPA does not prohibit gift-giving. Rather, just like its domestic bribery counterparts, the FCPA prohibits the payments of bribes, including those disguised as gifts.

Charitable Contributions

Companies often engage in charitable giving as part of legitimate local outreach. The FCPA does not prohibit charitable contributions or prevent corporations from acting as good corporate citizens. Companies, however, cannot use the pretense of charitable contributions as a way to funnel bribes to government officials.

For example, a pharmaceutical company used charitable donations to a small local castle restoration charity headed by a foreign government official to induce the official to direct business to the company. Although the charity was a bona fide charitable organization, internal documents at the pharmaceutical company's subsidiary established that the payments were not viewed as charitable contributions but rather as "dues" the subsidiary was required to pay for assistance from the government official. The payments constituted a significant portion of the subsidiary's total promotional donations budget and were structured to allow the subsidiary to exceed its authorized limits. The payments also were not in compliance with the company's internal policies, which provided that charitable donations generally should be made to healthcare institutions and relate to the practice of medicine.[102]

Hypothetical: Gifts, Travel, and Entertainment

Company A is a large U.S. engineering company with global operations in more than 50 countries, including a number that have a high risk of corruption, such as Foreign Country. Company A's stock is listed on a national U.S. stock exchange. In conducting its business internationally, Company A's officers and employees come into regular contact with foreign officials, including officials in various ministries and state-owned entities. At a trade show, Company A has a booth at which it offers free pens, hats, t-shirts, and other similar promotional items with Company A's logo. Company A also serves free coffee, other beverages, and snacks at the booth. Some of the visitors to the booth are foreign officials.

Is Company A in violation of the FCPA?

No. These are legitimate, bona fide expenditures made in connection with the promotion, demonstration, or explanation of Company A's products or services. There is nothing to suggest corrupt intent here. The FCPA does not prevent companies from promoting their businesses in this way or providing legitimate hospitality, including to foreign officials.

Providing promotional items with company logos or free snacks as set forth above is an appropriate means of providing hospitality and promoting business Such conduct has never formed the basis for an FCPA enforcement action.

At the trade show, Company A invites a dozen current and prospective customers out for drinks, and pays the moderate bar tab. Some of the current and prospective customers are foreign officials under the FCPA. Is Company A in violation of the FCPA?

No. Again, the FCPA was not designed to prohibit all forms of hospitality to foreign officials. While the cost here may be more substantial than the beverages, snacks, and promotional items provided at the booth, and the invitees specifically selected, there is still nothing to suggest corrupt intent.

Two years ago, Company A won a long-term contract to supply goods and services to the state-owned Electricity Commission in Foreign Country. The Electricity Commission is 100% owned, controlled, and operated by the government of Foreign Country, and employees of the Electricity Commission are subject to Foreign Country's domestic bribery laws. Some Company A executives are in Foreign Country for meetings with officials of the Electricity Commission. The General Manager of the Electricity Commission was recently married, and during the trip Company A executives present a moderately priced crystal vase to the General Manager as a wedding gift and token of esteem. Is Company A in violation of the FCPA?

No. It is appropriate to provide reasonable gifts to foreign officials as tokens of esteem or gratitude. It is important that such gifts be made openly and transparently, properly recorded in a company's books and records, and given only where appropriate under local law, customary where given, and reasonable for the occasion.

During the course of the contract described above, Company A periodically provides training to Electricity Commission employees at its facilities in Michigan. The training is paid for by the Electricity Commission as part of the contract. Senior officials of the Electricity Commission inform Company A that they want to inspect the faciliti and ensure that the training is working well. Company A pays for the airfare, hotel, and transportation for the.Electricity Commission senior officials to travel to Michigan to inspect Company A's facilities.

Because it is a lengthy international flight, Company A agrees to pay for business class airfare, to which its own employees are entitled for lengthy flights. The foreign officials visit Michigan for several days, during which the senior officials perform an appropriate inspection. Company A executives take the officials to a moderately priced dinner, a baseball game, and a play. Do any of these actions violate the FCPA?

No. Neither the costs associated with training the employees nor the trip for the senior officials to the Company's facilities in order to inspect them violates the FCPA. Reasonable and bona fide promotional expenditures do not violate the FCPA. Here, Company A is providing training to the Electricity Commission's employees and is hosting the Electricity Commission senior officials. Their review of the execution and performance of the contract is a legitimate business purpose. Even the provision of business class airfare is reasonable under the circumstances, as are the meals and entertainment, which are only a small component of the business trip.

Would this analysis be different if Company A instead paid for the senior officials to travel first-class with their spouses for an all-expenses-paid, week-long trip to Las Vegas, where Company A has no facilities?

Yes. This conduct almost certainly violates the FCPA because it evinces a corrupt intent. Here, the trip does not appear to be designed for any legitimate business purpose, is extravagant, includes expenses for the officials' spouses, and therefore appears to be designed to corruptly curry favor with the foreign government officials. Moreover, if the trip were booked as a legitimate business expense—such as the provision of training at its facilities—Company A would also be in violation of the FCPA's accounting provisions. Furthermore, this conduct suggests deficiencies in Company A's internal controls.

Company A's contract with the Electricity Commission is going to expire, and the Electricity Commission is offering the next contract through its tender process. An employee of the Electricity Commission contacts Company A and offers to provide Company A with confidential, non-public bid information from Company A's competitors if Company A will pay for a vacation to Paris for him and his girlfriend. Employees of Company A accede to the official's request, pay for the vacation, receive the confidential bid information, and yet still do not win the contract.

Has Company A violated the FCPA?

Yes. Company A has provided things of value to a foreign official for the purpose of inducing the official to misuse his office and to gain an improper advantage. It does not matter that it was the foreign official who first suggested the illegal conduct or that Company A ultimately was not successful in winning the contract. This conduct would also violate the FCPA's accounting provisions if the trip were booked as a legitimate business expense and suggests deficiencies in Company A's internal controls.

Proper due diligence and controls are critical for charitable giving. In general, the adequacy of measures taken to prevent misuse of charitable donations will depend on a risk-based analysis and the specific facts at hand. In Opinion Procedure Release No. 10-02, DOJ described the due diligence and controls that can minimize the likelihood of an FCPA violation. In that matter, a Eurasian-based subsidiary of a U.S. non-governmental organization was asked by an agency of a foreign government to make a grant to a local microfinance institution (MFI) as a prerequisite to the subsidiary's transformation to bank status. The subsidiary proposed contributing $1.42 million to a local MFI to satisfy the request. The subsidiary undertook an extensive, three-stage due diligence process to select the proposed grantee and imposed significant controls on the proposed grant, including ongoing monitoring and auditing, earmarking funds for capacity building, prohibiting compensation of board members, and implementing anti-corruption compliance provisions. DOJ explained that it would not take any enforcement action because the company's due diligence and the controls it planned to put in place sufficed to prevent an FCPA violation.

Other opinion releases also address charitable-type grants or donations. Under the facts presented in those releases, DOJ approved the proposed grant or donation,[103] based on due diligence measures and controls such as:

- certifications by the recipient regarding compliance with the FCPA;[104]
- due diligence to confirm that none of the recipient's officers were affiliated with the foreign government at issue;[105]
- a requirement that the recipient provide audited financial statements;[106]
- a written agreement with the recipient restricting the use of funds;[107]
- steps to ensure that the funds were transferred to a valid bank account;[108]

- confirmation that the charity's commitments were met before funds were disbursed;[109] and
- on-going monitoring of the efficacy of the program.[110]

Legitimate charitable giving does not violate the FCPA. Compliance with the FCPA merely requires that charitable giving not be used as a vehicle to conceal payments made to corruptly influence foreign officials.

Five Questions to Consider When Making Charitable Payments in a Foreign Country:

1) What is the purpose of the payment?
2) Is the payment consistent with the company's internal guidelines on charitable giving?
3) Is the payment at the request of a foreign official?
4) Is a foreign official associated with the charity and, if so, can the foreign official make decisions regarding your business in that country?
5) Is the payment conditioned upon receiving business or other benefits?

Who Is a Foreign Official?

The FCPA's anti-bribery provisions apply to corrupt payments made to (1) "any foreign official"; (2) "any foreign political party or official thereof"; (3) "any candidate for foreign political office"; or (4) any person, while knowing that all or a portion of the payment will be offered, given, or promised to an individual falling within one of these three categories.[111] Although the statute distinguishes between a "foreign official," "foreign political party or official thereof," and "candidate for foreign political office," the term "foreign official" in this guide generally refers to an individual falling within any of these three categories.

The FCPA defines "foreign official" to include:

> any officer or employee of a foreign government or any department, agency, or instrumentality thereof, or of a public international organization, or any person acting in an official capacity for or on behalf of any such

government or department, agency, or instrumentality, or for or on behalf of any such public international organization.[112]

As this language makes clear, the FCPA broadly applies to corrupt payments to "any" officer or employee of a foreign government and to those acting on the foreign government's behalf.[113] The FCPA thus covers corrupt payments to low-ranking employees and high-level officials alike.[114]

The FCPA prohibits payments to foreign *officials*, not to foreign *governments*.[115] That said, companies contemplating contributions or donations to foreign governments should take steps to ensure that no monies are used for corrupt purposes, such as the personal benefit of individual foreign officials.

Department, Agency, or Instrumentality of a Foreign Government

Foreign officials under the FCPA include officers or employees of a department, agency, or instrumentality of a foreign government. When a foreign government is organized in a fashion similar to the U.S. system, what constitutes a government department or agency is typically clear (e.g., a ministry of energy, national security agency, or transportation authority).[116] However, governments can be organized in very different ways.[117] Many operate through state-owned and state-controlled entities, particularly in such areas as aerospace and defense manufacturing, banking and finance, healthcare and life sciences, energy and extractive industries, telecommunications, and transportation.[118] By including officers or employees of agencies and instrumentalities within the definition of "foreign official," the FCPA accounts for this variability.

The term "instrumentality" is broad and can include state-owned or state-controlled entities. Whether a particular entity constitutes an "instrumentality" under the FCPA requires a fact-specific analysis of an entity's ownership, control, status, and function.[119] A number of courts have approved final jury instructions providing a non-exclusive list of factors to be considered:

- the foreign state's extent of ownership of the entity;
- the foreign state's degree of control over the entity (including whether key officers and directors of the entity are, or are appointed by, government officials);
- the foreign state's characterization of the entity and its employees;
- the circumstances surrounding the entity's creation;
- the purpose of the entity's activities;

- the entity's obligations and privileges under the foreign state's law;
- the exclusive or controlling power vested in the entity to administer its designated functions;
- the level of financial support by the foreign state (including subsidies, special tax treatment, government-mandated fees, and loans);
- the entity's provision of services to the jurisdiction's residents;
- whether the governmental end or purpose sought to be achieved is expressed in the policies of the foreign government; and
- the general perception that the entity is performing official or governmental functions.[120]

Companies should consider these factors when evaluating the risk of FCPA violations and designing compliance programs.

DOJ and SEC have pursued cases involving instrumentalities since the time of the FCPA's enactment and have long used an analysis of ownership, control, status, and function to determine whether a particular entity is an agency or instrumentality of a foreign government. For example, the second-ever FCPA case charged by DOJ involved a California company that paid bribes through a Mexican corporation to two executives of a state-owned Mexican national oil company. [121] And in the early 1980s, DOJ and SEC brought cases involving a $1 million bribe to the chairman of Trinidad and Tobago's racing authority.[122]

DOJ and SEC continue to regularly bring FCPA cases involving bribes paid to employees of agencies and instrumentalities of foreign governments. In one such case, the subsidiary of a Swiss engineering company paid bribes to officials of a state-owned and controlled electricity commission. The commission was created by, owned by, and controlled by the Mexican government, and it had a monopoly on the transmission and distribution of electricity in Mexico.

Many of the commission's board members were cabinet-level government officials, and the director was appointed by Mexico's president.[123] Similarly, in another recent case, Miami telecommunications executives were charged with paying bribes to employees of Haiti's state-owned and controlled telecommunications company. The telecommunications company was 97% owned and 100% controlled by the Haitian government, and its director was appointed by Haiti's president.[124]

While no one factor is dispositive or necessarily more important than another, as a practical matter, an entity is unlikely to qualify as an instrumentality if a government does not own or control a majority of its shares. However, there are circumstances in which an entity would qualify as an instrumentality absent 50% or greater foreign government ownership, which is reflected in the limited number of DOJ or SEC enforcement actions brought in such situations.

For example, in addition to being convicted of funneling millions of dollars in bribes to two sitting presidents in two different countries, a French issuer's three subsidiaries were convicted of paying bribes to employees of a Malaysian telecommunications company that was 43% owned by Malaysia's Ministry of Finance. There, notwithstanding its minority ownership stake in the company, the Ministry held the status of a "special shareholder," had veto power over all major expenditures, and controlled important operational decisions.[125]

In addition, most senior company officers were political appointees, including the Chairman and Director, the Chairman of the Board of the Tender Committee, and the Executive Director.[126] Thus, despite the Malaysian government having a minority shareholder position, the company was an instrumentality of the Malaysian government as the government nevertheless had substantial control over the company.

Companies and individuals should also remember that, whether an entity is an instrumentality of a foreign government or a private entity, commercial (i.e., privateto-private) bribery may still violate the FCPA's accounting provisions, the Travel Act, anti-money laundering laws, and other federal or foreign laws. Any type of corrupt payment thus carries a risk of prosecution.

Public International Organizations

In 1998, the FCPA was amended to expand the definition of "foreign official" to include employees and representatives of public international organizations.[127] A "public international organization" is any organization designated as such by Executive Order under the International Organizations Immunities Act, 22 U.S.C. § 288, or any other organization that the President so designates.[128] Currently, public international organizations include entities such as the World Bank, the International Monetary Fund, the World Intellectual Property Organization, the World Trade Organization, the OECD, the Organization of American States, and numerous others. A comprehensive list of organizations designated as "public international organizations" is contained in 22 U.S.C. § 288 and can also be found on the U.S. Government Printing Office website at http://www.gpo.gov/fdsys/.

How Are Payments to Third Parties Treated?

The FCPA expressly prohibits corrupt payments made through third parties or intermediaries.[129] Specifically, it covers payments made to "any person, while knowing that all or a portion of such money or thing of value will be offered, given, or promised, directly or indirectly,"[130] to a foreign official. Many companies doing business in a foreign country retain a local individual or company to help them conduct business. Although these foreign agents may provide entirely legitimate advice regarding local customs and procedures and may help facilitate business transactions, companies should be aware of the risks involved in engaging third-party agents or intermediaries. The fact that a bribe is paid by a third party does not eliminate the potential for criminal or civil FCPA liability.[131]

For instance, a four-company joint venture used two agents—a British lawyer and a Japanese trading company—to bribe Nigerian government officials in order to win a series of liquefied natural gas construction projects.[132] Together, the four multi-national corporations and the Japanese trading company paid a combined $1.7 billion in civil and criminal sanctions for their decade-long bribery scheme. In addition, the subsidiary of one of the companies pleaded guilty and a number of individuals, including the British lawyer and the former CEO of one of the companies' subsidiaries, received significant prison terms. Similarly, a medical device manufacturer entered into a deferred prosecution agreement as the result of corrupt payments it authorized its local Chinese distributor to pay to Chinese officials.[133] Another company, a manufacturer of specialty chemicals, committed multiple FCPA violations through its agents in Iraq: a Canadian national and the Canadian's companies. Among other acts, the Canadian national paid and promised to pay more than $1.5 million in bribes to officials of the Iraqi Ministry of Oil to secure sales of a fuel additive. Both the company and the Canadian national pleaded guilty to criminal charges and resolved civil enforcement actions by SEC.[134] In another case, the U.S. subsidiary of a Swiss freight forwarding company was charged with paying bribes on behalf of its customers in several countries.[135] Although the U.S. subsidiary was not an issuer under the FCPA, it was an "agent" of several U.S. issuers and was thus charged directly with violating the FCPA. Charges against the freight forwarding company and seven of its customers resulted in over $236.5 million in sanctions.[136]

Because Congress anticipated the use of third-party agents in bribery schemes—for example, to avoid actual knowledge of a bribe—it defined the term "knowing" in a way that prevents individuals and businesses from avoiding liability by putting "any person" between themselves and the foreign officials.[137] Under the FCPA, a person's state of mind is "knowing" with respect to conduct, a circumstance, or a result if the person:

- is aware that [he] is engaging in such conduct, that such circumstance exists, or that such result is substantially certain to occur; or
- has a firm belief that such circumstance exists or that such result is substantially certain to occur.[138]

Thus, a person has the requisite knowledge when he is aware of a high probability of the existence of such circumstance, unless the person actually believes that such circumstance does not exist.[139] As Congress made clear, it meant to impose liability not only on those with actual knowledge of wrongdoing, but also on those who purposefully avoid actual knowledge:

> [T]he so-called "head-in-the-sand" problem—variously described in the pertinent authorities as "conscious disregard," "willful blindness" or "deliberate ignorance"—should be covered so that management officials could not take refuge from the Act's prohibitions by their unwarranted obliviousness to any action (or inaction), language or other "signaling device" that should reasonably alert them of the "high probability" of an FCPA violation.[140]

Common red flags associated with third parties include:

- excessive commissions to third-party agents or consultants;
- unreasonably large discounts to third-party distributors;
- third-party "consulting agreements" that include only vaguely described services;
- the third-party consultant is in a different line of business than that for which it has been engaged;
- the third party is related to or closely associated with the foreign official;
- the third party became part of the transaction at the express request or insistence of the foreign official;
- the third party is merely a shell company incorporated in an offshore jurisdiction; and
- the third party requests payment to offshore bank accounts.

Businesses may reduce the FCPA risks associated with third-party agents by implementing an effective compliance program, which includes due diligence of any prospective foreign agents.

United States v. Kozeny, *et al.*

In December 2011, the U S Court of Appeals for the Second Circuit upheld a conscious avoidance instruction given during the 2009 trial of a businessman who was convicted of conspiring to violate the FCPA's anti-bribery provisions by agreeing to make payments to Azeri officials in a scheme to encourage the privatization of the Azerbaijan Republic's state oil company. The court of appeals found that the instruction did not lack a factual predicate, citing evidence and testimony at trial demonstrating that the defendant knew corruption was pervasive in Azerbaijan; that he was aware of his business partner's reputation for misconduct; that he had created two U.S. companies in order to shield himself and other investors from potential liability for payments made in violation of the FCPA; and that the defendant expressed concerns during a conference call about whether his business partner and company were bribing officials.

The court of appeals also rejected the defendant's contention that the conscious avoidance charge had improperly permitted the jury to convict him based on negligence, explaining that ample evidence in the record showed that the defendant had "serious concerns" about the legality of his partner's business practices "and worked to avoid learning exactly what [he] was doing," and noting that the district court had specifically instructed the jury not to convict based on negligence.

What Affirmative Defenses Are Available?

The FCPA's anti-bribery provisions contain two affirmative defenses: (1) that the payment was lawful under the written laws of the foreign country (the "local law" defense), and (2) that the money was spent as part of demonstrating a product or performing a contractual obligation (the "reasonable and bona fide business expenditure" defense). Because these are affirmative defenses, the defendant bears the burden of proving them.

The Local Law Defense

For the local law defense to apply, a defendant must establish that "the payment, gift, offer, or promise of anything of value that was made, was lawful under the written laws and regulations of the foreign official's, political party's, party official's, or candidate's country."[141] The defendant must establish that the payment was lawful under the foreign country's written laws and regulations at the time of the offense. In creating the local law defense in 1988, Congress sought "to make clear that the absence of written laws in a foreign official's country would not by itself be sufficient to satisfy this defense."[142] Thus, the fact that bribes may not be prosecuted under local law is insufficient to establish the defense. In practice, the local law defense arises infrequently, as the written laws and regulations of countries rarely, if ever, permit corrupt payments. Nevertheless, if a defendant can establish that conduct that otherwise falls within the scope of the FCPA's anti-bribery provisions was lawful under written, local law, he or she would have a defense to prosecution.

In *United States v. Kozeny*, the defendant unsuccessfully sought to assert the local law defense regarding the law of Azerbaijan. The parties disputed the contents and applicability of Azeri law, and each presented expert reports and testimony on behalf of their conflicting interpretations. The court ruled that the defendant could not invoke the FCPA's affirmative defense because Azeri law did not actually legalize the bribe payment. The court concluded that an exception under Azeri law relieving bribe payors who voluntarily disclose bribe payments to the authorities of criminal liability did not make the bribes legal.[143]

Reasonable and Bona Fide Expenditures

The FCPA allows companies to provide reasonable and bona fide travel and lodging expenses to a foreign official, and it is an affirmative defense where expenses are directly related to the promotion, demonstration, or explanation of a company's products or services, or are related to a company's execution or performance of a contract with a foreign government or agency.[144] Trips that are primarily for personal entertainment purposes, however, are not bona fide business expenses and may violate the FCPA's anti-bribery provisions.[145] Moreover, when expenditures, bona fide or not, are mischaracterized in a company's books and records, or where unauthorized or improper expenditures occur due to a failure to implement adequate internal controls, they may also violate the FCPA's accounting provisions. Purposeful mischaracterization of expenditures may also, of course, indicate a corrupt intent.

DOJ and SEC have consistently recognized that businesses, both foreign and domestic, are permitted to pay for reasonable expenses associated with the promotion of their products and services or the execution of existing contracts. In addition, DOJ has frequently provided guidance about legitimate promotional and contract-related expenses— addressing travel and lodging expenses in particular— through several opinion procedure releases. Under the circumstances presented in those releases,[146] DOJ opined that the following types of expenditures on behalf of foreign officials did not warrant FCPA enforcement action:

- travel and expenses to visit company facilities or operations;
- travel and expenses for training; and
- product demonstration or promotional activities, including travel and expenses for meetings.

Whether any particular payment is a bona fide expenditure necessarily requires a fact-specific analysis. But the following non-exhaustive list of safeguards, compiled from several releases, may be helpful to businesses in evaluating whether a particular expenditure is appropriate or may risk violating the FCPA:

- Do not select the particular officials who will participate in the party's proposed trip or program[147] or else select them based on pre-determined, merit-based criteria.[148]
- Pay all costs directly to travel and lodging vendors and/or reimburse costs only upon presentation of a receipt.[149]
- Do not advance funds or pay for reimbursements in cash.[150]
- Ensure that any stipends are reasonable approximations of costs likely to be incurred[151] and/or that expenses are limited to those that are necessary and reasonable.[152]
- Ensure the expenditures are transparent, both within the company and to the foreign government.[153]
- Do not condition payment of expenses on any action by the foreign official.[154]
- Obtain written confirmation that payment of the expenses is not contrary to local law.[155]

- Provide no additional compensation, stipends, or spending money beyond what is necessary to pay for actual expenses incurred.[156]
- Ensure that costs and expenses on behalf of the foreign officials will be accurately recorded in the company's books and records.[157]

In sum, while certain expenditures are more likely to raise red flags, they will not give rise to prosecution if they are (1) reasonable, (2) bona fide, and (3) directly related to (4) the promotion, demonstration, or explanation of products or services or the execution or performance of a contract.[158]

What Are Facilitating or Expediting Payments?

The FCPA's bribery prohibition contains a narrow exception for "facilitating or expediting payments" made in furtherance of routine governmental action.[159] The facilitating payments exception applies only when a payment is made to further "routine governmental action" that involves non-discretionary acts.[160] Examples of "routine governmental action" include processing visas, providing police protection or mail service, and supplying utilities like phone service, power, and water. Routine government action does *not* include a decision to award new business or to continue business with a particular party.[161] Nor does it include acts that are within an official's discretion or that would constitute misuse of an official's office.[162] Thus, paying an official a small amount to have the power turned on at a factory might be a facilitating payment; paying an inspector to ignore the fact that the company does not have a valid permit to operate the factory would not be a facilitating payment.

Examples of "Routine Governmental Action"

An action which is ordinarily and commonly performed by a foreign official in—

- obtaining permits, licenses, or other official documents to qualify a person to do business in a foreign country;
- processing governmental papers, such as visas and work orders;
- providing police protection, mail pickup and delivery, or scheduling inspections associated with contract performance or inspections related to transit of goods across country;

- providing phone service, power and water supply, loading and unloading cargo, or protecting perishable products or commodities from deterioration; or
- actions of a similar nature

Whether a payment falls within the exception is not dependent on the size of the payment, though size can be telling, as a large payment is more suggestive of corrupt intent to influence a non-routine governmental action. But, like the FCPA's anti-bribery provisions more generally, the facilitating payments exception focuses on the *purpose* of the payment rather than its value. For instance, an Oklahoma-based corporation violated the FCPA when its subsidiary paid Argentine customs officials approximately $166,000 to secure customs clearance for equipment and materials that lacked required certifications or could not be imported under local law and to pay a lower-than-applicable duty rate. The company's Venezuelan subsidiary had also paid Venezuelan customs officials approximately $7,000 to permit the importation and exportation of equipment and materials not in compliance with local regulations and to avoid a full inspection of the imported goods.[163] In another case, three subsidiaries of a global supplier of oil drilling products and services were criminally charged with authorizing an agent to make at least 378 corrupt payments (totaling approximately $2.1 million) to Nigerian Customs Service officials for preferential treatment during the customs process, including the reduction or elimination of customs duties.[164]

Labeling a bribe as a "facilitating payment" in a company's books and records does not make it one. A Swiss offshore drilling company, for example, recorded payments to its customs agent in the subsidiary's "facilitating payment" account, even though company personnel believed the payments were, in fact, bribes. The company was charged with violating both the FCPA's anti-bribery and accounting provisions.[165]

Although true facilitating payments are not illegal under the FCPA, they may still violate local law in the countries where the company is operating, and the OECD's Working Group on Bribery recommends that all countries encourage companies to prohibit or discourage facilitating payments, which the United States has done regularly.[166] In addition, other countries' foreign bribery laws, such as the United Kingdom's, may not contain an exception for facilitating payments.[167] Individuals and companies should therefore be aware that although true facilitating payments are permissible under the FCPA, they may still subject a company or individual to sanctions. As with any expenditure, facilitating payments may still violate the FCPA if they are not properly recorded in an issuer's books and records.[168]

Hypothetical: Facilitating Payments

Company A is a large multi-national mining company with operations in Foreign Country, where it recently identified a significant new ore deposit. It has ready buyers for the new ore but has limited capacity to get it to market. In order to increase the size and speed of its ore export, Company A will need to build a new road from its facility to the port that can accommodate larger trucks. Company A retains an agent in Foreign Country to assist it in obtaining the required permits, including an environmental permit, to build the road. The agent informs Company A's vice president for international operations that he plans to make a one-time small cash payment to a clerk in the relevant government office to ensure that the clerk files and stamps the permit applications expeditiously, as the agent has experienced delays of three months when he has not made this "grease" payment. The clerk has no discretion about whether to file and stamp the permit applications once the requisite filing fee has been paid. The vice president authorizes the payment.

A few months later, the agent tells the vice president that he has run into a problem obtaining a necessary environmental permit. It turns out that the planned road construction would adversely impact an environmentally sensitive and protected local wetland. While the problem could be overcome by rerouting the road, such rerouting would cost Company A $1 million more and would slow down construction by six months. It would also increase the transit time for the ore and reduce the number of monthly shipments. The agent tells the vice president that he is good friends with the director of Foreign Country's Department of Natural Resources and that it would only take a modest cash payment to the director and the "problem would go away." The vice president authorizes the payment, and the agent makes it. After receiving the payment, the director issues the permit, and Company A constructs its new road through the wetlands.

Was the payment to the clerk a violation of the FCPA?

No Under these circumstances, the payment to the clerk would qualify as a facilitating payment, since it is a one-time, small payment to obtain a routine, non-discretionary governmental service that Company A is entitled to receive (i e , the stamping and filing of the permit application).

However, while the payment may qualify as an exception to the FCPA's anti-bribery provisions, it may violate other laws, both in Foreign Country and elsewhere In addition, if the payment is not accurately recorded, it could violate the FCPA's books and records provision.

Was the payment to the director a violation of the FCPA?

Yes. The payment to the director of the Department of Natural Resources was in clear violation of the FCPA, since it was designed to corruptly influence a foreign official into improperly approving a permit. The issuance of the environmental permit was a discretionary act, and indeed, Company A should not have received it. Company A, its vice president, and the local agent may all be prosecuted for authorizing and paying the bribe.

Does the FCPA Apply to Cases of Extortion or Duress?

Situations involving extortion or duress will not give rise to FCPA liability because a payment made in response to true extortionate demands under imminent threat of physical harm cannot be said to have been made with corrupt intent or for the purpose of obtaining or retaining business.[169] In enacting the FCPA, Congress recognized that real-world situations might arise in which a business is compelled to pay an official in order to avoid threats to health and safety. As Congress explained, "a payment to an official to keep an oil rig from being dynamited should not be held to be made with the requisite corrupt purpose."[170]

Mere *economic* coercion, however, does not amount to extortion. As Congress noted when it enacted the FCPA: "The defense that the payment was demanded on the part of a government official as a price for gaining entry into a market or to obtain a contract would not suffice since at some point the U.S. company would make a conscious decision whether or not to pay a bribe."[171] The fact that the payment was "first proposed by the recipient ... does not alter the corrupt purpose on the part of the person paying the bribe."[172]

This distinction between extortion and economic coercion was recognized by the court in *United States v. Kozeny*. There, the court concluded that although an individual who makes a payment under duress (i.e., upon threat of physical harm) will not be criminally liable under the FCPA,[173] a bribe payor who claims payment was demanded as a price for gaining market entry or obtaining a contract "cannot argue that he lacked the intent to bribe the official because he made the 'conscious decision' to pay the official."[174] While the bribe payor in this situation "could have turned his back and walked away," in the oil rig example, "he could not."[175]

Businesses operating in high-risk countries may face real threats of violence or harm to their employees, and payments made in response to imminent threats to health or safety do not violate the FCPA.[176] If such a situation arises, and to ensure the safety of its employees, companies should immediately contact the appropriate U.S. embassy for assistance.

Principles of Corporate Liability for Anti-Bribery Violations

General principles of corporate liability apply to the FCPA. Thus, a company is liable when its directors, officers, employees, or agents, acting within the scope of their employment, commit FCPA violations intended, at least in part, to benefit the company.[177] Similarly, just as with any other statute, DOJ and SEC look to principles of parent-subsidiary and successor liability in evaluating corporate liability.

Parent-Subsidiary Liability

There are two ways in which a parent company may be liable for bribes paid by its subsidiary. First, a parent may have participated sufficiently in the activity to be directly liable for the conduct—as, for example, when it directed its subsidiary's misconduct or otherwise directly participated in the bribe scheme.

Second, a parent may be liable for its subsidiary's conduct under traditional agency principles. The fundamental characteristic of agency is control.[178] Accordingly, DOJ and SEC evaluate the parent's control—including the parent's knowledge and direction of the subsidiary's actions, both generally and in the context of the specific transaction— when evaluating whether a subsidiary is an agent of the parent. Although the formal relationship between the parent and subsidiary is important in this analysis, so are the practical realities of how the parent and subsidiary actually interact.

If an agency relationship exists, a subsidiary's actions and knowledge are imputed to its parent.[179] Moreover, under traditional principles of *respondeat superior*, a company is liable for the acts of its agents, including its employees, undertaken within the scope of their employment and intended, at least in part, to benefit the company.[180] Thus, if an agency relationship exists between a parent and a subsidiary, the parent is liable for bribery committed by the subsidiary's employees. For example, SEC brought an administrative action against a parent for bribes paid by the president of its indirect, wholly owned subsidiary. In that matter, the subsidiary's president reported directly to the CEO of the parent issuer, and the issuer routinely identified the president as a member of its senior management in its annual filing with SEC and in annual reports. Additionally, the parent's legal department approved the retention of the third-party agent through whom the bribes were arranged despite a lack of documented due diligence and an agency agreement that violated corporate policy; also, an official of the parent approved one of the payments to the third-party agent.[181] Under these circumstances, the parent company had sufficient knowledge and control of its subsidiary's actions to be liable under the FCPA.

Successor Liability

Companies acquire a host of liabilities when they merge with or acquire another company, including those arising out of contracts, torts, regulations, and statutes. As a general legal matter, when a company merges with or acquires another company, the successor company assumes the predecessor company's liabilities.[182] Successor liability is an integral component of corporate law and, among other things, prevents companies from avoiding liability by reorganizing.[183] Successor liability applies to all kinds of civil and criminal liabilities,[184] and FCPA violations are no exception. Whether successor liability applies to a particular corporate transaction depends on the facts and the applicable state, federal, and foreign law. Successor liability does not, however, create liability where none existed before. For example, if an issuer were to acquire a foreign company that was not previously subject to the FCPA's jurisdiction, the mere acquisition of that foreign company would not retroactively create FCPA liability for the acquiring issuer.

DOJ and SEC encourage companies to conduct pre-acquisition due diligence and improve compliance programs and internal controls after acquisition for a variety of reasons. First, due diligence helps an acquiring company to accurately value the target company. Contracts obtained through bribes may be legally unenforceable, business obtained illegally may be lost when bribe payments are stopped, there may be liability for prior illegal conduct, and the prior corrupt acts may harm the acquiring company's reputation and future business prospects. Identifying these issues before an acquisition allows companies to better evaluate any potential post-acquisition liability and thus properly assess the target's value.[185] Second, due diligence reduces the risk that the acquired company will continue to pay bribes. Proper pre-acquisition due diligence can identify business and regional risks and can also lay the foundation for a swift and successful post-acquisition integration into the acquiring company's corporate control and compliance environment. Third, the consequences of potential violations uncovered through due diligence can be handled by the parties in an orderly and efficient manner through negotiation of the costs and responsibilities for the investigation and remediation. Finally, comprehensive due diligence demonstrates a genuine commitment to uncovering and preventing FCPA violations.

In a significant number of instances, DOJ and SEC have declined to take action against companies that voluntarily disclosed and remediated conduct and cooperated with DOJ and SEC in the merger and acquisition context.[186] And DOJ and SEC have only taken action against successor companies in limited circumstances, generally in cases involving egregious and sustained violations or where the successor company directly participated in the violations or failed to stop the misconduct from continuing after the acquisition.

In one case, a U.S.-based issuer was charged with books and records and internal controls violations for continuing a kickback scheme originated by its predecessor.[187] Another recent case involved a merger between two tobacco leaf merchants, where prior to the merger each company committed FCPA violations through its foreign subsidiaries, involving multiple countries over the course of many years. At each company, the bribes were directed by the parent company's senior management. The two issuers then merged to form a new public company.

Under these circumstances—the merger of two public companies that had each engaged in bribery—both the new entity and the foreign subsidiaries were liable under the FCPA. The new parent entered into a non-prosecution agreement with DOJ and settled a civil action with SEC, while the company's subsidiaries, which also merged, pleaded guilty.[188]

Practical Tips to Reduce FCPA Risk in Mergers and Acquisitions

Companies pursuing mergers or acquisitions can take certain steps to identify and potentially reduce FCPA risks:

- M&A Opinion Procedure Release Requests: One option is to seek an opinion from DOJ in anticipation of a potential acquisition, such as occurred with Opinion Release 08-02.

That case involved special circumstances, namely, severely limited pre-acquisition due diligence available to the potential acquiring company, and, because it was an opinion release (i e , providing certain assurances by DOJ concerning prospective conduct), it necessarily imposed demanding standards and prescriptive timeframes in return for specific assurances from DOJ, which SEC, as a matter of discretion, also honors. Thus, obtaining an opinion from DOJ can be a good way to address specific due diligence challenges, but, because of the nature of such an opinion, it will likely contain more stringent requirements than may be necessary in all circumstances.

- M&A Risk-Based FCPA Due Diligence and Disclosure: As a practical matter, most acquisitions will typically not require the type of prospective assurances contained in an opinion from DOJ DOJ and SEC encourage companies engaging in mergers and acquisitions to: (1) conduct thorough risk-based FCPA and anti-corruption due diligence on potential new business acquisitions; (2) ensure that the acquiring company's code of conduct and compliance policies and procedures regarding the FCPA and other anti-corruption laws apply as quickly as is practicable to newly acquired businesses or merged entities; (3) train the directors, officers, and employees of newly acquired businesses or merged entities, and when appropriate, train agents and business partners, on the FCPA and other relevant anti-corruption laws and the company's code of conduct and compliance policies and procedures; (4) conduct an FCPA-specific audit of all newly acquired or merged businesses as quickly as practicable; and (5) disclose any corrupt payments discovered as part of its due diligence of newly acquired entities or merged entities. DOJ and SEC will give meaningful credit to companies who undertake these actions, and, in appropriate circumstances, DOJ and SEC may consequently decline to bring enforcement actions.

More often, DOJ and SEC have pursued enforcement actions against the predecessor company (rather than the acquiring company), particularly when the acquiring company uncovered and timely remedied the violations or when the government's investigation of the predecessor company preceded the acquisition. In one such case, an Ohio-based health care company's due diligence of an acquisition target uncovered FCPA violations by the target's subsidiary, and, before the merger was completed, the subsidiary's violations were disclosed to DOJ and SEC. The subsidiary pleaded guilty and paid a $2 million criminal fine,[189] the acquisition target settled with SEC and paid a $500,000 civil penalty,[190] and no successor liability was sought against the acquiring entity. In another case, a Pennsylvania-based issuer that supplied heating and air conditioning products and services was subject to an ongoing investigation by DOJ and SEC at the time that it was acquired; DOJ and SEC resolved enforcement actions only against the predecessor company, which had by that time become a wholly owned subsidiary of the successor company.[191] DOJ and SEC have also brought actions only against a predecessor company where its FCPA violations are discovered after acquisition. For example, when a Florida-based U.S. company discovered in post-acquisition due diligence that the telecommunications company (a domestic concern) it had acquired had engaged in foreign bribery, the successor company disclosed the FCPA violations to DOJ. It then conducted an internal investigation, cooperated fully with DOJ, and took appropriate remedial action— including terminating senior management at the acquired company. No enforcement action was taken against the successor, but the predecessor company pleaded guilty to one count of violating the FCPA and agreed to pay a $2 million fine.[192] Later, four executives from the predecessor company were convicted of FCPA violations, three of whom received terms of imprisonment.[193] On occasion, when an enforcement action has been taken against a predecessor company, the successor seeks assurances that it will not be subject to a future enforcement action. In one such case, a Dutch predecessor resolved FCPA charges with DOJ through a deferred prosecution agreement.[194] While both the predecessor and successor signed the agreement, which included a commitment to ongoing cooperation and an improved compliance program, only the predecessor company was charged; in signing the agreement, the successor company gained the certainty of conditional release from criminal liability, even though it was not being pursued for FCPA violations.[195] In another case, after a Connecticut-based company uncovered FCPA violations by a California company it sought to acquire, both companies voluntarily disclosed the conduct to DOJ and SEC.[196] The predecessor company resolved its criminal liability through a non-prosecution agreement with DOJ that included an $800,000 monetary penalty and also settled with SEC, paying a total of $1.1 million in disgorgement, pre-judgment interest, and civil penalties. The successor company proceeded with the acquisition and separately entered into a non-prosecution agreement with DOJ in which it agreed, among other things, to ensure full performance of the predecessor company's non-prosecution agreement. This agreement provided certainty to the successor concerning its FCPA liability.[197] Importantly, a successor company's voluntary disclosure, appropriate due diligence, and implementation of an effective compliance program may also decrease the likelihood of an enforcement action regarding an acquired company's post-acquisition conduct when pre-acquisition due diligence is not possible.[198]

Hypothetical: Successor Liability Where Acquired Company Was Not Previously Subject to the FCPA

Company A is a Delaware corporation with its principal offices in the United States and whose shares are listed on a national U S exchange. Company A is considering acquiring Foreign Company, which is not an issuer or a domestic concern. Foreign Company takes no actions within the United States that would make it subject to territorial jurisdiction. Company A's proposed acquisition would make Foreign Company a subsidiary of Company A.

Scenario 1:

Prior to acquiring Foreign Company, Company A engages in extensive due diligence of Foreign Company, including: (1) having its legal, accounting, and compliance departments review Foreign Company's sales and financial data, its customer contracts, and its third-party and distributor agreements; (2) performing a risk-based analysis of Foreign Company's customer base; (3) performing an audit of selected transactions engaged in by Foreign Company; and (4) engaging in discussions with Foreign Company's general counsel, vice president of sales, and head of internal audit regarding all corruption risks, compliance efforts, and any other corruption-related issues that have surfaced at Foreign Company over the past ten years. This due diligence aims to determine whether Foreign Company has appropriate anti-corruption and compliance policies in place, whether Foreign Company's employees have been adequately trained regarding those policies, how Foreign Company ensures that those policies are followed, and what remedial actions are taken if the policies are violated. During the course of its due diligence, Company A learns that Foreign Company has made several potentially improper payments in the form of an inflated commission to a third-party agent in connection with a government contract with Foreign Country.

Immediately after the acquisition, Company A discloses the conduct to DOJ and SEC, suspends and terminates those employees and the third-party agent responsible for the payments, and makes certain that the illegal payments have stopped. It also quickly integrates Foreign Company into Company A's own robust internal controls, including its anti-corruption and compliance policies, which it communicates to its new employees through required online and in-person training in the local language. Company A also requires Foreign Company's third-party distributors and other agents to sign anti-corruption certifications, complete training, and sign new contracts that incorporate FCPA and anticorruption representations and warranties and audit rights.

Based on these facts, could DOJ or SEC prosecute Company A?

No. Although DOJ and SEC have jurisdiction over Company A because it is an issuer, neither could pursue Company A for conduct that occurred prior to its acquisition of Foreign Company. As Foreign Company was neither an issuer nor a domestic concern and was not subject to U.S. territorial jurisdiction, DOJ and SEC have no jurisdiction over its pre-acquisition misconduct. The acquisition of a company does not create jurisdiction where none existed before. Importantly, Company A's extensive pre-acquisition due diligence allowed it to identify and halt the corruption. As there was no continuing misconduct post-acquisition, the FCPA was not violated.

Scenario 2:

Company A performs only minimal and pro forma pre-acquisition due diligence. It does not conduct a risk-based analysis, and its review of Foreign Company's data, contracts, and third-party and distributor agreements is cursory. Company A acquires Foreign Company and makes it a wholly owned subsidiary. Although Company A circulates its compliance policies to all new personnel after the acquisition, it does not translate the compliance policies into the local language or train its new personnel or third-party agents on anti-corruption issues. A few months after the acquisition, an employee in Company A's international sales office (Sales Employee) learns from a legacy Foreign Company employee that for years the government contract that generated most of Foreign Company's revenues depended on inflated commissions to a third-party agent "to make the right person happy at Foreign Government Agency."

Sales Employee is told that unless the payments continue the business will likely be lost, which would mean that Company A's new acquisition would quickly become a financial failure. The payments continue for two years after the acquisition. After another employee of Company A reports the long-running bribe scheme to a director at Foreign Government Agency, Company A stops the payments and DOJ and SEC investigate.

Based on these facts, would DOJ or SEC charge Company A?

Yes. DOJ and SEC have prosecuted companies like Company A in similar circumstances. Any charges would not, however, be premised upon successor liability, but rather on Company A's post-acquisition bribe payments, which themselves created criminal and civil liability for Company A.

Scenario 3:

Under local law, Company A's ability to conduct pre-acquisition due diligence on Foreign Company is limited. In the due diligence it does conduct, Company A determines that Foreign Company is doing business in high-risk countries and in high-risk industries but finds no red flags specific to Foreign Company's operations. Post-acquisition, Company A conducts extensive due diligence and determines that Foreign Company had paid bribes to officials with Foreign Government Agency. Company A takes prompt action to remediate the problem, including following the measures set forth in Opinion Procedure Release No. 08-02. Among other actions, it voluntarily discloses the misconduct to DOJ and SEC, ensures all bribes are immediately stopped, takes remedial action against all parties involved in the corruption, and quickly incorporates Foreign Company into a robust compliance program and Company A's other internal controls.

Based on these facts, would DOJ or SEC prosecute Company A?

DOJ and SEC have declined to prosecute companies like Company A in similar circumstances Companies can follow the measures set forth in Opinion Procedure Release No 08-02, or seek their own opinions, where adequate pre-acquisition due diligence is not possible.

Hypothetical: Successor Liability Where Acquired Company Was Already Subject to the FCPA.

Both Company A and Company B are Delaware corporations with their principal offices in the United States Both companies' shares are listed on a national U S exchange.

Scenario 1:

Company A is considering acquiring several of Company B's business lines. Prior to the acquisition, Company A engages in extensive due diligence, including: (1) having its legal, accounting, and compliance departments review Company B's sales and financial data, its customer contracts, and its third-party and distributor agreements; (2) performing a risk-based analysis of Company B's customer base; (3) performing an audit of selected transactions engaged in by Company B; and (4) engaging in discussions with Company B's general counsel, vice president of sales, and head of internal audit regarding all corruption risks, compliance efforts, and any other major corruption-related issues that have surfaced at Company B over the past ten years. This due diligence aims to determine whether Company B has appropriate anti-corruption and compliance policies in place, whether Company B's employees have been adequately trained regarding those policies, how Company B ensures that those policies are followed, and what remedial actions are taken if the policies are violated.

During the course of its due diligence, Company A learns that Company B has made several potentially improper payments in connection with a government contract with Foreign Country. As a condition of the acquisition, Company A requires Company B to disclose the misconduct to the government. Company A makes certain that the illegal payments have stopped and quickly integrates Company B's business lines into Company A's own robust internal controls, including its anti-corruption and compliance policies, which it communicates to its new employees through required online and in-person training in the local language. Company A also requires Company B's third-party distributors and other agents to sign anti-corruption certifications, complete training, and sign new contracts that incorporate FCPA and anti-corruption representations and warranties and audit rights.

Based on these facts, would DOJ or SEC prosecute?

DOJ and SEC have declined to prosecute companies like Company A in similar circumstances. DOJ and SEC encourage companies like Company A to conduct extensive FCPA due diligence. By uncovering the corruption, Company A put itself in a favorable position, and, because the corrupt payments have stopped, Company A has no continuing liability. Whether DOJ and SEC might charge Company B depends on facts and circumstances beyond the scope of this hypothetical.

DOJ would consider its *Principles of Federal Prosecution of Business Organizations* and SEC would consider the factors contained in the *Seaboard Report*, both of which are discussed in Chapter 5. In general, the more egregious and long-standing the corruption, the more likely it is that DOJ and SEC would prosecute Company B.

In certain limited circumstances, DOJ and SEC have in the past declined to bring charges against acquired companies, recognizing that acquiring companies may bear much of the reputational damage and costs associated with such charges.

Scenario 2:

Company A plans to acquire Company B Although, as in Scenario 1, Company A conducts extensive due diligence, it does not uncover the bribery until after the acquisition Company A then makes certain that the illegal payments stop and voluntarily discloses the misconduct to DOJ and SEC It quickly integrates Company B into Company A's own robust internal controls, including its anti-corruption and compliance policies, which it communicates to its new employees through required online and in-person training in the local language Company A also requires Company B's third-party distributors and other agents to sign anti-corruption certifications, complete training, and sign new contracts that incorporate FCPA and anticorruption representations and warranties and audit rights.

Based on these facts, would DOJ or SEC prosecute?

Absent unusual circumstances not contemplated by this hypothetical, DOJ and SEC are unlikely to prosecute Company A for the pre-acquisition misconduct of Company B, provided that Company B still exists in a form that would allow it to be prosecuted separately (e.g., Company B is a subsidiary of Company A.) DOJ and SEC understand that no due diligence is perfect and that society benefits when companies with strong compliance programs acquire and improve companies with weak ones.

At the same time, however, neither the liability for corruption—nor the harms caused by it— are eliminated when one company acquires another. Whether DOJ and SEC will pursue a case against Company B (or, in unusual circumstances, Company A) will depend on consideration of all the factors in the *Principles of Federal Prosecution of Business Organizations* and the *Seaboard Report*, respectively.

Scenario 3:

Company A merges with Company B, which is in the same line of business and interacts with the same Foreign Government customers, and forms Company C Due diligence before the merger reveals that both Company A and Company B have been engaging in similar bribery In both cases, the bribery was extensive and known by high-level management within the companies.

Based on these facts, would DOJ or SEC prosecute?

Yes. DOJ and SEC have prosecuted companies like Company C on the basis of successor liability. Company C is a combination of two companies that both violated the FCPA, and their merger does not eliminate their liability. In addition, since Company C is an ongoing concern, DOJ and SEC may impose a monitorship to ensure that the bribery has ceased and a compliance program is developed to prevent future misconduct.

Additional Principles of Criminal Liability for Anti-Bribery Violations: Aiding and Abetting and Conspiracy

Under federal law, individuals or companies that aid or abet a crime, including an FCPA violation, are as guilty as if they had directly committed the offense themselves. The aiding and abetting statute provides that whoever "commits an offense against the United States or aids, abets, counsels, commands, induces or procures its commission," or "willfully causes an act to be done which if directly performed by him or another would be an offense against the United States," is punishable as a principal.[199] Aiding and abetting is not an independent crime, and the government must prove that an underlying FCPA violation was committed.[200]

Individuals and companies, including foreign nationals and companies, may also be liable for conspiring to violate the FCPA—i.e., for *agreeing* to commit an FCPA violation—even if they are not, or could not be, independently charged with a substantive FCPA violation. For instance, a foreign, non-issuer company could be convicted of conspiring with a domestic concern to violate the FCPA. Under certain circumstances, it could also be held liable for the domestic concern's substantive FCPA violations under *Pinkerton v. United States*, which imposes liability on a defendant for reasonably foreseeable crimes committed by a co-conspirator in furtherance of a conspiracy that the defendant joined.[201]

A foreign company or individual may be held liable for aiding and abetting an FCPA violation or for conspiring to violate the FCPA, even if the foreign company or individual did not take any act in furtherance of the corrupt payment while in the territory of the United States. In conspiracy cases, the United States generally has jurisdiction over all the conspirators where at least one conspirator is an issuer, domestic concern, or commits a reasonably foreseeable overt act within the United States.[202] For example, if a foreign company or individual conspires to violate the FCPA with someone who commits an overt act within the United States, the United States can prosecute the foreign company or individual for the conspiracy. The same principle applies to aiding and abetting violations. For instance, even though they took no action in the United States, Japanese and European companies were charged with conspiring with and aiding and abetting a domestic concern's FCPA violations.[203]

Additional Principles of Civil Liability for Anti-Bribery Violations: Aiding and Abetting and Causing

Both companies and individuals can be held civilly liable for aiding and abetting FCPA anti-bribery violations if they knowingly or recklessly provide substantial assistance to a violator.[204] Similarly, in the administrative proceeding context, companies and individuals may be held liable for causing FCPA violations.[205] This liability extends to the subsidiaries and agents of U.S. issuers. In one case, the U.S. subsidiary of a Swiss freight forwarding company was held civilly liable for paying bribes on behalf of its customers in several countries.[206] Although the U.S. subsidiary was not an issuer for purposes of the FCPA, it was an "agent" of several U.S. issuers. By paying bribes on behalf of its issuers' customers, the subsidiary both directly violated and aided and abetted the issuers' FCPA violations.

What Is the Applicable Statute of Limitations?

Statute of Limitations in Criminal Cases

The FCPA's anti-bribery and accounting provisions do not specify a statute of limitations for criminal actions. Accordingly, the general five-year limitations period set forth in 18 U.S.C. § 3282 applies to substantive criminal violations of the Act.[207]

In cases involving FCPA conspiracies, the government may be able to reach conduct occurring before the five-year limitations period applicable to conspiracies under 18 U.S.C. § 371. For conspiracy offenses, the government generally need prove only that one act in furtherance of the conspiracy occurred during the limitations period, thus enabling the government to prosecute bribes paid or accounting violations occurring more than five years prior to the filing of formal charges.[208]

There are at least two ways in which the applicable limitations period is commonly extended. First, companies or individuals cooperating with DOJ may enter into a tolling agreement that voluntarily extends the limitations period. Second, under 18 U.S.C. § 3292, the government may seek a court order suspending the statute of limitations posed in a criminal case for up to three years in order to obtain evidence from foreign countries. Generally, the suspension period begins when the official request is made by the U.S. government to the foreign authority and ends on the date on which the foreign authority takes final action on the request.[209]

Statute of Limitations in Civil Actions

In civil cases brought by SEC, the statute of limitations is set by 28 U.S.C. § 2462, which provides for a five-year limitation on any "suit or proceeding for the enforcement of any civil fine, penalty, or forfeiture." The five-year period begins to run "when the claim first accrued." The five-year limitations period applies to SEC actions seeking civil penalties, but it does not prevent SEC from seeking equitable remedies, such as an injunction or the disgorgement of ill-gotten gains, for conduct pre-dating the five-year period. In cases against individuals who are not residents of the United States, the statute is tolled for any period when the defendants are not "found within the United States in order that proper service may be made thereon."[210] Furthermore, companies or individuals cooperating with SEC may enter into tolling agreements that voluntarily extend the limitations period.

THE FCPA: ACCOUNTING PROVISIONS

In addition to the anti-bribery provisions, the FCPA contains accounting provisions applicable to public companies. The FCPA's accounting provisions operate in tandem with the anti-bribery provisions[211] and prohibit off-the-books accounting. Company management and investors rely on a company's financial statements and internal accounting controls to ensure transparency in the financial health of the business, the risks undertaken, and the transactions between the company and its customers and business partners. The accounting provisions are designed to "strengthen the accuracy of the corporate books and records and the reliability of the audit process which constitute the foundations of our system of corporate disclosure."[212]

The accounting provisions consist of two primary components. First, under the "books and records" provision, issuers must make and keep books, records, and accounts that, in reasonable detail, accurately and fairly reflect an issuer's transactions and dispositions of an issuer's assets.[213] Second, under the "internal controls" provision, issuers must devise and maintain a system of internal accounting controls sufficient to assure management's control, authority, and responsibility over the firm's assets.[214]

These components, and other aspects of the accounting provisions, are discussed in greater detail below.

Although the accounting provisions were originally enacted as part of the FCPA, they do not apply only to bribery-related violations. Rather, the accounting provisions ensure that all public companies account for all of their assets and liabilities accurately and in reasonable detail, and they form the backbone for most accounting fraud and issuer disclosure cases brought by DOJ and SEC.[215]

> In the past, "corporate bribery has been concealed by the falsification of corporate books and records" and the accounting provisions "remove[] this avenue of coverup "
>
> *Senate Report No. 95-114, at 3 (1977)*

What Is Covered by the Accounting Provisions?

Books and Records Provision

Bribes, both foreign and domestic, are often mischaracterized in companies' books and records. Section 13(b)(2)(A) of the Exchange Act (15 U.S.C. § 78m(b)(2)(A)), commonly called the "books and records" provision, requires issuers to "make and keep books, records, and accounts, which, in reasonable detail, accurately and fairly reflect the transactions and dispositions of the assets of the issuer."[216] The "in reasonable detail" qualification was adopted by Congress "in light of the concern that such a standard, if unqualified, might connote a degree of exactitude and precision which is unrealistic."[217] The addition of this phrase was intended to make clear "that the issuer's records should reflect transactions in conformity with accepted methods of recording economic events and effectively prevent off-the-books slush funds and payments of bribes."[218]

The term "reasonable detail" is defined in the statute as the level of detail that would "satisfy prudent officials in the conduct of their own affairs."[219] Thus, as Congress noted when it adopted this definition, "[t]he concept of reasonableness of necessity contemplates the weighing of a number of relevant factors, including the costs of compliance."[220]

Although the standard is one of reasonable detail, it is never appropriate to mischaracterize transactions in a company's books and records.[221] Bribes are often concealed under the guise of legitimate payments, such as commissions or consulting fees.

In instances where all the elements of a violation of the anti-bribery provisions are not met—where, for example, there was no use of interstate commerce—companies nonetheless may be liable if the improper payments are inaccurately recorded. Consistent with the FCPA's approach to prohibiting payments of any value that are made with a corrupt purpose, there is no materiality threshold under the books and records provision. In combination with the internal controls provision, the requirement that issuers maintain books and records that accurately and fairly reflect the corporation's transactions "assure[s], among other things, that the assets of the issuer are used for proper corporate purpose[s]."[222] As with the anti-bribery provisions, DOJ's and SEC's enforcement of the books and records provision has typically involved misreporting of either large bribe payments or widespread inaccurate recording of smaller payments made as part of a systemic pattern of bribery.

Bribes Have Been Mischaracterized as:

- Commissions or Royalties
- Consulting Fees
- Sales and Marketing Expenses
- Scientific Incentives or Studies
- Travel and Entertainment Expenses
- Rebates or Discounts
- After Sales Service Fees
- Miscellaneous Expenses
- Petty Cash Withdrawals

- Free Goods
- Intercompany Accounts
- Supplier / Vendor Payments
- Write-offs
- "Customs Intervention" Payments

Internal Controls Provision

The payment of bribes often occurs in companies that have weak internal control environments. Internal controls over financial reporting are the processes used by companies to provide reasonable assurances regarding the reliability of financial reporting and the preparation of financial statements. They include various components, such as: a control environment that covers the tone set by the organization regarding integrity and ethics; risk assessments; control activities that cover policies and procedures designed to ensure that management directives are carried out (e.g., approvals, authorizations, reconciliations, and segregation of duties); information and communication; and monitoring. Section 13(b)(2)(B) of the Exchange Act (15 U.S.C. § 78m(b)(2)(B)), commonly called the "internal controls" provision, requires issuers to:

> devise and maintain a system of internal accounting controls sufficient to provide reasonable assurances that—
>
> (i) transactions are executed in accordance with management's general or specific authorization;
>
> (ii) transactions are recorded as necessary (I) to permit preparation of financial statements in conformity with generally accepted accounting principles or any other criteria applicable to such statements, and (II) to maintain accountability for assets;
>
> (iii) access to assets is permitted only in accordance with management's general or specific authorization; and
>
> (iv) the recorded accountability for assets is compared with the existing assets at reasonable intervals and appropriate action is taken with respect to any differences ....[223]

Like the "reasonable detail" requirement in the books and records provision, the Act defines "reasonable assurances" as "such level of detail and degree of assurance as would satisfy prudent officials in the conduct of their own affairs."[224]

The Act does not specify a particular set of controls that companies are required to implement. Rather, the internal controls provision gives companies the flexibility to develop and maintain a system of controls that is appropriate to their particular needs and circumstances.

An effective compliance program is a critical component of an issuer's internal controls. Fundamentally, the design of a company's internal controls must take into account the operational realities and risks attendant to the company's business, such as: the nature of its products or services; how the products or services get to market; the nature of its work force; the degree of regulation; the extent of its government interaction; and the degree to which it has operations in countries with a high risk of corruption. A company's compliance program should be tailored to these differences. Businesses whose operations expose them to a high risk of corruption will necessarily devise and employ different internal controls than businesses that have a lesser exposure to corruption, just as a financial services company would be expected to devise and employ different internal controls than a manufacturer.

A 2008 case against a German manufacturer of industrial and consumer products illustrates a systemic internal controls problem involving bribery that was unprecedented in scale and geographic reach. From 2001 to 2007, the company created elaborate payment schemes—including slush funds, off-the-books accounts, and systematic payments to business consultants and other intermediaries—to facilitate bribery. Payments were made in ways that obscured their purpose and the ultimate recipients of the money. In some cases, employees obtained large amounts of cash from cash desks and then transported the cash in suitcases across international borders. Authorizations for some payments were placed on sticky notes and later removed to avoid any permanent record. The company made payments totaling approximately $1.36 billion through various mechanisms, including $805.5 million as bribes and $554.5 million for unknown purposes.[225] The company was charged with internal controls and books and records violations, along with anti-bribery violations, and paid over $1.6 billion to resolve the case with authorities in the United States and Germany.[226]

> Companies with ineffective internal controls often face risks of embezzlement and self-dealing by employees, commercial bribery, export control problems, and violations of other U.S. and local laws.

The types of internal control failures identified in the above example exist in many other cases where companies were charged with internal controls violations.[227] A 2010 case against a multi-national automobile manufacturer involved bribery that occurred over a long period of time in multiple countries.[228] In that case, the company used dozens of ledger accounts, known internally as "internal third party accounts," to maintain credit balances for the benefit of government officials.[229] The accounts were funded through several bogus pricing mechanisms, such as "price surcharges," "price inclusions," or excessive commissions.[230] The company also used artificial discounts or rebates on sales contracts to generate the money to pay the bribes.[231] The bribes also were made through phony sales intermediaries and corrupt business partners, as well as through the use of cash desks.[232] Sales executives would obtain cash from the company in amounts as high as hundreds of thousands of dollars, enabling the company to obscure the purpose and recipients of the money paid to government officials.[233] In addition to bribery charges, the company was charged with internal controls and books and records violations.

Good internal controls can prevent not only FCPA violations, but also other illegal or unethical conduct by the company, its subsidiaries, and its employees. DOJ and SEC have repeatedly brought FCPA cases that also involved other types of misconduct, such as financial fraud,[234] commercial bribery,[235] export controls violations,[236] and embezzlement or self-dealing by company employees.[237]

Potential Reporting and Anti-Fraud Violations

Issuers have reporting obligations under Section 13(a) of the Exchange Act, which requires issuers to file an annual report that contains comprehensive information about the issuer. Failure to properly disclose material information about the issuer's business, including material revenue, expenses, profits, assets, or liabilities related to bribery of foreign government officials, may give rise to anti-fraud and reporting violations under Sections 10(b) and 13(a) of the Exchange Act.

For example, a California-based technology company was charged with reporting violations, in addition to violations of the FCPA's anti-bribery and accounting provisions, when its bribery scheme led to material misstatements in its SEC filings.[238] The company was awarded contracts procured through bribery of Chinese officials that generated material revenue and profits. The revenue and profits helped the company offset losses incurred to develop new products expected to become the company's future source of revenue growth. The company improperly recorded the bribe payments as sales commission expenses in its books and records.

Companies engaged in bribery may also be engaged in activity that violates the anti-fraud and reporting provisions. For example, an oil and gas pipeline company and its employees engaged in a long-running scheme to use the company's petty cash accounts in Nigeria to make a variety of corrupt payments to Nigerian tax and court officials using false invoices.[239] The company and its employees also engaged in a fraudulent scheme to minimize the company's tax obligations in Bolivia by using false invoices to claim false offsets to its value-added tax obligations. The scheme resulted in material overstatements of the company's net income in the company's financial statements, which violated the Exchange Act's anti-fraud and reporting provisions. Both schemes also violated the books and records and internal controls provisions.

What Are Management's Other Obligations?

Sarbanes-Oxley Act of 2002

In 2002, in response to a series of accounting scandals involving U.S. companies, Congress enacted the SarbanesOxley Act (Sarbanes-Oxley or SOX),[240] which strengthened the accounting requirements for issuers. All issuers must comply with Sarbanes-Oxley's requirements, several of which have FCPA implications.

SOX Section 302 (15 U.S.C. § 7241)—Responsibility of Corporate Officers for the Accuracy and Validity of Corporate Financial Reports

Section 302 of Sarbanes-Oxley requires that a company's "principal officers" (typically the Chief Executive Officer (CEO) and Chief Financial Officer (CFO)) take responsibility for and certify the integrity of their company's financial reports on a quarterly basis. Under Exchange Act Rule 13a-14, which is commonly called the "SOX certification" rule, each periodic report filed by an issuer must include a certification signed by the issuer's principal executive officer and principal financial officer that, among other things, states that: (i) based on the officer's knowledge, the report contains no material misstatements or omissions; (ii) based on the officer's knowledge, the relevant financial statements are accurate in all material respects; (iii) internal controls are properly designed; and (iv) the certifying officers have disclosed to the issuer's audit committee and auditors all significant internal control deficiencies.

SOX Section 404 (15 U.S.C. § 7262)—Reporting on the State of a Company's Internal Controls over Financial Reporting

Sarbanes-Oxley also strengthened a company's required disclosures concerning the state of its internal control over financial reporting. Under

Section 404, issuers are required to present in their annual reports management's conclusion regarding the effectiveness of the company's internal controls over financial reporting. This statement must also assess the effectiveness of such internal controls and procedures. In addition, the company's independent auditor must attest to and report on its assessment of the effectiveness of the company's internal controls over financial reporting.

As directed by Section 404, SEC has adopted rules requiring issuers and their independent auditors to report to the public on the effectiveness of the company's internal controls over financial reporting.[241] These internal controls include those related to illegal acts and fraud—including acts of bribery—that could result in a material misstatement of the company's financial statements.[242] In 2007, SEC issued guidance on controls over financial reporting.[243]

SOX Section 802 (18 U.S.C. §§ 1519 and 1520)— Criminal Penalties for Altering Documents

Section 802 of Sarbanes-Oxley prohibits altering, destroying, mutilating, concealing, or falsifying records, documents, or tangible objects with the intent to obstruct, impede, or influence a potential or actual federal investigation. This section also prohibits any accountant from knowingly and willfully violating the requirement that all audit or review papers be maintained for a period of five years.

Who Is Covered by the Accounting Provisions?

Civil Liability for Issuers, Subsidiaries, and Affiliates

The FCPA's accounting provisions apply to every issuer that has a class of securities registered pursuant to Section 12 of the Exchange Act or that is required to file annual or other periodic reports pursuant to Section 15(d) of the Exchange Act.[244] These provisions apply to any issuer whose securities trade on a national securities exchange in the United States, including foreign issuers with exchange-traded American Depository Receipts.[245] They also apply to companies whose stock trades in the over-the-counter market in the United States and which file periodic reports with the Commission, such as annual and quarterly reports. Unlike the FCPA's anti-bribery provisions, the accounting provisions do not apply to private companies.[246]

Although the FCPA's accounting requirements are directed at "issuers," an issuer's books and records include those of its consolidated subsidiaries and affiliates. An issuer's responsibility thus extends to ensuring that subsidiaries or affiliates under its control, including foreign subsidiaries and joint ventures, comply with the accounting provisions. For instance, DOJ and SEC brought enforcement actions against a California company for violating the FCPA's accounting provisions when two Chinese joint ventures in which it was a partner paid more than $400,000 in bribes over a four-year period to obtain business in China.[247] Sales personnel in China made the illicit payments by obtaining cash advances from accounting personnel, who recorded the payments on the books as "business fees" or "travel and entertainment" expenses. Although the payments were made exclusively in China by Chinese employees of the joint venture, the California company failed to have adequate internal controls and failed to act on red flags indicating that its affiliates were engaged in bribery. The California company paid $1.15 million in civil disgorgement and a criminal monetary penalty of $1.7 million.

Companies may not be able to exercise the same level of control over a minority-owned subsidiary or affiliate as they do over a majority or wholly owned entity. Therefore, if a parent company owns 50% or less of a subsidiary or affiliate, the parent is only required to use good faith efforts to cause the minority-owned subsidiary or affiliate to devise and maintain a system of internal accounting controls consistent with the issuer's own obligations under the FCPA.[248] In evaluating an issuer's good faith efforts, all the circumstances—including "the relative degree of the issuer's ownership of the domestic or foreign firm and the laws and practices governing the business operations of the country in which such firm is located"—are taken into account.[249]

Civil Liability for Individuals and Other Entities

Companies (including subsidiaries of issuers) and individuals may also face civil liability for aiding and abetting or causing an issuer's violation of the accounting provisions.[250] For example, in April 2010, SEC charged four individuals—a Country Manager, a Senior Vice President of Sales, a Regional Financial Director, and an International Controller of a U.S. issuer—for their roles in schemes to bribe Kyrgyz and Thai government officials to purchase tobacco from their employer. The complaint alleged that, among other things, the individuals aided and abetted the issuer company's violations of the books and records and internal controls provisions by "knowingly provid[ing] substantial assistance to" the parent company.[251] All four executives settled the charges against them, consenting to the entry of final judgments permanently enjoining them from violating the accounting and anti-bribery provisions, with two executives paying civil penalties.[252] As in other areas of federal securities law, corporate officers also can be held liable as control persons.[253]

Similarly, in October 2011, SEC brought an administrative action against a U.S. water valve manufacturer and a former employee of the company's Chinese subsidiary for violations of the FCPA's accounting provisions.[254] The Chinese subsidiary had made improper payments to employees of certain design institutes to create design specifications that favored the company's valve products. The payments were disguised as sales commissions in the subsidiary's books and records, thereby causing the U.S. issuer's books and records to be inaccurate. The general manager of the subsidiary, who approved the payments and knew or should have known that they were improperly recorded, was ordered to cease-and-desist from committing or causing violations of the accounting provisions, among other charges.[255]

Additionally, individuals and entities can be held directly civilly liable for falsifying an issuer's books and records or for circumventing internal controls. Exchange Act Rule 13b2-1 provides: "No person shall, directly or indirectly, falsify or cause to be falsified, any book, record or account subject to [the books and records provision] of the Securities Exchange Act."[256] And Section 13(b)(5) of the Exchange Act (15 U.S.C. § 78m(b)(5)) provides that "[n]o person shall knowingly circumvent or knowingly fail to implement a system of internal accounting controls or knowingly falsify any book, record, or account …."[257] The Exchange Act defines "person" to include a "natural person, company, government, or political subdivision, agency, or instrumentality of a government."[258]

An issuer's officers and directors may also be held civilly liable for making false statements to a company's auditor. Exchange Act Rule 13b2-2 prohibits officers and directors from making (or causing to be made) materially false or misleading statements, including an omission of material facts, to an accountant. This liability arises in connection with any audit, review, or examination of a company's financial statements or in connection with the filing of any document with SEC.[259]

Finally, the principal executive and principal financial officer, or persons performing similar functions, can be held liable for violating Exchange Act Rule 13a-14 by signing false personal certifications required by SOX. Thus, for example, in January 2011, SEC charged the former CEO of a U.S. issuer for his role in schemes to bribe Iraqi government officials in connection with the United Nations Oil-For-Food Programme and to bribe Iraqi and Indonesian officials to purchase the company's fuel additives. There, the company used false invoices and sham consulting contracts to support large bribes that were passed on to foreign officials through an agent, and the bribes were mischaracterized as legitimate commissions and travel fees in the company's books and records. The officer directed and authorized the bribe payments and their false recording in the books and records. He also signed annual and quarterly SOX certifications in which he falsely represented that the company's financial statements were fairly presented and the company's internal controls sufficiently designed, as well as annual representations to the company's external auditors where he falsely stated that he complied with the company's code of ethics and was unaware of any violations of the code of ethics by anyone else. The officer was charged with aiding and abetting violations of the books and records and internal controls provisions, circumventing internal controls, falsifying books and records, making false statements to accountants, and signing false certifications.[260] He consented to the entry of an injunction and paid disgorgement and a civil penalty.[261] He also later pleaded guilty in the United Kingdom to conspiring to corrupt Iraqi and Indonesian officials.[262]

Criminal Liability for Accounting Violations

Criminal liability can be imposed on companies and individuals for knowingly failing to comply with the FCPA's books and records or internal controls provisions.[263] As with the FCPA's anti-bribery provisions, individuals are only subject to the FCPA's criminal penalties for violations of the accounting provisions if they acted "willfully."[264]

For example, a French company was criminally charged with failure to implement internal controls and failure to keep accurate books and records, among other violations.[265] As part of its deferred prosecution agreement, the company admitted to numerous internal control failures, including failure to implement sufficient anti-bribery compliance policies, maintain a sufficient system for the selection and approval of consultants, and conduct appropriate audits of payments to purported "business consultants."[266] Likewise, a German company pleaded guilty to internal controls and books and records violations where, from 2001 through 2007, it made payments totaling approximately $1.36 billion through various mechanisms, including $805.5 million as bribes and $554.5 million for unknown purposes.[267]

Individuals can be held criminally liable for accounting violations. For example, a former managing director of a U.S. bank's real estate business in China pleaded guilty to conspiring to evade internal accounting controls in order to transfer a multi-million dollar ownership interest in a Shanghai building to himself and a Chinese public official with whom he had a personal friendship. The former managing director repeatedly made false representations to his employer about the transaction and the ownership interests involved.[268]

Conspiracy and Aiding and Abetting Liability

As with the FCPA's anti-bribery provisions, companies (including subsidiaries of issuers) and individuals may face criminal liability for conspiring to commit or for aiding and abetting violations of the accounting provisions.

For example, the subsidiary of a Houston-based company pleaded guilty both to conspiring to commit and to aiding and abetting the company's books and records and anti-bribery violations.[269] The subsidiary paid bribes of over $4 million and falsely characterized the payments as "commissions," "fees," or "legal services," consequently causing the company's books and records to be inaccurate. Although the subsidiary was not an issuer and therefore could not be charged directly with an accounting violation, it was criminally liable for its involvement in the parent company's accounting violation.

Similarly, a U.S. subsidiary of a Swiss freight forwarding company that was not an issuer was charged with conspiring to commit and with aiding and abetting the books and records violations of its customers, who were issuers and therefore subject to the FCPA's accounting provisions.[270] The U.S. subsidiary substantially assisted the issuer-customers in violating the FCPA's books and records provision by masking the true nature of the bribe payments in the invoices it submitted to the issuer-customers.[271] The subsidiary thus faced criminal liability for its involvement in the issuer-customers' FCPA violations even though it was not itself subject to the FCPA's accounting provisions.

Auditor Obligations

All public companies in the United States must file annual financial statements that have been prepared in conformity with U.S. Generally Accepted Accounting Principles (U.S. GAAP). These accounting principles are among the most comprehensive in the world. U.S. GAAP requires an accounting of all assets, liabilities, revenue, and expenses as well as extensive disclosures concerning the company's operations and financial condition. A company's financial statements should be complete and fairly represent the company's financial condition.[272] Thus, under U.S. GAAP, any payments to foreign government officials must be properly accounted for in a company's books, records, and financial statements.

U.S. laws, including SEC Rules, require issuers to undergo an annual external audit of their financial statements and to make those audited financial statements available to the public by filing them with SEC. SEC Rules and the rules and standards issued by the Public Company Accounting Oversight Board (PCAOB) under SEC oversight, require external auditors to be independent of the companies that they audit. Independent auditors must comply with the rules and standards set forth by the PCAOB when they perform an audit of a public company. These audit standards govern, for example, the auditor's responsibility concerning material errors, irregularities, or illegal acts by a client and its officers, directors, and employees. Additionally, the auditor has a responsibility to obtain an understanding of an entity's internal controls over financial reporting as part of its audit and must communicate all significant deficiencies and material weaknesses identified during the audit to management and the audit committee.[273]

Under Section 10A of the Exchange Act, independent auditors who discover an illegal act, such as the payment of bribes to domestic or foreign government officials, have certain obligations in connection with their audits of public companies. [274] Generally, Section 10A requires auditors who become aware of illegal acts to report such acts to appropriate levels within the company and, if the company fails to take appropriate action, to notify SEC.

Other Related U.S. Laws

Businesses and individuals should be aware that conduct that violates the FCPA's anti-bribery or accounting provisions may also violate other statutes or regulations. Moreover, payments to foreign government officials and intermediaries may violate these laws even if all of the elements of an FCPA violation are not present.

Travel Act

The Travel Act, 18 U.S.C. § 1952, prohibits travel in interstate or foreign commerce or using the mail or any facility in interstate or foreign commerce, with the intent to distribute the proceeds of any unlawful activity or to promote, manage, establish, or carry on any unlawful activity.[275] "Unlawful activity" includes violations of not only the FCPA, but also state commercial bribery laws. Thus, bribery between private commercial enterprises may, in some circumstances, be covered by the Travel Act. Said differently, if a company pays kickbacks to an employee of a private company who is not a foreign official, such privateto-private bribery could possibly be charged under the Travel Act.

DOJ has previously charged both individual and corporate defendants in FCPA cases with violations of the Travel Act.[276] For instance, an individual investor was convicted of conspiracy to violate the FCPA and the Travel Act in 2009 where the relevant "unlawful activity" under the Travel Act was an FCPA violation involving a bribery scheme in Azerbaijan.[277] Also in 2009, a California company that engaged in both bribery of foreign officials in violation of the FCPA and commercial bribery in violation of California state law pleaded guilty to conspiracy to violate the FCPA and the Travel Act, among other charges.[278]

Money Laundering

Many FCPA cases also involve violations of anti-money laundering statutes.[279] For example, two Florida executives of a Miami-based telecommunications company were convicted of FCPA and money laundering conduct where they conducted financial transactions involving the proceeds of specified unlawful activities—violations of the FCPA, the criminal bribery laws of Haiti, and wire fraud— in order to conceal and disguise these proceeds. Notably, although foreign officials cannot be prosecuted for FCPA violations,[280] three former Haitian officials involved in the same scheme were convicted of money laundering.[281]

Mail and Wire Fraud

The mail and wire fraud statutes may also apply. In 2006, for example, a wholly owned foreign subsidiary of a U.S. issuer pleaded guilty to both FCPA and wire fraud counts where the scheme included overbilling the subsidiary's customers—both government and private—and using part of the overcharged money to pay kickbacks to the customers' employees. The wire fraud charges alleged that the subsidiary had funds wired from its parent's Oregon bank account to off-the-books bank accounts in South Korea that were controlled by the subsidiary. The funds, amounting to almost $2 million, were then paid to managers of state-owned and private steel production companies in China and South Korea as illegal commission payments and kickbacks that were disguised as refunds, commissions, and other seemingly legitimate expenses.[282]

Certification and Reporting Violations

Certain other licensing, certification, and reporting requirements imposed by the U.S. government can also be implicated in the foreign bribery context. For example, as a condition of its facilitation of direct loans and loan guarantees to a foreign purchaser of U.S. goods and services, the Export-Import Bank of the United States requires the U.S. supplier to make certifications concerning commissions, fees, or other payments paid in connection with the financial assistance and that it has not and will not violate the FCPA.[283] A false certification may give rise to criminal liability for false statements.[284]

Similarly, manufacturers, exporters, and brokers of certain defense articles and services are subject to registration, licensing, and reporting requirements under the Arms Export Control Act (AECA), 22 U.S.C. § 2751, *et seq.*, and its implementing regulations, the International Traffic in Arms Regulations (ITAR), 22 C.F.R. § 120, *et seq.* For example, under AECA and ITAR, all manufacturers and exporters of defense articles and services must register with the Directorate of Defense Trade Controls. The sale of defense articles and services valued at $500,000 or more triggers disclosure requirements concerning fees and commissions, including bribes, in an aggregate amount of $100,000 or more.[285] Violations of AECA and ITAR can result in civil and criminal penalties.[286]

Tax Violations

Individuals and companies who violate the FCPA may also violate U.S. tax law, which explicitly prohibits tax deductions for bribes, such as false sales "commissions" deductions intended to conceal corrupt payments.[287] Internal Revenue Service-Criminal Investigation has been involved in a number of FCPA investigations involving tax violations, as well as other financial crimes like money laundering.

GUIDING PRINCIPLES OF ENFORCEMENT

What Does DOJ Consider When Deciding Whether to Open an Investigation or Bring Charges?

Whether and how DOJ will commence, decline, or otherwise resolve an FCPA matter is guided by the *Principles of Federal Prosecution* in the case of individuals, and the *Principles of Federal Prosecution of Business Organizations* in the case of companies.

DOJ Principles of Federal Prosecution

The *Principles of Federal Prosecution*, set forth in Chapter 9-27.000 of the U.S. Attorney's Manual,[288] provide guidance for DOJ prosecutors regarding initiating or declining prosecution, selecting charges, and plea-bargaining. The *Principles of Federal Prosecution* provide that prosecutors should recommend or commence federal prosecution if the putative defendant's conduct constitutes a federal offense and the admissible evidence will probably be sufficient to obtain and sustain a conviction unless (1) no substantial federal interest would be served by prosecution; (2) the person is subject to effective prosecution in another jurisdiction; or (3) an adequate non-criminal alternative to prosecution exists. In assessing the existence of a substantial federal interest, the prosecutor is advised to "weigh all relevant considerations," including the nature and seriousness of the offense; the deterrent effect of prosecution; the person's culpability in connection with the offense; the person's history with respect to criminal activity; the person's willingness to cooperate in the investigation or prosecution of others; and the probable sentence or other consequences if the person is convicted. The *Principles of Federal Prosecution* also set out the considerations to be weighed when deciding whether to enter into a plea agreement with an individual defendant, including the nature and seriousness of the offense and the person's willingness to cooperate, as well as the desirability of prompt and certain disposition of the case and the expense of trial and appeal.[289]

DOJ Principles of Federal Prosecution of Business Organizations

The *Principles of Federal Prosecution of Business Organizations*, set forth in Chapter 9-28.000 of the U.S. Attorney's Manual,[290] provide guidance regarding the resolution of cases involving corporate wrongdoing. The *Principles of Federal Prosecution of Business Organizations* recognize that resolution of corporate criminal cases by means other than indictment, including non-prosecution and deferred prosecution agreements, may be appropriate in certain circumstances. Nine factors are considered in conducting an investigation, determining whether to charge a corporation, and negotiating plea or other agreements:

- the nature and seriousness of the offense, including the risk of harm to the public;
- the pervasiveness of wrongdoing within the corporation, including the complicity in, or the condoning of, the wrongdoing by corporate management;
- the corporation's history of similar misconduct, including prior criminal, civil, and regulatory enforcement actions against it;
- the corporation's timely and voluntary disclosure of wrongdoing and its willingness to cooperate in the investigation of its agents;
- the existence and effectiveness of the corporation's pre-existing compliance program;
- the corporation's remedial actions, including any efforts to implement an effective corporate compliance program or improve an existing one, replace responsible management, discipline or terminate wrongdoers, pay restitution, and cooperate with the relevant government agencies;
- collateral consequences, including whether there is disproportionate harm to shareholders, pension holders, employees, and others not proven personally culpable, as well as impact on the public arising from the prosecution;
- the adequacy of the prosecution of individuals responsible for the corporation's malfeasance; and
- the adequacy of remedies such as civil or regulatory enforcement actions.

As these factors illustrate, in many investigations it will be appropriate for a prosecutor to consider a corporation's pre-indictment conduct, including voluntary disclosure, cooperation, and remediation, in determining whether to seek an indictment. In assessing a corporation's cooperation, prosecutors are prohibited from requesting attorney-client privileged materials with two exceptions—when a corporation or its employee asserts an advice-of-counsel defense and when the attorney-client communications were in furtherance of a crime or fraud. Otherwise, an organization's cooperation may only be assessed on the basis of whether it disclosed the *relevant facts* underlying an investigation—and not on the basis of whether it has waived its attorney-client privilege or work product protection.[291]

What Does SEC Consider When Deciding Whether to Open an Investigation or Bring Charges?

SEC's *Enforcement Manual*, published by SEC's Enforcement Division and available on SEC's website,[292] sets forth information about how SEC conducts investigations, as well as the guiding principles that SEC staff considers when determining whether to open or close an investigation and whether civil charges are merited. There are various ways that potential FCPA violations come to the attention of SEC staff, including: tips from informants or whistleblowers; information developed in other investigations; self-reports or public disclosures by companies; referrals from other offices or agencies; public sources, such as media reports and trade publications; and proactive investigative techniques, including risk-based initiatives. Investigations can be formal, such as where SEC has issued a formal order of investigation that authorizes its staff to issue investigative subpoenas for testimony and documents, or informal, such as where the staff proceeds with the investigation without the use of investigative subpoenas.

In determining whether to open an investigation and, if so, whether an enforcement action is warranted, SEC staff considers a number of factors, including: the statutes or rules potentially violated; the egregiousness of the potential violation; the potential magnitude of the violation; whether the potentially harmed group is particularly vulnerable or at risk; whether the conduct is ongoing; whether the conduct can be investigated efficiently and within the statute of limitations period; and whether other authorities, including federal or state agencies or regulators, might be better suited to investigate the conduct. SEC staff also may consider whether the case involves a possibly widespread industry practice that should be addressed, whether the case involves a recidivist, and whether the matter gives SEC an opportunity to be visible in a community that might not otherwise be familiar with SEC or the protections afforded by the securities laws.

For more information about the Enforcement Division's procedures concerning investigations, enforcement actions, and cooperation with other regulators, see the *Enforcement Manual* at http://www.sec.gov/divisions/enforce.shtml.

Self-Reporting, Cooperation, and Remedial Efforts

While the conduct underlying any FCPA investigation is obviously a fundamental and threshold consideration in deciding what, if any, action to take, both DOJ and SEC place a high premium on self-reporting, along with cooperation and remedial efforts, in determining the appropriate resolution of FCPA matters.

Criminal Cases

Under DOJ's *Principles of Federal Prosecution of Business Organizations*, federal prosecutors consider a company's cooperation in determining how to resolve a corporate criminal case. Specifically, prosecutors consider whether the company made a voluntary an d timely disclosure as well as the company's willingness to provide relevant information and evidence and identify relevant actors inside and outside the company, including senior executives. In addition, prosecutors may consider a company's remedial actions, including efforts to improve an existing compliance program or appropriate disciplining of wrongdoers.[293] A company's remedial measures should be meaningful and illustrate its recognition of the seriousness of the misconduct, for example, by taking steps to implement the personnel, operational, and organizational changes necessary to establish an awareness among employees that criminal conduct will not be tolerated.[294]

The *Principles of Federal Prosecution* similarly provide that prosecutors may consider an individual's willingness to cooperate in deciding whether a prosecution should be undertaken and how it should be resolved. Although a willingness to cooperate will not, by itself, generally relieve a person of criminal liability, it may be given "serious consideration" in evaluating whether to enter into a plea agreement with a defendant, depending on the nature and value of the cooperation offered.[295]

The U.S. Sentencing Guidelines similarly take into account an individual defendant's cooperation and voluntary disclosure. Under § 5K1.1, a defendant's cooperation, if sufficiently substantial, may justify the government filing a motion for a reduced sentence. And under § 5K2.16, a defendant's voluntary disclosure of an offense prior to its discovery—if the offense was unlikely to have been discovered otherwise—may warrant a downward departure in certain circumstances.

Chapter 8 of the Sentencing Guidelines, which governs the sentencing of organizations, takes into account an organization's remediation as part of an "effective compliance and ethics program." One of the seven elements of such a program provides that after the detection of criminal conduct, "the organization shall take reasonable steps to respond appropriately to the criminal conduct and to prevent further similar criminal conduct, including making any necessary modifications to the organization's compliance and ethics program."[296] Having an effective compliance and ethics program may lead to a three-point reduction in an organization's culpability score under § 8C2.5, which affects the fine calculation under the Guidelines. Similarly, an organization's self-reporting, cooperation, and acceptance of responsibility may lead to fine reductions under § 8C2.5(g) by decreasing the culpability score. Conversely, an organization will not qualify for the compliance program reduction when it unreasonably delayed reporting the offense.[297] Similar to § 5K1.1 for individuals, organizations can qualify for departures pursuant to § 8C4.1 of the Guidelines for cooperating in the prosecution of others.

Civil Cases

SEC's Framework for Evaluating Cooperation by Companies

SEC's framework for evaluating cooperation by companies is set forth in its 2001 Report of Investigation Pursuant to Section 21(a) of the Securities Exchange Act of 1934 and Commission Statement on the Relationship of Cooperation to Agency Enforcement Decisions, which is commonly known as the Seaboard Report.[298] The report, which explained the Commission's decision not to take enforcement action against a public company for certain accounting violations caused by its subsidiary, details the many factors SEC considers in determining whether, and to what extent, it grants leniency to companies for cooperating in its investigations and for related good corporate citizenship. Specifically, the report identifies four broad measures of a company's cooperation:

- self-policing prior to the discovery of the misconduct, including establishing effective compliance procedures and an appropriate tone at the top;
- self-reporting of misconduct when it is discovered, including conducting a thorough review of the nature, extent, origins, and consequences of the misconduct, and promptly, completely, and effectively disclosing the misconduct to the public, to regulatory agencies, and to self-regulatory organizations;
- remediation, including dismissing or appropriately disciplining wrongdoers, modifying and improving internal controls and

procedures to prevent recurrence of the misconduct, and appropriately compensating those adversely affected; and

- cooperation with law enforcement authorities, including providing SEC staff with all information relevant to the underlying violations and the company's remedial efforts.

Since every enforcement matter is different, this analytical framework sets forth general principles but does not limit SEC's broad discretion to evaluate every case individually on its own unique facts and circumstances. Similar to SEC's treatment of cooperating individuals, credit for cooperation by companies may range from taking no enforcement action to pursuing reduced sanctions in connection with enforcement actions.

SEC's Framework for Evaluating Cooperation by Individuals

In 2010, SEC announced a new cooperation program for individuals.[299] SEC staff has a wide range of tools to facilitate and reward cooperation by individuals, from taking no enforcement action to pursuing reduced sanctions in connection with enforcement actions. Although the evaluation of cooperation depends on the specific circumstances, SEC generally evaluates four factors to determine whether, to what extent, and in what manner to credit cooperation by individuals:

- the assistance provided by the cooperating individual in SEC's investigation or related enforcement actions, including, among other things: the value and timeliness of the cooperation, including whether the individual was the first to report the misconduct to SEC or to offer his or her cooperation; whether the investigation was initiated based upon the information or other cooperation by the individual; the quality of the cooperation, including whether the individual was truthful and the cooperation was complete; the time and resources conserved as a result of the individual's cooperation; and the nature of the cooperation, such as the type of assistance provided;
- the importance of the matter in which the individual provided cooperation;
- the societal interest in ensuring that the cooperating individual is held accountable for his or her misconduct, including the severity of the individual's misconduct, the culpability of the individual, and the efforts undertaken by the individual to remediate the harm; and

- the appropriateness of a cooperation credit in light of the profile of the cooperating individual.

Corporate Compliance Program

In a global marketplace, an effective compliance program is a critical component of a company's internal controls and is essential to detecting and preventing FCPA violations.[300] Effective compliance programs are tailored to the company's specific business and to the risks associated with that business. They are dynamic and evolve as the business and the markets change.

An effective compliance program promotes "an organizational culture that encourages ethical conduct and a commitment to compliance with the law."[301] Such a program protects a company's reputation, ensures investor value and confidence, reduces uncertainty in business transactions, and secures a company's assets.[302] A well-constructed, thoughtfully implemented, and consistently enforced compliance and ethics program helps prevent, detect, remediate, and report misconduct, including FCPA violations.

In addition to considering whether a company has self-reported, cooperated, and taken appropriate remedial actions, DOJ and SEC also consider the adequacy of a company's compliance program when deciding what, if any, action to take. The program may influence whether or not charges should be resolved through a deferred prosecution agreement (DPA) or non-prosecution agreement (NPA), as well as the appropriate length of any DPA or NPA, or the term of corporate probation. It will often affect the penalty amount and the need for a monitor or self-reporting.[303] As discussed above, SEC's *Seaboard Report* focuses, among other things, on a company's self-policing prior to the discovery of the misconduct, including whether it had established effective compliance procedures.[304] Likewise, three of the nine factors set forth in DOJ's *Principles of Federal Prosecution of Business Organizations* relate, either directly or indirectly, to a compliance program's design and implementation, including the pervasiveness of wrongdoing within the company, the existence and effectiveness of the company's pre-existing compliance program, and the company's remedial actions.[305] DOJ also considers the U.S.

Sentencing Guidelines' elements of an effective compliance program, as set forth in § 8B2.1 of the Guidelines.

These considerations reflect the recognition that a company's failure to prevent every single violation does not necessarily mean that a particular company's compliance program was not generally effective. DOJ and SEC understand that "no compliance program can ever prevent all criminal activity by a corporation's employees,"[306] and they do not hold companies to a standard of perfection. An assessment of a company's compliance program, including its design and good faith implementation and enforcement, is an important part of the government's assessment of whether a violation occurred, and if so, what action should be taken. In appropriate circumstances, DOJ and SEC may decline to pursue charges against a company based on the company's effective compliance program, or may otherwise seek to reward a company for its program, even when that program did not prevent the particular underlying FCPA violation that gave rise to the investigation.[307]

DOJ and SEC have no formulaic requirements regarding compliance programs. Rather, they employ a common-sense and pragmatic approach to evaluating compliance programs, making inquiries related to three basic questions:

- Is the company's compliance program well designed?
- Is it being applied in good faith?
- Does it work?[308]

This guide contains information regarding some of the basic elements DOJ and SEC consider when evaluating compliance programs. Although the focus is on compliance with the FCPA, given the existence of anti-corruption laws in many other countries, businesses should consider designing programs focused on anti-corruption compliance more broadly.[309]

Hallmarks of Effective Compliance Programs

Individual companies may have different compliance needs depending on their size and the particular risks associated with their businesses, among other factors. When it comes to compliance, there is no one-size-fits-all program. Thus, the discussion below is meant to provide insight into the aspects of compliance programs that DOJ and SEC assess, recognizing that companies may consider a variety of factors when making their own determination of what is appropriate for their specific business needs.[310] Indeed, small- and medium-size enterprises likely will have different compliance programs from large multi-national corporations, a fact DOJ and SEC take into account when evaluating companies' compliance programs.

Compliance programs that employ a "check-the-box" approach may be inefficient and, more importantly, ineffective. Because each compliance program should be tailored to an organization's specific needs, risks, and challenges, the information provided below should not be considered a substitute for a company's own assessment of the corporate compliance program most appropriate for that particular business organization. In the end, if designed carefully, implemented earnestly, and enforced fairly, a company's compliance program—no matter how large or small the organization—will allow the company generally to prevent violations, detect those that do occur, and remediate them promptly and appropriately.

Commitment from Senior Management and a Clearly Articulated Policy Against Corruption

Within a business organization, compliance begins with the board of directors and senior executives setting the proper tone for the rest of the company. Managers and employees take their cues from these corporate leaders. Thus, DOJ and SEC consider the commitment of corporate leaders to a "culture of compliance"[311] and look to see if this high-level commitment is also reinforced and implemented by middle managers and employees at all levels of a business. A well-designed compliance program that is not enforced in good faith, such as when corporate management explicitly or implicitly encourages employees to engage in misconduct to achieve business objectives, will be ineffective. DOJ and SEC have often encountered companies with compliance programs that are strong on paper but that nevertheless have significant FCPA violations because management has failed to effectively implement the program even in the face of obvious signs of corruption. This may be the result of aggressive sales staff preventing compliance personnel from doing their jobs effectively and of senior management, more concerned with securing a valuable business opportunity than enforcing a culture of compliance, siding with the sales team. The higher the financial stakes of the transaction, the greater the temptation for management to choose profit over compliance.

A strong ethical culture directly supports a strong compliance program. By adhering to ethical standards, senior managers will inspire middle managers to reinforce those standards. Compliant middle managers, in turn, will encourage employees to strive to attain those standards throughout the organizational structure.[312]

In short, compliance with the FCPA and ethical rules must start at the top. DOJ and SEC thus evaluate whether senior management has clearly articulated company standards, communicated them in unambiguous terms, adhered to them scrupulously, and disseminated them throughout the organization.

Code of Conduct and Compliance Policies and Procedures

A company's code of conduct is often the foundation upon which an effective compliance program is built. As DOJ has repeatedly noted in its charging documents, the most effective codes are clear, concise, and accessible to all employees and to those conducting business on the company's behalf. Indeed, it would be difficult to effectively implement a compliance program if it was not available in the local language so that employees in foreign subsidiaries can access and understand it. When assessing a compliance program, DOJ and SEC will review whether the company has taken steps to make certain that the code of conduct remains current and effective and whether a company has periodically reviewed and updated its code. Whether a company has policies and procedures that outline responsibilities for compliance within the company, detail proper internal controls, auditing practices, and documentation policies, and set forth disciplinary procedures will also be considered by DOJ and SEC. These types of policies and procedures will depend on the size and nature of the business and the risks associated with the business. Effective policies and procedures require an in-depth understanding of the company's business model, including its products and services, third-party agents, customers, government interactions, and industry and geographic risks. Among the risks that a company may need to address include the nature and extent of transactions with foreign governments, including payments to foreign officials; use of third parties; gifts, travel, and entertainment expenses; charitable and political donations; and facilitating and expediting payments. For example, some companies with global operations have created web-based approval processes to review and approve routine gifts, travel, and entertainment involving foreign officials and private customers with clear monetary limits and annual limitations. Many of these systems have built-in flexibility so that senior management, or in-house legal counsel, can be apprised of and, in appropriate circumstances, approve unique requests. These types of systems can be a good way to conserve corporate resources while, if properly implemented, preventing and detecting potential FCPA violations.

Regardless of the specific policies and procedures implemented, these standards should apply to personnel at all levels of the company.

Oversight, Autonomy, and Resources

In appraising a compliance program, DOJ and SEC also consider whether a company has assigned responsibility for the oversight and implementation of a company's compliance program to one or more specific senior executives within an organization.[313] Those individuals must have appropriate authority within the organization, adequate autonomy from management, and sufficient resources to ensure that the company's compliance program is implemented effectively.[314] Adequate autonomy generally includes direct access to an organization's governing authority, such as the board of directors and committees of the board of directors (e.g., the audit committee).[315] Depending on the size and structure of an organization, it may be appropriate for day-to-day operational responsibility to be delegated to other specific individuals within a company.[316] DOJ and SEC recognize that the reporting structure will depend on the size and complexity of an organization. Moreover, the amount of resources devoted to compliance will depend on the company's size, complexity, industry, geographical reach, and risks associated with the business. In assessing whether a company has reasonable internal controls, DOJ and SEC typically consider whether the company devoted adequate staffing and resources to the compliance program given the size, structure, and risk profile of the business.

Risk Assessment

Assessment of risk is fundamental to developing a strong compliance program, and is another factor DOJ and SEC evaluate when assessing a company's compliance program.[317] One-size-fits-all compliance programs are generally ill-conceived and ineffective because resources inevitably are spread too thin, with too much focus on low-risk markets and transactions to the detriment of high-risk areas. Devoting a disproportionate amount of time policing modest entertainment and gift-giving instead of focusing on large government bids, questionable payments to third-party consultants, or excessive discounts to resellers and distributors may indicate that a company's compliance program is ineffective. A $50 million contract with a government agency in a high-risk country warrants greater scrutiny than modest and routine gifts and entertainment. Similarly, performing identical due diligence on all third-party agents, irrespective of risk factors, is often counter-productive, diverting attention and resources away from those third parties that pose the most significant risks. DOJ and SEC will give meaningful credit to a company that implements in good faith a comprehensive, risk-based compliance program, even if that program does not prevent an infraction in a low risk area because greater attention and resources had been devoted to a higher risk area. Conversely, a company that fails to prevent an FCPA violation on an economically significant, high-risk transaction because it failed to perform a level of due diligence commensurate with the size and risk of the transaction is likely to receive reduced credit based on the quality and effectiveness of its compliance program.

As a company's risk for FCPA violations increases, that business should consider increasing its compliance procedures, including due diligence and periodic internal audits. The degree of appropriate due diligence is fact-specific and should vary based on industry, country, size, and nature of the transaction, and the method and amount of third-party compensation. Factors to consider, for instance, include risks presented by: the country and industry sector, the business opportunity, potential business partners, level of involvement with governments, amount of government regulation and oversight, and exposure to customs and immigration in conducting business affairs. When assessing a company's compliance program, DOJ and SEC take into account whether and to what degree a company analyzes and addresses the particular risks it faces.

Training and Continuing Advice

Compliance policies cannot work unless effectively communicated throughout a company. Accordingly, DOJ and SEC will evaluate whether a company has taken steps to ensure that relevant policies and procedures have been communicated throughout the organization, including through periodic training and certification for all directors, officers, relevant employees, and, where appropriate, agents and

business partners.[318] For example, many larger companies have implemented a mix of web-based and in-person training conducted at varying intervals. Such training typically covers company policies and procedures, instruction on applicable laws, practical advice to address real-life scenarios, and case studies. Regardless of how a company chooses to conduct its training, however, the information should be presented in a manner appropriate for the targeted audience, including providing training and training materials in the local language. For example, companies may want to consider providing different types of training to their sales personnel and accounting personnel with hypotheticals or sample situations that are similar to the situations they might encounter. In addition to the existence and scope of a company's training program, a company should develop appropriate measures, depending on the size and sophistication of the particular company, to provide guidance and advice on complying with the company's ethics and compliance program, including when such advice is needed urgently. Such measures will help ensure that the compliance program is understood and followed appropriately at all levels of the company.

Incentives and Disciplinary Measures

In addition to evaluating the design and implementation of a compliance program throughout an organization, enforcement of that program is fundamental to its effectiveness.[319] A compliance program should apply from the board room to the supply room—no one should be beyond its reach. DOJ and SEC will thus consider whether, when enforcing a compliance program, a company has appropriate and clear disciplinary procedures, whether those procedures are applied reliably and promptly, and whether they are commensurate with the violation. Many companies have found that publicizing disciplinary actions internally, where appropriate under local law, can have an important deterrent effect, demonstrating that unethical and unlawful actions have swift and sure consequences.

DOJ and SEC recognize that positive incentives can also drive compliant behavior. These incentives can take many forms such as personnel evaluations and promotions, rewards for improving and developing a company's compliance program, and rewards for ethics and compliance leadership.[320] Some organizations, for example, have made adherence to compliance a significant metric for management's bonuses so that compliance becomes an integral part of management's everyday concern. Beyond financial incentives, some companies have highlighted compliance within their organizations by recognizing compliance professionals and internal audit staff. Others have made working in the company's compliance organization a way to advance an employee's career. SEC, for instance, has encouraged companies to embrace methods to incentivize ethical and lawful behavior:

> [M]ake integrity, ethics and compliance part of the promotion, compensation and evaluation processes as well. For at the end of the day, the most effective way to communicate that "doing the right thing" is a priority, is to reward it. Conversely, if employees are led to believe that, when it comes to compensation and career advancement, all that counts is short-term profitability, and that cutting ethical corners is an acceptable way of getting there, they'll perform to that measure. To cite an example from a different walk of life: a college football coach can be told that the graduation rates of his players are what matters, but he'll know

differently if the sole focus of his contract extension talks or the decision to fire him is his win-loss record.[321]

No matter what the disciplinary scheme or potential incentives a company decides to adopt, DOJ and SEC will consider whether they are fairly and consistently applied across the organization. No executive should be above compliance, no employee below compliance, and no person within an organization deemed too valuable to be disciplined, if warranted. Rewarding good behavior and sanctioning bad behavior reinforces a culture of compliance and ethics throughout an organization.

Third-Party due Diligence and Payments

DOJ's and SEC's FCPA enforcement actions demonstrate that third parties, including agents, consultants, and distributors, are commonly used to conceal the payment of bribes to foreign officials in international business transactions. Risk-based due diligence is particularly important with third parties and will also be considered by DOJ and SEC in assessing the effectiveness of a company's compliance program. Although the degree of appropriate due diligence may vary based on industry, country, size and nature of the transaction, and historical relationship with the third-party, some guiding principles always apply.

First, as part of risk-based due diligence, companies should understand the qualifications and associations of its third-party partners, including its business reputation, and relationship, if any, with foreign officials. The degree of scrutiny should increase as red flags surface.

Second, companies should have an understanding of the business rationale for including the third party in the transaction. Among other things, the company should understand the role of and need for the third party and ensure that the contract terms specifically describe the services to be performed. Additional considerations include payment terms and how those payment terms compare to typical terms in that industry and country, as well as the timing of the third party's introduction to the business. Moreover, companies may want to confirm and document that the third party is actually performing the work for which it is being paid and that its compensation is commensurate with the work being provided.

Third, companies should undertake some form of ongoing monitoring of third-party relationships.[322] Where appropriate, this may include updating due diligence periodically, exercising audit rights, providing periodic training, and requesting annual compliance certifications by the third party.

In addition to considering a company's due diligence on third parties, DOJ and SEC also assess whether the company has informed third parties of the company's compliance program and commitment to ethical and lawful business practices and, where appropriate, whether it has sought assurances from third parties, through certifications and otherwise, of reciprocal commitments. These can be meaningful ways to mitigate third-party risk.

Compliance Program Case Study

Recent DOJ and SEC actions relating to a financial institution's real estate transactions with a government agency in China illustrate the benefits of implementing and enforcing a comprehensive risk-based compliance program. The case involved a joint venture real estate investment in the Luwan District of Shanghai, China, between a U S -based financial institution and a state-owned entity that functioned as the District's real estate arm. The government entity conducted the transactions through two special purpose vehicles ("SPVs"), with the second SPV purchasing a 12% stake in a real estate project. The financial institution, through a robust compliance program, frequently trained its employees, imposed a comprehensive payment-approval process designed to prevent bribery, and staffed a compliance department with a direct reporting line to the board of directors.

As appropriate given the industry, market, and size and structure of the transactions, the financial institution (1) provided extensive FCPA training to the senior executive responsible for the transactions and (2) conducted extensive due diligence on the transactions, the local government entity, and the SPVs.

Due diligence on the entity included reviewing Chinese government records; speaking with sources familiar with the Shanghai real estate market; checking the government entity's payment records and credit references; conducting an on-site visit and placing a pretextual telephone call to the entity's offices; searching media sources; and conducting background checks on the entity's principals. The financial institution vetted the SPVs by obtaining a letter with designated bank account information from a Chinese official associated with the government entity (the "Chinese Official"); using an international law firm to request and review 50 documents from the SPVs' Canadian attorney; interviewing the attorney; and interviewing the SPVs' management.

Notwithstanding the financial institution's robust compliance program and good faith enforcement of it, the company failed to learn that the Chinese Official personally owned nearly 50% of the second SPV (and therefore a nearly 6% stake in the joint venture) and that the SPV was used as a vehicle for corrupt payments. This failure was due, in large part, to misrepresentations by the Chinese Official, the financial institution's executive in charge of the project, and the SPV's attorney that the SPV was 100% owned and controlled by the government entity. DOJ and SEC declined to take enforcement action against the financial institution, and its executive pleaded guilty to conspiracy to violate the FCPA's internal control provisions and also settled with SEC.

Confidential Reporting and Internal Investigation

An effective compliance program should include a mechanism for an organization's employees and others to report suspected or actual misconduct or violations of the company's policies on a confidential basis and without fear of retaliation.[323] Companies may employ, for example, anonymous hotlines or ombudsmen. Moreover, once an allegation is made, companies should have in place an efficient, reliable, and properly funded process for investigating the allegation and documenting the company's response, including any disciplinary or remediation measures taken. Companies will want to consider taking "lessons learned" from any reported violations and the outcome of any resulting investigation to update their internal controls and compliance program and focus future training on such issues, as appropriate.

Continuous Improvement: Periodic Testing and Review

Finally, a good compliance program should constantly evolve. A company's business changes over time, as do the environments in which it operates, the nature of its customers, the laws that govern its actions, and the standards of its industry.

In addition, compliance programs that do not just exist on paper but are followed in practice will inevitably uncover compliance weaknesses and require enhancements. Consequently, DOJ and SEC evaluate whether companies regularly review and improve their compliance programs and not allow them to become stale.

According to one survey, 64% of general counsel whose companies are subject to the FCPA say there is room for improvement in their FCPA training and compliance programs.[324] An organization should take the time to review and test its controls, and it should think critically about its potential weaknesses and risk areas. For example, some companies have undertaken employee surveys to measure their compliance culture and strength of internal controls, identify best practices, and detect new risk areas. Other companies periodically test their internal controls with targeted audits to make certain that controls on paper are working in practice. DOJ and SEC will give meaningful credit to thoughtful efforts to create a sustainable compliance program if a problem is later discovered. Similarly, undertaking proactive evaluations before a problem strikes can lower the applicable penalty range under the U.S. Sentencing Guidelines.[325] Although the nature and the frequency of proactive evaluations may vary depending on the size and complexity of an organization, the idea behind such efforts is the same: continuous improvement and sustainability.[326]

Mergers and Acquisitions: Pre-Acquisition due Diligence and Post-Acquisition Integration

In the context of the FCPA, mergers and acquisitions present both risks and opportunities. A company that does not perform adequate FCPA due diligence prior to a merger or acquisition may face both legal and business risks.[327] Perhaps most commonly, inadequate due diligence can allow a course of bribery to continue—with all the attendant harms to a business's profitability and reputation, as well as potential civil and criminal liability.

In contrast, companies that conduct effective FCPA due diligence on their acquisition targets are able to evaluate more accurately each target's value and negotiate for the costs of the bribery to be borne by the target. In addition, such actions demonstrate to DOJ and SEC a company's commitment to compliance and are taken into account when evaluating any potential enforcement action. For example, DOJ and SEC declined to take enforcement action against an acquiring issuer when the issuer, among other things, uncovered the corruption at the company being acquired as part of due diligence, ensured that the corruption was voluntarily disclosed to the government, cooperated with the investigation, and incorporated the acquired company into its compliance program and internal controls. On the other hand, SEC took action against the acquired company, and DOJ took action against a subsidiary of the acquired company.[328] When pre-acquisition due diligence is not possible, DOJ has described procedures, contained in Opinion Procedure Release No. 08-02, pursuant to which companies can nevertheless be rewarded if they choose to conduct thorough post-acquisition FCPA due diligence.[329]

FCPA due diligence, however, is normally only a portion of the compliance process for mergers and acquisitions. DOJ and SEC evaluate whether the acquiring company promptly incorporated the acquired company into all of its internal controls, including its compliance program. Companies should consider training new employees, reevaluating third parties under company standards, and, where appropriate, conducting audits on new business units.

For example, as a result of due diligence conducted by a California-based issuer before acquiring the majority interest in a joint venture, the issuer learned of corrupt payments to obtain business. However, the issuer only implemented its internal controls "halfway" so as not to "choke the sales engine and cause a distraction for the sales guys." As a result, the improper payments continued, and the issuer was held liable for violating the FCPA's internal controls and books and records provisions.[330]

Other Guidance on Compliance and International Best Practices

In addition to this guide, the U.S. Departments of Commerce and State have both issued publications that contain guidance regarding compliance programs. The Department of Commerce's International Trade Administration has published *Business Ethics: A Manual for Managing a Responsible Business Enterprise in Emerging Market Economies*,[331] and the Department of State has published *Fighting Global Corruption: Business Risk Management*.[332] There is also an emerging international consensus on compliance best practices, and a number of inter-governmental and non-governmental organizations have issued guidance regarding best practices for compliance.[333] Most notably, the OECD's 2009 Anti-Bribery Recommendation and its Annex II, *Good Practice Guidance on Internal Controls, Ethics, and Compliance*,[334] published in February 2010, were drafted based on consultations with the private sector and civil society and set forth specific good practices for ensuring effective compliance programs and measures for preventing and detecting foreign bribery. In addition, businesses may wish to refer to the following resources:

- Asia-Pacific Economic Cooperation—AntiCorruption Code of Conduct for Business;[335]
- International Chamber of Commerce—ICC Rules on Combating Corruption;[336]
- Transparency International—Business Principles for Countering Bribery;[337]

- United Nations Global Compact—The Ten Principles;[338]
- World Bank—Integrity Compliance Guidelines;[339] and
- World Economic Forum—Partnering Against Corruption–Principles for Countering Bribery.[340]

Hypothetical: Third-Party Vetting Part 1: Consultants

Company A, a U S issuer headquartered in Delaware, wants to start doing business in a country that poses high risks of corruption. Company A learns about a potential $50 million contract with the country's Ministry of Immigration. This is a very attractive opportunity to Company A, both for its profitability and to open the door to future projects with the government. At the suggestion of the company's senior vice president of international sales (Sales Executive), Company A hires a local businessman who assures them that he has strong ties to political and government leaders in the country and can help them win the contract. Company A enters into a consulting contract with the local businessman (Consultant). The agreement requires Consultant to use his best efforts to help the company win the business and provides for Consultant to receive a significant monthly retainer as well as a success fee of 3% of the value of any contract the company wins.

What steps should Company A consider taking before hiring Consultant?

There are several factors here that might lead Company A to perform heightened FCPA-related due diligence prior to retaining Consultant: (1) the market (high-risk country); (2) the size and significance of the deal to the company; (3) the company's first time use of this particular consultant; (4) the consultant's strong ties to political and government leaders; (5) the success fee structure of the contract; and (6) the vaguely-defined services to be provided.

In order to minimize the likelihood of incurring FCPA liability, Company A should carefully vet Consultant and his role in the transaction, including close scrutiny of the relationship between Consultant and any Ministry of Immigration officials or other government officials. Although there is nothing inherently illegal about contracting with a third party that has close connections to politicians and government officials to perform legitimate services on a transaction, this type of relationship can be susceptible to corruption.

Among other things, Company A may consider conducting due diligence on Consultant, including background and reference checks; ensuring that the contract spells out exactly what services and deliverables (such as written status reports or other documentation) Consultant is providing; training Consultant on the FCPA and other anti-corruption laws; requiring Consultant to represent that he will abide by the FCPA and other anti-corruption laws; including audit rights in the contract (and exercising those rights); and ensuring that payments requested by Consultant have the proper supporting documentation before they are approved for payment

Part 2: Distributors and Local Partners

Assume the following alternative facts:

Instead of hiring Consultant, Company A retains an often-used local distributor (Distributor) to sell Company A's products to the Ministry of Immigration In negotiating the pricing structure, Distributor, which had introduced the project to Company A, claims that the standard discount price to Distributor creates insufficient margin for Distributor to cover warehousing, distribution, installation, marketing, and training costs and requests an additional discount or rebate, or, in the alternative, a contribution to its marketing efforts, either in the form of a lump sum or as a percentage of the total contract.

The requested discount/allowance is significantly larger than usual, although there is precedent at Company A for granting this level of discount in unique circumstances.

Distributor further advises Company A that the Ministry's procurement officials responsible for awarding the contract have expressed a strong preference for including a particular local company (Local Partner) in the transaction as a subcontractor of Company A to perform installation, training, and other services that would normally have been performed by Distributor or Company A.

According to Distributor, the Ministry has a solid working relationship with Local Partner, and it would cause less disruption for Local Partner to perform most of the on-site work at the Ministry. One of the principals (Principal 1) of the Local Partner is an official in another government ministry.

What additional compliance considerations do these alternative facts raise?

As with Consultant in the first scenario above, Company A should carefully vet Distributor and Local Partner and their roles in the transaction in order to minimize the likelihood of incurring FCPA liability. While Company A has an established relationship with Distributor, the fact that Distributor has requested an additional discount warrants further inquiry into the economic justification for the change, particularly where, as here, the proposed transaction structure contemplates paying Local Partner to provide many of the same services that Distributor would otherwise provide. In many cases, it may be appropriate for distributors to receive larger discounts to account for unique circumstances in particular transactions. That said, a common mechanism to create additional margin for bribe payments is through excessive discounts or rebates to distributors. Accordingly, when a company has pre-existing relationships with distributors and other third parties, transaction-specific due diligence—including an analysis of payment terms to confirm that the payment is commensurate with the work being performed—can be critical even in circumstances where due diligence of the distributor or other third party raises no initial red flags.

Company A should carefully scrutinize the relationship among Local Partner, Distributor, and Ministry of Immigration officials. While there is nothing inherently illegal about contracting with a third party that is recommended by the end-user, or even hiring a government official to perform legitimate services on a transaction unrelated to his or her government job, these facts raise additional red flags that warrant significant scrutiny. Among other things, Company A would be well-advised to require Principal 1 to verify that he will have no role in the Ministry of Immigration's decision to award the contract to Company A, notify the Ministry of Immigration and his own ministry of his proposed involvement in the transaction, and certify that he will abide by the FCPA and other anti-corruption laws and that his involvement in the transaction is permitted under local law.

Assume the following additional facts:

Under its company policy for a government transaction of this size, Company A requires both finance and compliance approval. The finance officer is concerned that the discounts to Distributor are significantly larger than what they have approved for similar work and will cut too deeply into Company A's profit margin.

The finance officer is also skeptical about including Local Partner to perform some of the same services that Company A is paying Distributor to perform. Unsatisfied with Sales Executive's explanation, she requests a meeting with Distributor and Principal 1. At the meeting, Distributor and Principal 1 offer vague and inconsistent justifications for the payments and fail to provide any supporting analysis, and Principal 1 seems to have no real expertise in the industry. During a coffee break, Distributor comments to Sales Executive that the finance officer is naïve about "how business is done in my country." Following the meeting, Sales Executive dismisses the finance officer's concerns, assuring her that the proposed transaction structure is reasonable and legitimate. Sales Executive also reminds the finance officer that "the deal is key to their growth in the industry "

The compliance officer focuses his due diligence on vetting Distributor and Local Partner and hires a business investigative firm to conduct a background check. Distributor appears reputable, capable, and financially stable and is willing to take on real risk in the project, financial and otherwise. However, the compliance officer learns that Distributor has established an off-shore bank account for the transaction. The compliance officer further learns that Local Partner's business was organized two years ago and appears financially stable but has no expertise in the industry and has established an off-shore shell company and bank account to conduct this transaction. The background check also reveals that Principal 1 is a former college roommate of a senior official of the Ministry of Immigration. The Sales Executive dismisses the compliance officer's concerns, commenting that what Local Partner does with its payments "isn't our problem." Sales Executive also strongly objects to the compliance officer's request to meet with Principal 1 to discuss the off-shore company and account, assuring him that it was done for legitimate tax purposes and complaining that if Company A continues to "harass" Local Partner and Distributor, they would partner with Company A's chief competitor. The compliance officer and the finance officer discuss their concerns with each other but ultimately sign off on the deal even though their questions had not been answered. Their decision is motivated in large part by their conversation with Sales Executive, who told them that this was the region's most important contract and that the detailed FCPA questionnaires and robust anti-corruption representations in the contracts placed the burden on Distributor and Local Partner to act ethically.

Company A goes forward with the Distributor and Local Partner agreements and wins the contract after six months. The finance officer approves Company A's payments to Local Partner via the offshore account, even though Local Partner's invoices did not contain supporting detail or documentation of any services provided. Company A recorded the payments as legitimate operational expenses on its books and records. Sales Executive received a large year-end bonus due to the award of the contract. In fact, Local Partner and Distributor used part of the payments and discount margin, respectively, to funnel bribe payments to several Ministry of Immigration officials, including Principal 1's former college roommate, in exchange for awarding the contract to Company A. Thousands of dollars are also wired to the personal offshore bank account of Sales Executive.

How would DOJ and SEC evaluate the potential FCPA liability of Company A and its employees?

This is not the case of a single "rogue employee" circumventing an otherwise robust compliance program. Although Company A's finance and compliance officers had the correct instincts to scrutinize the structure and economics of the transaction and the role of the third parties, their due diligence was incomplete. When the initial inquiry identified significant red flags, they approved the transaction despite knowing that their concerns were unanswered or the answers they received raised additional concerns and red flags. Relying on due diligence questionnaires and anti-corruption representations is insufficient, particularly when the risks are readily apparent. Nor can Company A or its employees shield themselves from liability because it was Distributor and Local Partner—rather than Company A directly—that made the payments. The facts suggest that Sales Executive had actual knowledge of or was willfully blind to the consultant's payment of the bribes. He also personally profited from the scheme (both from the kickback and from the bonus he received from the company) and intentionally discouraged the finance and compliance officers from learning the full story. Sales Executive is therefore subject to liability under the anti-bribery, books and records, and internal controls provisions of the FCPA, and others may be as well. Company A may also be liable for violations of the anti-bribery, books and records, and internal controls provisions of the FCPA given the number and significance of red flags that established a high probability of bribery and the role of employees and agents acting on the company's behalf.

FCPA PENALTIES, SANCTIONS, AND REMEDIES

What Are the Potential Consequences for Violations of the FCPA?

The FCPA provides for different criminal and civil penalties for companies and individuals.

Criminal Penalties

For each violation of the anti-bribery provisions, the FCPA provides that corporations and other business entities are subject to a fine of up to $2 million.[341] Individuals, including officers, directors, stockholders, and agents of companies, are subject to a fine of up to $100,000 and imprisonment for up to five years.[342]

For each violation of the accounting provisions, the FCPA provides that corporations and other business entities are subject to a fine of up to $25 million.[343] Individuals are subject to a fine of up to $5 million and imprisonment for up to 20 years.[344]

Under the Alternative Fines Act, 18 U.S.C. § 3571(d), courts may impose significantly higher fines than those provided by the FCPA—up to twice the benefit that the defendant sought to obtain by making the corrupt payment, as long as the facts supporting the increased fines are included in the indictment and either proved to the jury beyond a reasonable doubt or admitted in a guilty plea proceeding.[345]

Fines imposed on individuals may not be paid by their employer or principal.[346]

U.S. Sentencing Guidelines

When calculating penalties for violations of the FCPA, DOJ focuses its analysis on the U.S. Sentencing Guidelines (Guidelines)[347] in all of its resolutions, including guilty pleas, DPAs, and NPAs. The Guidelines provide a very detailed and predictable structure for calculating penalties for all federal crimes, including violations of the FCPA. To determine the appropriate penalty, the "offense level" is first calculated by examining both the severity of the crime and facts specific to the crime, with appropriate reductions for cooperation and acceptance of responsibility, and, for business entities, additional factors such as voluntary disclosure, cooperation, preexisting compliance programs, and remediation.

The Guidelines provide for different penalties for the different provisions of the FCPA. The initial offense level for violations of the anti-bribery provisions is determined under § 2C1.1, while violations of the accounting provisions are assessed under § 2B1.1. For individuals, the initial offense level is modified by factors set forth in Chapters 3, 4, and 5 of the Guidelines[348] to identify a final offense level. This final offense level, combined with other factors, is used to determine whether the Guidelines would recommend that incarceration is appropriate, the length of any term of incarceration, and the appropriate amount of any fine. For corporations, the offense level is modified by factors particular to organizations as described in Chapter 8 to determine the applicable organizational penalty.

For example, violations of the anti-bribery provisions are calculated pursuant to § 2C1.1. The offense level is determined by first identifying the base offense level;[349] adding additional levels based on specific offense characteristics, including whether the offense involved more than one bribe, the value of the bribe or the benefit that was conferred, and the level of the public official;[350] adjusting the offense level based on the defendant's role in the offense;[351] and using the total offense level as well as the defendant's criminal history category to determine the advisory guideline range.[352] For violations of the accounting provisions assessed under § 2B1.1, the procedure is generally the same, except that the specific offense characteristics differ. For instance, for violations of the FCPA's accounting provisions, the offense level may be increased if a substantial part of the scheme occurred outside the United States or if the defendant was an officer or director of a publicly traded company at the time of the offense.[353]

For companies, the offense level is calculated pursuant to §§ 2C1.1 or 2B1.1 in the same way as for an individual—by starting with the base offense level and increasing it as warranted by any applicable specific offense characteristics. The organizational guidelines found in Chapter 8, however, provide the structure for determining the final advisory guideline fine range for organizations. The base fine consists of the greater of the amount corresponding to the total offense level, calculated pursuant to the Guidelines, or the pecuniary gain or loss from the offense.[354] This base fine is then multiplied by a culpability score that can either reduce the fine to as little as five percent of the base fine or increase the recommended fine to up to four times the amount of the base fine.[355] As described in § 8C2.5, this culpability score is calculated by taking into account numerous factors such as the size of the organization committing the criminal acts; the involvement in or tolerance of criminal activity by high-level personnel within the organization; and prior misconduct or obstructive behavior.

The culpability score is reduced if the organization had an effective pre-existing compliance program to prevent violations and if the organization voluntarily disclosed the offense, cooperated in the investigation, and accepted responsibility for the criminal conduct.[356]

Civil Penalties

Although only DOJ has the authority to pursue criminal actions, both DOJ and SEC have civil enforcement authority under the FCPA. DOJ may pursue civil actions for anti-bribery violations by domestic concerns (and their officers, directors, employees, agents, or stockholders) and foreign nationals and companies for violations while in the United States, while SEC may pursue civil actions against issuers and their officers, directors, employees, agents, or stockholders for violations of the anti-bribery and the accounting provisions.[357]

For violations of the anti-bribery provisions, corporations and other business entities are subject to a civil penalty of up to $16,000 per violation.[358] Individuals, including officers, directors, stockholders, and agents of companies, are similarly subject to a civil penalty of up to $16,000 per violation,[359] which may not be paid by their employer or principal.[360]

For violations of the accounting provisions, SEC may obtain a civil penalty not to exceed the greater of (a) the gross amount of the pecuniary gain to the defendant as a result of the violations or (b) a specified dollar limitation. The specified dollar limitations are based on the egregiousness of the violation, ranging from $7,500 to $150,000 for an individual and $75,000 to $725,000 for a company.[361] SEC may obtain civil penalties both in actions filed in federal court and in administrative proceedings.[362]

Collateral Consequences

In addition to the criminal and civil penalties described above, individuals and companies who violate the FCPA may face significant collateral consequences, including suspension or debarment from contracting with the federal government, cross-debarment by multilateral development banks, and the suspension or revocation of certain export privileges.

Debarment

Under federal guidelines governing procurement, an individual or company that violates the FCPA or other criminal statutes may be barred from doing business with the federal government. The Federal Acquisition Regulations (FAR) provide for the potential suspension or debarment of companies that contract with the government upon conviction of or civil judgment for bribery, falsification or destruction of records, the making of false statements, or "[c]ommission of any other offense indicating a lack of business integrity or business honesty that seriously and directly affects the present responsibility of a Government contractor or subcontractor."[363] These measures are not intended to be punitive and may be imposed only if "in the public's interest for the Government's protection."[364]

Under the FAR, a decision to debar or suspend is discretionary. The decision is not made by DOJ prosecutors or SEC staff, but instead by independent debarment authorities within each agency, such as the Department of Defense or the General Services Administration, which analyze a number of factors to determine whether a company should be suspended, debarred, or otherwise determined to be ineligible for government contracting. Such factors include whether the contractor has effective internal control systems in place, self-reported the misconduct in a timely manner, and has taken remedial measures.[365] If a cause for debarment exists, the contractor has the burden of demonstrating to the satisfaction of the debarring official that it is presently responsible and that debarment is not necessary.[366] Each federal department and agency determines the eligibility of contractors with whom it deals. However, if one department or agency debars or suspends a contractor, the debarment or suspension applies to the entire executive branch of the federal government, unless a department or agency shows compelling reasons not to debar or suspend the contractor.[367]

Although guilty pleas, DPAs, and NPAs do not result in automatic debarment from U.S. government contracting, committing a federal crime and the factual admissions underlying a resolution are factors that the independent debarment authorities may consider. Moreover, indictment alone can lead to suspension of the right to do business with the government.[368] The U.S. Attorney's Manual also provides that when a company engages in fraud against the government, a prosecutor may not negotiate away an agency's right to debar or delist the company as part of the plea bargaining process.[369] In making debarment determinations, contracting agencies, including at the state and local level, may consult with DOJ in advance of awarding a contract. Depending on the circumstances, DOJ may provide information to contracting authorities in the context of the corporate settlement about the facts and circumstances underlying the criminal conduct and remediation measures undertaken by the company, if any. This information sharing is not advocacy, and the ultimate debarment decisions are squarely within the purview of the independent debarment authorities. In some situations, the contracting agency may impose its own oversight requirements in order for a company that has admitted to violations of federal law to be awarded federal contracts, such as the Corporate Integrity Agreements often required by the Department of Health and Human Services.

Cross-Debarment by Multilateral Development Banks

Multilateral Development Banks (MDBs), like the World Bank, also have the ability to debar companies and individuals for corrupt practices.[370] Each MDB has its own process for evaluating alleged corruption in connection with MDB-funded projects. When appropriate, DOJ and SEC work with MDBs to share evidence and refer cases. On April 9, 2010, the African Development Bank Group, the Asian Development Bank, the European Bank for Reconstruction and Development, the Inter-American Development Bank Group, and the World Bank Group entered into an agreement under which entities debarred by one MDB will be sanctioned for the same misconduct by other signatory MDBs.[371] This cross-debarment agreement means that if a company is debarred by one MDB, it is debarred by all.[372]

Loss of Export Privileges

Companies and individuals who violate the FCPA may face consequences under other regulatory regimes, such as the Arms Export Control Act (AECA), 22 U.S.C. § 2751, *et seq.*, and its implementing regulations, the International Traffic in Arms Regulations (ITAR), 22 C.F.R. § 120, *et seq.* AECA and ITAR together provide for the suspension, revocation, amendment, or denial of an arms export license if an applicant has been indicted or convicted for violating the FCPA.[373] They also set forth certain factors for the Department of State's Directorate of Defense Trade Controls (DDTC)[374] to consider when determining whether to grant, deny, or return without action license applications for certain types of defense materials. One of those factors is whether there is reasonable cause to believe that an applicant for a license has violated (or conspired to violate) the FCPA; if so, the Department of State "may disapprove the application."[375] In addition, it is the policy of the Department of State not to consider applications for licenses involving any persons who have been convicted of violating the AECA or convicted of conspiracy to violate the AECA.[376] In an action related to the criminal resolution of a U.K. military products manufacturer, the DDTC imposed a "policy of denial" for export licenses on three of the company's subsidiaries that were involved in violations of AECA and ITAR.[377]

When Is a Compliance Monitor or Independent Consultant Appropriate?

One of the primary goals of both criminal prosecutions and civil enforcement actions against companies that violate the FCPA is ensuring that such conduct does not occur again. As a consequence, enhanced compliance and reporting requirements may be part of criminal and civil resolutions of FCPA matters. The amount of enhanced compliance and kind of reporting required varies according to the facts and circumstances of individual cases.

In criminal cases, a company's sentence, or a DPA or NPA with a company, may require the appointment of an independent corporate monitor. Whether a monitor is appropriate depends on the specific facts and circumstances of the case. In 2008, DOJ issued internal guidance regarding the selection and use of corporate monitors in DPAs and NPAs with companies. Additional guidance has since been issued.[378] A monitor is an independent third party who assesses and monitors a company's adherence to the compliance requirements of an agreement that was designed to reduce the risk of recurrence of the company's misconduct. Appointment of a monitor is not appropriate in all circumstances, but it may be appropriate, for example, where a company does not already have an effective internal compliance program or needs to establish necessary internal controls. In addition, companies are sometimes allowed to engage in self-monitoring, typically in cases when the company has made a voluntary disclosure, has been fully cooperative, and has demonstrated a genuine commitment to reform.

In civil cases, a company may similarly be required to retain an independent compliance consultant or monitor to provide an independent, third-party review of the company's internal controls. The consultant recommends improvements, to the extent necessary, which the company must adopt. When both DOJ and SEC require a company to retain a monitor, the two agencies have been able to coordinate their requirements so that the company can retain one monitor to fulfill both sets of requirements.

The most successful monitoring relationships are those in which the company embraces the monitor or consultant. If the company takes the recommendations and suggestions seriously and uses the monitoring period as a time to find and fix any outstanding compliance issues, the company can emerge from the monitorship with a stronger, long-lasting compliance program.

Factors DOJ and SEC Consider When Determining Whether a Compliance Monitor Is Appropriate Include:

- Seriousness of the offense - Duration of the misconduct
- Pervasiveness of the misconduct, including whether the conduct cuts across geographic and/ or product lines
- Nature and size of the company
- Quality of the company's compliance program at the time of the misconduct
- Subsequent remediation efforts

RESOLUTIONS

What Are the Different Types of Resolutions with DOJ?

Criminal Complaints, Informations, and Indictments

Charges against individuals and companies are brought in three different ways under the Federal Rules of Criminal Procedure: criminal complaints, criminal informations, and indictments.

DOJ may agree to resolve criminal FCPA matters against companies either through a declination or, in appropriate cases, a negotiated resolution resulting in a plea agreement, deferred prosecution agreement, or non-prosecution agreement. For individuals, a negotiated resolution will generally take the form of a plea agreement, which may include language regarding cooperation, or a non-prosecution cooperation agreement. When negotiated resolutions cannot be reached with companies or individuals, the matter may proceed to trial.

Plea Agreements

Plea agreements—whether with companies or individuals—are governed by Rule 11 of the Federal Rules of Criminal Procedure. The defendant generally admits to the facts supporting the charges, admits guilt, and is convicted of the charged crimes when the plea agreement is presented to and accepted by a court.

The plea agreement may jointly recommend a sentence or fine, jointly recommend an analysis under the U.S. Sentencing Guidelines, or leave such items open for argument at the time of sentencing.

Deferred Prosecution Agreements

Under a deferred prosecution agreement, or a DPA as it is commonly known, DOJ files a charging document with the court,[379] but it simultaneously requests that the prosecution be deferred, that is, postponed for the purpose of allowing the company to demonstrate its good conduct. DPAs generally require a defendant to agree to pay a monetary penalty, waive the statute of limitations, cooperate with the government, admit the relevant facts, and enter into certain compliance and remediation commitments, potentially including a corporate compliance monitor. DPAs describe the company's conduct, cooperation, and remediation, if any, and provide a calculation of the penalty pursuant to the U.S. Sentencing Guidelines. In addition to being publicly filed, DOJ places all of its DPAs on its website. If the company successfully completes the term of the agreement (typically two or three years), DOJ will then move to dismiss the filed charges. A company's successful completion of a DPA is not treated as a criminal conviction.

Non-Prosecution Agreements

Under a non-prosecution agreement, or an NPA as it is commonly known, DOJ maintains the right to file charges but refrains from doing so to allow the company to demonstrate its good conduct during the term of the NPA. Unlike a DPA, an NPA is not filed with a court but is instead maintained by the parties. In circumstances where an NPA is with a company for FCPA-related offenses, it is made available to the public through DOJ's website. The requirements of an NPA are similar to those of a DPA, and generally require a waiver of the statute of limitations, ongoing cooperation, admission of the material facts, and compliance and remediation commitments, in addition to payment of a monetary penalty. If the company complies with the agreement throughout its term, DOJ does not file criminal charges. If an individual complies with the terms of his or her NPA, namely, truthful and complete cooperation and continued law-abiding conduct, DOJ will not pursue criminal charges.

Declinations

As discussed above, DOJ's decision to bring or decline to bring an enforcement action under the FCPA is made pursuant to the *Principles of Federal Prosecution*, in the case of individuals, and the *Principles of Federal Prosecution of Business Organizations*, in the case of companies. As described, in the case of individuals, the *Principles of Federal Prosecution* advise prosecutors to weigh all relevant considerations, including:

- federal law enforcement priorities;
- the nature and seriousness of the offense;
- the deterrent effect of prosecution;
- the person's culpability in connection with the offense;
- the person's history of criminal activity;
- the person's willingness to cooperate in the investigation or prosecution of others; and
- the probable sentence or other consequences if the person is convicted.[380]

The *Principles of Federal Prosecution* provide additional commentary about each of these factors. For instance, they explain that prosecutors should take into account federal law enforcement priorities because federal law enforcement and judicial resources are not sufficient to permit prosecution of every alleged offense over which federal jurisdiction exists. The deterrent effect of prosecution should also be kept in mind because some offenses, "although seemingly not of great importance by themselves, if commonly committed would have a substantial cumulative impact on the community."[381]

As discussed above, the *Principles of Federal Prosecution of Business Organizations* require prosecutors to consider nine factors when determining whether to prosecute a corporate entity for an FCPA violation, including the nature and seriousness of the offense; the pervasiveness of wrongdoing within the company; the company's history of similar conduct; the existence and effectiveness of the company's pre-existing compliance program; and the adequacy of remedies, such as civil or regulatory enforcement actions.

Pursuant to these guidelines, DOJ has declined to prosecute both individuals and corporate entities in numerous cases based on the particular facts and circumstances presented in those matters, taking into account the available evidence.[382] To protect the privacy rights and other interests of the uncharged and other potentially interested parties, DOJ has a long-standing policy not to provide, without the party's consent, non-public information on matters it has declined to prosecute. To put DOJ's declinations in context, however, in the past two years alone, DOJ has declined several dozen cases against companies where potential FCPA violations were alleged.

As mentioned above, there are rare occasions in which, in conjunction with the public filing of charges against an individual, it is appropriate to disclose that a company is not also being prosecuted. That was done in a recent case where a former employee was charged but the former corporate employer was not.[383]

What Are the Different Types of Resolutions with SEC?

Civil Injunctive Actions and Remedies

In a civil injunctive action, SEC seeks a court order compelling the defendant to obey the law in the future. Violating such an order can result in civil or criminal contempt proceedings. Civil contempt sanctions, brought by SEC, are remedial rather than punitive in nature and serve one of two purposes: to compensate the party injured as a result of the violation of the injunction or force compliance with the terms of the injunction.

Where a defendant has profited from a violation of law, SEC can obtain the equitable relief of disgorgement of ill-gotten gains and pre-judgment interest and can also obtain civil money penalties pursuant to Sections 21(d)(3) and 32(c) of the Exchange Act. SEC may also seek ancillary relief (such as an accounting from a defendant). Pursuant to Section 21(d)(5), SEC also may seek, and any federal court may grant, any other equitable relief that may be appropriate or necessary for the benefit of investors, such as enhanced remedial measures or the retention of an independent compliance consultant or monitor.

Civil Administrative Actions and Remedies

SEC has the ability to institute various types of administrative proceedings against a person or an entity that it believes has violated the law. This type of enforcement action is brought by SEC's Enforcement Division and is litigated before an SEC administrative law judge (AUJ). The AUJ's decision is subject to appeal directly to the Securities and Exchange Commission itself, and the Commission's decision is in turn subject to review by a U.S. Court of Appeals.

Administrative proceedings provide for a variety of relief. For regulated persons and entities, such as broker-dealers and investment advisers and persons associated with them, sanctions include censure, limitation on activities, suspension of up to twelve months, and bar from association or revocation of registration. For professionals such as attorneys and accountants, SEC can order in Rule 102(e) proceedings that the professional be censured, suspended, or barred from practicing before SEC.[384] SEC staff can seek an order from an administrative law judge requiring the respondent to cease and desist from any current or future violations of the securities laws. In addition, SEC can obtain disgorgement, pre-judgment interest, and civil money penalties in administrative proceedings under Section 21B of the Exchange Act, and also can obtain other equitable relief, such as enhanced remedial measures or the retention of an independent compliance consultant or monitor.

Deferred Prosecution Agreements

A deferred prosecution agreement is a written agreement between SEC and a potential cooperating individual or company in which SEC agrees to forego an enforcement action against the individual or company if the individual or company agrees to, among other things: (1) cooperate truthfully and fully in SEC's investigation and related enforcement actions; (2) enter into a long-term tolling agreement; (3) comply with express prohibitions and/ or undertakings during a period of deferred prosecution; and (4) under certain circumstances, agree either to admit or not to contest underlying facts that SEC could assert to establish a violation of the federal securities laws. If the agreement is violated during the period of deferred prosecution, SEC staff may recommend an enforcement action to the Commission against the individual or company for the original misconduct as well as any additional misconduct. Furthermore, if the Commission authorizes the enforcement action, SEC staff may use any factual admissions made by the cooperating individual or company in support of a motion for summary judgment, while maintaining the ability to bring an enforcement action for any additional misconduct at a later date.

In May of 2011, SEC entered into its first deferred prosecution agreement against a company for violating the FCPA.[385] In that case, a global manufacturer of steel pipe products violated the FCPA by bribing Uzbekistan government officials during a bidding process to supply pipelines for transporting oil and natural gas. The company made almost $5 million in profits when it was subsequently awarded several contracts by the Uzbekistan government. The company discovered the misconduct during a worldwide review of its operations and brought it to the government's attention. In addition to self-reporting, the company conducted a thorough internal investigation; provided complete, real-time cooperation with SEC and DOJ staff; and undertook extensive remediation, including enhanced anti-corruption procedures and training. Under the terms of the DPA, the company paid $5.4 million in disgorgement and prejudgment interest. The company also paid a $3.5 million monetary penalty to resolve a criminal investigation by DOJ through an NPA.[386]

For further information about deferred prosecution agreements, see SEC's *Enforcement Manual.*[387]

Non-Prosecution Agreements

A non-prosecution agreement is a written agreement between SEC and a potential cooperating individual or company, entered into in limited and appropriate circumstances, that provides that SEC will not pursue an enforcement action against the individual or company if the individual or company agrees to, among other things: (1) cooperate truthfully and fully in SEC's investigation and related enforcement actions; and (2) comply, under certain circumstances, with express undertakings. If the agreement is violated, SEC staff retains its ability to recommend an enforcement action to the Commission against the individual or company.

For further information about non-prosecution agreements, see SEC's *Enforcement Manual.*[388]

Termination Letters and Declinations

As discussed above, SEC's decision to bring or decline to bring an enforcement action under the FCPA is made pursuant to the guiding principles set forth in SEC's *Enforcement Manual*. The same factors that apply to SEC staff's determination of whether to recommend an enforcement action against an individual or entity apply to the decision to close an investigation without recommending enforcement action.[389]

Generally, SEC staff considers, among other things:

- the seriousness of the conduct and potential violations;
- the resources available to SEC staff to pursue the investigation;
- the sufficiency and strength of the evidence;
- the extent of potential investor harm if an action is not commenced; and
- the age of the conduct underlying the potential violations.

SEC has declined to take enforcement action against both individuals and companies based on the facts and circumstances present in those matters, where, for example, the conduct was not egregious, the company fully cooperated, and the company identified and remediated the misconduct quickly. SEC Enforcement Division policy is to notify individuals and entities at the earliest opportunity when the staff has determined not to recommend an enforcement action against them to the Commission. This notification takes the form of a termination letter. In order to protect the privacy rights and other interests of the uncharged and other potentially interested parties, SEC does not provide non-public information on matters it has declined to prosecute.

What Are Some Examples of Past Declinations by DOJ and SEC?

Neither DOJ nor SEC typically publicizes declinations but, to provide some insight into the process, the following are recent, anonymized examples of matters DOJ and SEC have declined to pursue:

Example 1: Public Company Declination

DOJ and SEC declined to take enforcement action against a public U.S. company. Factors taken into consideration included:

- The company discovered that its employees had received competitor bid information from a third party with connections to the foreign government.
- The company began an internal investigation, withdrew its contract bid, terminated the employees involved, severed ties to the third-party agent, and voluntarily disclosed the conduct to DOJ's Antitrust Division, which also declined prosecution.
- During the internal investigation, the company uncovered various FCPA red flags, including prior concerns about the third-party agent, all of which the company voluntarily disclosed to DOJ and SEC.
- The company immediately took substantial steps to improve its compliance program.

Example 2: Public Company Declination

DOJ and SEC declined to take enforcement action against a public U.S. company. Factors taken into consideration included:

- With knowledge of employees of the company's subsidiary, a retained construction company paid relatively small bribes, which were wrongly approved by the company's local law firm, to foreign building code inspectors.
- When the company's compliance department learned of the bribes, it immediately ended the conduct, terminated its relationship with the construction company and law firm, and terminated or disciplined the employees involved.
- The company completed a thorough internal investigation and voluntarily disclosed to DOJ and SEC.
- The company reorganized its compliance department, appointed a new compliance officer dedicated to anti-corruption, improved the training and compliance program, and undertook a review of all of the company's international third-party relationships.

Example 3: Public Company Declination

DOJ and SEC declined to take enforcement action against a U.S. publicly held industrial services company for bribes paid by a small foreign subsidiary. Factors taken into consideration included:

- The company self-reported the conduct to DOJ and SEC.
- The total amount of the improper payments was relatively small, and the activity appeared to be an isolated incident by a single employee at the subsidiary.
- The profits potentially obtained from the improper payments were very small.
- The payments were detected by the company's existing internal controls. The company's audit committee conducted a thorough independent internal investigation. The results of the investigation were provided to the government.
- The company cooperated fully with investigations by DOJ and SEC.
- The company implemented significant remedial actions and enhanced its internal control structure.

Example 4: Public Company Declination

DOJ and SEC declined to take enforcement action against a U.S. publicly held oil-and-gas services company for small bribes paid by a foreign subsidiary's customs agent. Factors taken into consideration included:

- The company's internal controls timely detected a potential bribe before a payment was made.
- When company management learned of the potential bribe, management immediately reported the issue to the company's General Counsel and Audit Committee and prevented the payment from occurring.
- Within weeks of learning of the attempted bribe, the company provided in-person FCPA training to employees of the subsidiary and undertook an extensive internal investigation to determine whether any of the company's subsidiaries in the same region had engaged in misconduct.
- The company self-reported the misconduct and the results of its internal investigation to DOJ and SEC.
- The company cooperated fully with investigations by DOJ and SEC.
- In addition to the immediate training at the relevant subsidiary, the company provided comprehensive FCPA training to all of its employees and conducted an extensive review of its anti-corruption compliance program.
- The company enhanced its internal controls and record-keeping policies and procedures, including requiring periodic internal audits of customs payments.
- As part of its remediation, the company directed that local lawyers rather than customs agents be used to handle its permits, with instructions that "no matter what, we don't pay bribes"—a policy that resulted in a longer and costlier permit procedure.

Example 5: Public Company Declination

DOJ and SEC declined to take enforcement action against a U.S. publicly held consumer products company in connection with its acquisition of a foreign company. Factors taken into consideration included:

- The company identified the potential improper payments to local government officials as part of its pre-acquisition due diligence.
- The company promptly developed a comprehensive plan to investigate, correct, and remediate any FCPA issues after acquisition.
- The company promptly self-reported the issues prior to acquisition and provided the results of its investigation to the government on a real-time basis.

- The acquiring company's existing internal controls and compliance program were robust.
- After the acquisition closed, the company implemented a comprehensive remedial plan, ensured that all improper payments stopped, provided extensive FCPA training to employees of the new subsidiary, and promptly incorporated the new subsidiary into the company's existing internal controls and compliance environment.

Example 6: Private Company Declination

In 2011, DOJ declined to take prosecutorial action against a privately held U.S. company and its foreign subsidiary. Factors taken into consideration included:

- The company voluntarily disclosed bribes paid to social security officials in a foreign country.
- The total amount of the bribes was small.
- When discovered, the corrupt practices were immediately terminated.
- The conduct was thoroughly investigated, and the results of the investigation were promptly provided to DOJ.
- All individuals involved were either terminated or disciplined. The company also terminated its relationship with its foreign law firm.
- The company instituted improved training and compliance programs commensurate with its size and risk exposure.

WHISTLEBLOWER PROVISIONS AND PROTECTIONS

Assistance and information from a whistleblower who knows of possible securities law violations can be among the most powerful weapons in the law enforcement arsenal. Through their knowledge of the circumstances and individuals involved, whistleblowers can help SEC and DOJ identify potential violations much earlier than might otherwise have been possible, thus allowing SEC and DOJ to minimize the harm to investors, better preserve the integrity of the U.S. capital markets, and more swiftly hold accountable those responsible for unlawful conduct.

The Sarbanes-Oxley Act of 2002 and the Dodd-Frank Act of 2010 both contain provisions affecting whistleblowers who report FCPA violations. Sarbanes-Oxley prohibits issuers from retaliating against whistleblowers and provides that employees who are retaliated against for reporting possible securities law violations may file a complaint with the Department of Labor, for which they would be eligible to receive reinstatement, back pay, and other compensation.[390] Sarbanes-Oxley also prohibits retaliation against employee whistleblowers under the obstruction of justice statute.[391]

In 2010, the Dodd-Frank Act added Section 21F to the Exchange Act, addressing whistleblower incentives and protections. Section 21F authorizes SEC to provide monetary awards to eligible individuals who voluntarily come forward with high quality, original information that leads to an SEC enforcement action in which over $1,000,000 in sanctions is ordered. [392] The awards range is between 10% and 30% of the monetary sanctions recovered by the government. The Dodd-Frank Act also prohibits employers from retaliating against whistleblowers and creates a private right of action for employees who are retaliated against.[393]

Furthermore, businesses should be aware that retaliation against a whistleblower may also violate state, local, and foreign laws that provide protection of whistleblowers.

On August 12, 2011, the final rules for SEC's Whistleblower Program became effective. These rules set forth the requirements for whistleblowers to be eligible for awards consideration, the factors that SEC will use to determine the amount of the award, the categories of individuals who are excluded from award consideration, and the categories of individuals who are subject to limitations in award considerations.[394] The final rules strengthen incentives for employees to report the suspected violations internally through internal compliance programs when appropriate, although it does not require an employee to do so in order to qualify for an award.[395]

Individuals with information about a possible violation of the federal securities laws, including FCPA violations, should submit that information to SEC either online through SEC's Tips, Complaints, and Referrals (TCR) Intake and Resolution System (available at https://denebleo.sec.gov /TCRExternal/disclaimer.xhtml) or by mailing or faxing a completed Form TCR to the Commission's Office of the Whistleblower.

Whistleblowers can submit information anonymously. To be considered under SEC's whistleblower program as eligible for a reward, however, the information must be submitted on an anonymous whistleblower's behalf by an attorney.[396] Whether or not a whistleblower reports anonymously, SEC is committed to protecting the identity of a whistleblower to the fullest extent possible under the statute.[397] SEC's Office of the Whistleblower administers SEC's Whistleblower Program and answers questions from the public regarding the program. Additional information regarding SEC's

Whistleblower Program, including answers to frequently asked questions, is available online at http://www.sec.gov/whistleblower.

SEC Office of the Whistleblower
100 F Street NE, Mail Stop 5971
Washington, DC 20549
Facsimile: (703) 813-9322
Online Report Form: http://www.sec.gov/whistleblower

DOJ Opinion Procedure

DOJ's opinion procedure is a valuable mechanism for companies and individuals to determine whether proposed conduct would be prosecuted by DOJ under the FCPA.[398] Generally speaking, under the opinion procedure process, parties submit information to DOJ, after which DOJ issues an opinion about whether the proposed conduct falls within its enforcement policy. All of DOJ's prior opinions are available online.[399] Parties interested in obtaining such an opinion should follow these steps:[400]

First, those seeking an opinion should evaluate whether their question relates to actual, prospective conduct.[401] The opinion procedure cannot be used to obtain opinions on purely historical conduct or on hypothetical questions. DOJ will not consider a request unless that portion of the transaction for which an opinion is sought involves only prospective conduct, although the transaction as a whole may have components that already have occurred. An executed contract is not a prerequisite and, in most—if not all—instances, an opinion request should be made before the requestor commits to proceed with a transaction.[402] Those seeking requests should be aware that FCPA opinions relate only to the FCPA's anti-bribery provisions.[403]

Second, before making the request, the company or individual should check that they are either an issuer or a domestic concern, as only those categories of parties can receive an opinion.[404] If the transaction involves more than one issuer or domestic concern, consider making a request for an opinion jointly, as opinions only apply to the parties that request them.[405]

Third, those seeking an opinion must put their request in writing. The request must be specific and accompanied by all relevant and material information bearing on the conduct and circumstances for which an opinion is requested. Material information includes background information, complete copies of all operative documents, and detailed statements of all collateral or oral understandings, if any. Those seeking opinions are under an affirmative obligation to make full and true disclosures.[406] Materials disclosed to DOJ will not be made public without the consent of the party submitting them.[407]

Fourth, the request must be signed. For corporate requestors, the signatory should be an appropriate senior officer with operational responsibility for the conduct that is the subject of the request and who has been designated by the corporation's chief executive officer. In appropriate cases, DOJ also may require the chief executive officer to sign the request. Those signing the request must certify that it contains a true, correct, and complete disclosure with respect to the proposed conduct and the circumstances of the conduct. 408

Fifth, an original and five copies of the request should be addressed to the Assistant Attorney General in charge of the Criminal Division, Attention: FCPA Opinion Group.[409] The mailing address is P.O. Box 28188 Central Station, Washington, D.C. 20038. DOJ also asks that you send an electronic courtesy copy to FCPA.Fraud@usdoj.gov.

DOJ will evaluate the request for an FCPA opinion.[410] A party may withdraw a request for an opinion at any time prior to the release of an opinion.[411] If the request is complete and all the relevant information has been submitted, DOJ will respond to the request by issuing an opinion within 30 days.[412] If the request is incomplete, DOJ will identify for the requestor what additional information or documents are required for DOJ to review the request. Such information must be provided to DOJ promptly. Once the additional information has been received, DOJ will issue an opinion within 30 days of receipt of that additional information.[413] DOJ's FCPA opinions state whether, for purposes of DOJ's present enforcement policy, the prospective conduct would violate either the issuer or domestic concern anti-bribery provisions of the FCPA.[414] DOJ also may take other positions in the opinion as it considers appropriate.[415] To the extent that the opinion concludes that the proposed conduct would not violate the FCPA, a rebuttable presumption is created that the requestor's conduct that was the basis of the opinion is in compliance with the FCPA.[416] In order to provide non-binding guidance to the business community, DOJ makes versions of its opinions publicly available on its website.[417]

If, after receiving an opinion, a party is concerned about prospective conduct that is beyond the scope of conduct specified in a previous request, the party may submit an additional request for an opinion using the procedures outlined above.[418]

CONCLUSION

The FCPA was designed to prevent corrupt practices, protect investors, and provide a fair playing field for those honest companies trying to win business based on quality and price rather than bribes. Following Congress' leadership in enacting the FCPA 35 years ago, and through determined international diplomatic and law enforcement efforts in the time since, laws like the FCPA prohibiting foreign bribery have been enacted by most of the United States' major trading partners.

This guide is designed to provide practical advice about, and useful insights into, our enforcement considerations. For businesses desiring to compete fairly in foreign markets, it is our goal to maximize those businesses' ability to comply with the FCPA in the most effective and efficient way suitable to their business and the markets in which they operate. Through our ongoing efforts with the U.S. and international business and legal communities and non- governmental organizations, DOJ and SEC can continue effectively to protect the integrity of our markets and reduce corruption around the world.

APPENDIX: THE FOREIGN CORRUPT PRACTICES ACT

15 U .S .C . §§ 78dd-1, 78dd-2, 78dd-3, 78m, 78ff

15 U.S.C. § 78dd-1 [Section 30A of the Securities Exchange Act of 1934] Prohibited foreign trade practices by issuers

(a) Prohibition

It shall be unlawful for any issuer which has a class of securities registered pursuant to section 78l of this title or which is required to file reports under section 78o(d) of this title, or for any officer, director, employee, or agent of such issuer or any stockholder thereof acting on behalf of such issuer, to make use of the mails or any means or instrumentality of interstate commerce corruptly in furtherance of an offer, payment, promise to pay, or authorization of the payment of any money, or offer, gift, promise to give, or authorization of the giving of anything of value to—

(1) any foreign official for purposes of—

(A) (i) influencing any act or decision of such foreign official in his official capacity, (ii) inducing such foreign official to do or omit to do any act in violation of the lawful duty of such official, or (iii) securing any improper advantage; or

(B) inducing such foreign official to use his influence with a foreign government or instrumentality thereof to affect or influence any act or decision of such government or instrumentality, in order to assist such issuer in obtaining or retaining business for or with, or directing business to, any person;

(2) any foreign political party or official thereof or any candidate for foreign political office for purposes of—

(A) (i) influencing any act or decision of such party, official, or candidate in its or his official capacity, (ii) inducing such party, official, or candidate to do or omit to do an act in violation of the lawful duty of such party, official, or candidate, or (iii) securing any improper advantage; or

(B) inducing such party, official, or candidate to use its or his influence with a foreign government or instrumentality thereof to affect or influence any act or decision of such government or instrumentality, in order to assist such issuer in obtaining or retaining business for or with, or directing business to, any person; or

(3) any person, while knowing that all or a portion of such money or thing of value will be offered, given, or promised, directly or indirectly, to any foreign official, to any foreign political party or official thereof, or to any candidate for foreign political office, for purposes of—

(A) (i) influencing any act or decision of such foreign official, political party, party official, or candidate in his or its official capacity, (ii) inducing such foreign official, political party, party official, or candidate to do or omit to do any act in violation of the lawful duty of such foreign official, political party, party official, or candidate, or (iii) securing any improper advantage; or

(B) inducing such foreign official, political party, party official, or

candidate to use his or its influence with a foreign government or instrumentality thereof to affect or influence any act or decision of such government or instrumentality, in order to assist such issuer in obtaining or retaining business for or with, or directing business to, any person.

(b) Exception for routine governmental action

Subsections (a) and (g) of this section shall not apply to any facilitating or expediting payment to a foreign official, political party, or party official the purpose of which is to expedite or to secure the performance of a routine governmental action by a foreign official, political party, or party official.

(c) Affirmative defenses

It shall be an affirmative defense to actions under subsection (a) or (g) of this section that—

(1) the payment, gift, offer, or promise of anything of value that was made, was lawful under the written laws and regulations of the foreign official's, political party's, party official's, or candidate's country; or

(2) the payment, gift, offer, or promise of anything of value that was made, was a reasonable and bona fide expenditure, such as travel and lodging expenses, incurred by or on behalf of a foreign official, party, party official, or candidate and was directly related to—

(A) the promotion, demonstration, or explanation of products or services; or

(B) the execution or performance of a contract with a foreign government or agency thereof.

(d) Guidelines by Attorney General

Not later than one year after August 23, 1988, the Attorney General, after consultation with the Commission, the Secretary of Commerce, the United States Trade Representative, the Secretary of State, and the Secretary of the Treasury, and after obtaining the views of all interested persons through public notice and comment procedures, shall determine to what extent compliance with this section would be enhanced and the business community would be assisted by further clarification of the preceding provisions of this section and may, based on such determination and to the extent necessary and appropriate, issue—

(1) guidelines describing specific types of conduct, associated with common types of export sales arrangements and business contracts, which for purposes of the Department of Justice's present enforcement policy, the Attorney General determines would be in conformance with the preceding provisions of this section; and

(2) general precautionary procedures which issuers may use on a voluntary basis to conform their conduct to the Department of Justice's present enforcement policy regarding the preceding provisions of this section. The Attorney General shall issue the guidelines and procedures referred to in the preceding sentence in accordance with the provisions of subchapter II of chapter 5 of Title 5 and those guidelines and procedures shall be subject to the provisions of chapter 7 of that title.

(e) Opinions of Attorney General

(1) The Attorney General, after consultation with appropriate departments and agencies of the United States and after obtaining the views of all interested persons through public notice and comment procedures, shall establish a procedure to provide responses to specific inquiries by issuers concerning conformance of their conduct with the Department of Justice's present

enforcement policy regarding the preceding provisions of this section. The Attorney General shall, within 30 days after receiving such a request, issue an opinion in response to that request. The opinion shall state whether or not certain specified prospective conduct would, for purposes of the Department of Justice's present enforcement policy, violate the preceding provisions of this section. Additional requests for opinions may be filed with the Attorney General regarding other specified prospective conduct that is beyond the scope of conduct specified in previous requests. In any action brought under the applicable provisions of this section, there shall be a rebuttable presumption that conduct, which is specified in a request by an issuer and for which the Attorney General has issued an opinion that such conduct is in conformity with the Department of Justice's present enforcement policy, is in compliance with the preceding provisions of this section. Such a presumption may be rebutted by a preponderance of the evidence. In considering the presumption for purposes of this paragraph, a court shall weight all relevant factors, including but not limited to whether the information submitted to the Attorney General was accurate and complete and whether it was within the scope of the conduct specified in any request received by the Attorney General. The Attorney General shall establish the procedure required by this paragraph in accordance with the provisions of subchapter II of chapter 5 of Title 5 and that procedure shall be subject to the provisions of chapter 7 of that title.

(2) Any document or other material which is provided to, received by, or prepared in the Department of Justice or any other department or agency of the United States in connection with a request by an issuer under the procedure established under paragraph (1), shall be exempt from disclosure under section 552 of Title 5 and shall not, except with the consent of the issuer, be made publicly available, regardless of whether the Attorney General responds to such a request or the issuer withdraws such request before receiving a response.

(3) Any issuer who has made a request to the Attorney General under paragraph (1) may withdraw such request prior to the time the Attorney General issues an opinion in response to such request. Any request so withdrawn shall have no force or effect.

(4) The Attorney General shall, to the maximum extent practicable, provide timely guidance concerning the Department of Justice's present enforcement policy with respect to the preceding provisions of this section to potential exporters and small businesses that are unable to obtain specialized counsel on issues pertaining to such provisions. Such guidance shall be limited to responses to requests under paragraph (1) concerning conformity of

specified prospective conduct with the Department of Justice's present enforcement policy regarding the preceding provisions of this section and general explanations of compliance responsibilities and of potential liabilities under the preceding provisions of this section.

(f) Definitions

For purposes of this section:

(1)(A) The term "foreign official" means any officer or employee of a foreign government or any department, agency, or instrumentality thereof, or of a public international organization, or any person acting in an official capacity for or on behalf of any such government or department, agency, or instrumentality, or for or on behalf of any such public international organization.

(B) For purposes of subparagraph (A), the term "public international organization" means—

(i) an organization that is designated by Executive Order pursuant to section 1 of the International Organizations Immunities Act (22 U.S.C. § 288); or

(ii) any other international organization that is designated by the President by Executive order for the purposes of this section, effective as of the date of publication of such order in the Federal Register.

(2) (A) A person's state of mind is "knowing" with respect to conduct, a circumstance, or a result if—

(i) such person is aware that such person is engaging in such conduct, that such circumstance exists, or that such result is substantially certain to occur; or

(ii) such person has a firm belief that such circumstance exists or that such result is substantially certain to occur.

(B) When knowledge of the existence of a particular circumstance is required for an offense, such knowledge is established if a person is aware of a high probability of the existence of such circumstance, unless the person actually believes that such circumstance does not exist.

(3)(A) The term "routine governmental action" means only an action which is ordinarily and commonly performed by a foreign official in—

(i) obtaining permits, licenses, or other official documents to qualify a person to do business in a foreign country;

(ii) processing governmental papers, such as visas and work orders;

(iii) providing police protection, mail pick-up and delivery, or scheduling inspections associated with contract performance or inspections related to transit of goods across country;

(iv) providing phone service, power and water supply, loading and unloading cargo, or protecting perishable products or commodities from deterioration; or

(v) actions of a similar nature.

(B) The term "routine governmental action" does not include any decision by a foreign official whether, or on what terms, to award new business to or to continue business with a particular party, or any action taken by a foreign official involved in the decision-making process to encourage a decision to award new business to or continue business with a particular party.

(g) Alternative Jurisdiction

(1) It shall also be unlawful for any issuer organized under the laws of the United States, or a State, territory, possession, or commonwealth of the United States or a political subdivision thereof and which has a class of securities registered pursuant to section 78*l* of this title or which is required to file reports under section 78o(d)) of this title, or for any United States person that is an officer, director, employee, or agent of such issuer or a stockholder thereof acting on behalf of such issuer, to corruptly do any act outside the United States in furtherance of an offer, payment, promise to pay, or authorization of the payment of any money, or offer, gift, promise to give, or authorization of the giving of anything of value to any of the persons or entities set forth in paragraphs (1), (2), and (3) of this subsection (a) of this section for the purposes set forth therein, irrespective of whether such issuer or such officer, director, employee, agent, or stockholder makes use of the mails or any means or instrumentality of interstate commerce in furtherance of such offer, gift, payment, promise, or authorization.

(2) As used in this subsection, the term "United States person" means a national of the United States (as defined in section 101 of the Immigration and Nationality Act (8 U.S.C. § 1101)) or any corporation, partnership, association, joint-stock company, business trust, unincorporated organization, or sole proprietorship organized under the laws of the United States or any State, territory, possession, or commonwealth of the United States, or any political subdivision thereof.

15 U.S.C. § 78dd-2 Prohibited foreign trade practices by domestic concerns

(a) Prohibition

It shall be unlawful for any domestic concern, other than an issuer which is subject to section 78dd-1 of this title, or for any officer, director, employee, or agent of such domestic concern or any stockholder thereof acting on behalf of such domestic concern, to make use of the mails or any means or instrumentality of interstate commerce corruptly in furtherance of an offer, payment, promise to pay, or authorization of the payment of any money, or offer, gift, promise to give, or authorization of the giving of anything of value to—

(1) any foreign official for purposes of—

(A) (i) influencing any act or decision of such foreign official in his official capacity, (ii) inducing such foreign official to do or omit to do any act in violation of the lawful duty of such official, or (iii) securing any improper advantage; or

(B) inducing such foreign official to use his influence with a foreign government or instrumentality thereof to affect or influence any act or decision of such government or instrumentality, in order to assist such domestic concern in obtaining or retaining business for or with, or directing business to, any person; or

(2) any foreign political party or official thereof or any candidate for foreign political office for purposes of—

(A) (i) influencing any act or decision of such party, official, or candidate in its or his official capacity, (ii) inducing such party, official, or candidate to do or omit to do an act in violation of the lawful duty of such party, official, or candidate, or (iii) securing any improper advantage; or

inducing such party, official, or candidate to use its or his influence with a foreign government or instrumentality thereof to affect or influence any act or decision of such government or instrumentality, in order to assist such domestic concern in obtaining or retaining business for or with, or directing business to, any person;

(3) any person, while knowing that all or a portion of such money or thing of value will be offered, given, or promised, directly or indirectly, to any foreign official, to any foreign political party or official thereof, or to any candidate for foreign political office, for purposes of—

(A) (i) influencing any act or decision of such foreign official, political party, party official, or candidate in his or its official capacity, (ii) inducing such foreign official, political party, party official, or candidate to do or omit to do any act in violation of the lawful duty of such foreign official, political party, party official, or candidate, or (iii) securing any improper advantage; or

(B) inducing such foreign official, political party, party official, or candidate to use his or its influence with a foreign government or instrumentality thereof to affect or influence any act or decision of such government or instrumentality, in order to assist such domestic concern in obtaining or retaining business for or with, or directing business to, any person.

(b) Exception for routine governmental action

Subsections (a) and (i) of this section shall not apply to any facilitating or expediting payment to a foreign official, political party, or party official the purpose of which is to expedite or to secure the performance of a routine governmental action by a foreign official, political party, or party official.

(c) Affirmative defenses

It shall be an affirmative defense to actions under subsection (a) or (i) of this section that—

(1) the payment, gift, offer, or promise of anything of value that was made, was lawful under the written laws and regulations of the foreign official's, political party's, party official's, or candidate's country; or

(2) the payment, gift, offer, or promise of anything of value that was made, was a reasonable and bona fide expenditure, such as travel and lodging expenses, incurred by or on behalf of a foreign official, party, party official, or candidate and was directly related to—

(A) the promotion, demonstration, or explanation of products or services; or

(B) the execution or performance of a contract with a foreign government or agency thereof.

(d) Injunctive relief

(1) When it appears to the Attorney General that any domestic concern to which this section applies, or officer, director, employee, agent, or stockholder thereof, is engaged, or about to engage, in any act or practice constituting a violation of subsection (a) or (i) of this section, the Attorney General may, in his discretion, bring a civil action in an appropriate district court of the United States to enjoin such act or practice, and upon a proper showing, a permanent injunction or a temporary restraining order shall be granted without bond.

(2) For the purpose of any civil investigation which, in the opinion of the Attorney General, is necessary and proper to enforce this section, the Attorney General or his designee are empowered to administer oaths and affirmations, subpoena witnesses, take evidence, and require the production of any books, papers, or other documents which the Attorney General deems relevant or material to such investigation. The attendance of witnesses and the production of documentary evidence may be required from any place in the United States, or any territory, possession, or commonwealth of the United States, at any designated place of hearing.

(3) In case of contumacy by, or refusal to obey a subpoena issued to, any person, the Attorney General may invoke the aid of any court of the United States within the jurisdiction of which such investigation or proceeding is carried on, or where such person resides or carries on business, in requiring the attendance and testimony of witnesses and the production of books, papers, or other documents. Any such court may issue an order requiring such person to appear before the Attorney General or his designee, there to produce records, if so ordered, or to give testimony touching the matter under investigation. Any failure to obey such order of the court may be punished by such court as a contempt thereof. All process in any such case may be served in the judicial district in which such person resides or may be found. The Attorney General may make such rules relating to civil investigations as may be necessary or appropriate to implement the provisions of this subsection.

(e) Guidelines by Attorney General

Not later than 6 months after August 23, 1988, the Attorney General, after consultation with the Securities and Exchange Commission, the Secretary of Commerce, the United States Trade Representative, the Secretary of State, and the Secretary of the Treasury, and after obtaining the views of all interested persons through public notice and comment procedures, shall determine to what extent compliance with this section would be enhanced and the business community would be assisted by further clarification of the preceding provisions of this section and may, based on such determination and to the extent necessary and appropriate, issue—

(1) guidelines describing specific types of conduct, associated with common types of export sales arrangements and business contracts, which for purposes of the Department of Justice's present enforcement policy, the Attorney General determines would be in conformance with the preceding provisions of this section; and

(2) general precautionary procedures which domestic concerns may use on a voluntary basis to conform their conduct to the Department of Justice's present enforcement policy regarding the preceding provisions of this section.

The Attorney General shall issue the guidelines and procedures referred to in the preceding sentence in accordance with the provisions of subchapter II of chapter 5 of Title 5 and those guidelines and procedures shall be subject to the provisions of chapter 7 of that title.

(f) Opinions of Attorney General

(1) The Attorney General, after consultation with appropriate departments and agencies of the United States and after obtaining the views of all interested persons through public notice and comment procedures, shall establish a

procedure to provide responses to specific inquiries by domestic concerns concerning conformance of their conduct with the Department of Justice's present enforcement policy regarding the preceding provisions of this section. The Attorney General shall, within 30 days after receiving such a request, issue an opinion in response to that request. The opinion shall state whether or not certain specified prospective conduct would, for purposes of the Department of Justice's present enforcement policy, violate the preceding provisions of this section. Additional requests for opinions may be filed with the Attorney General regarding other specified prospective conduct that is beyond the scope of conduct specified in previous requests. In any action brought under the applicable provisions of this section, there shall be a rebuttable presumption that conduct, which is specified in a request by a domestic concern and for which the Attorney General has issued an opinion that such conduct is in conformity with the Department of Justice's present enforcement policy, is in compliance with the preceding provisions of this section. Such a presumption may be rebutted by a preponderance of the evidence. In considering the presumption for purposes of this paragraph, a court shall weigh all relevant factors, including but not limited to whether the information submitted to the Attorney General was accurate and complete and whether it was within the scope of the conduct specified in any request received by the Attorney General. The Attorney General shall establish the procedure required by this paragraph in accordance with the provisions of subchapter II of chapter 5 of Title 5 and that procedure shall be subject to the provisions of chapter 7 of that title.

(2) Any document or other material which is provided to, received by, or prepared in the Department of Justice or any other department or agency of the United States in connection with a request by a domestic concern under the procedure established under paragraph (1), shall be exempt from disclosure under section 552 of Title 5 and shall not, except with the consent of the domestic concern, by made publicly available, regardless of whether the Attorney General response to such a request or the domestic concern withdraws such request before receiving a response.

(3) Any domestic concern who has made a request to the Attorney General under paragraph (1) may withdraw such request prior to the time the Attorney General issues an opinion in response to such request. Any request so withdrawn shall have no force or effect.

(4) The Attorney General shall, to the maximum extent practicable, provide timely guidance concerning the Department of Justice's present enforcement policy with respect to the preceding provisions of this section to

potential exporters and small businesses that are unable to obtain specialized counsel on issues pertaining to such provisions. Such guidance shall be limited to responses to requests under paragraph (1) concerning conformity of specified prospective conduct with the Department of Justice's present enforcement policy regarding the preceding provisions of this section and general explanations of compliance responsibilities and of potential liabilities under the preceding provisions of this section.

(g) Penalties

(1)(A) Any domestic concern that is not a natural person and that violates subsection (a) or (i) of this section shall be fined not more than $2,000,000.

(B) Any domestic concern that is not a natural person and that violates subsection (a) or (i) of this section shall be subject to a civil penalty of not more than $10,000 imposed in an action brought by the Attorney General.

(2)(A) Any natural person that is an officer, director, employee, or agent of a domestic concern, or stockholder acting on behalf of such domestic concern, who willfully violates subsection (a) or (i) of this section shall be fined not more than $100,000 or imprisoned not more than 5 years, or both.

(B) Any natural person that is an officer, director, employee, or agent of a domestic concern, or stockholder acting on behalf of such domestic concern, who violates subsection (a) or (i) of this section shall be subject to a civil penalty of not more than $10,000 imposed in an action brought by the Attorney General.

(3) Whenever a fine is imposed under paragraph (2) upon any officer, director, employee, agent, or stockholder of a domestic concern, such fine may not be paid, directly or indirectly, by such domestic concern.

(h) Definitions

For purposes of this section:

(1) The term "domestic concern" means—

(A) any individual who is a citizen, national, or resident of the United States; and

(B) any corporation, partnership, association, joint-stock company, business trust, unincorporated organization, or sole proprietorship which has its principal place of business in the United States, or which is organized under the laws of a State of the United States or a territory, possession, or commonwealth of the United States.

(2)(A) The term "foreign official" means any officer or employee of a foreign government or any department, agency, or instrumentality thereof, or of a public international organization, or any person acting in an official capacity for or on behalf of any such government or department, agency, or instrumentality, or for or on behalf of any such public international organization.

(B) For purposes of subparagraph (A), the term "public international organization" means—

(i) an organization that has been designated by Executive order pursuant to Section 1 of the International Organizations Immunities Act (22 U.S.C. § 288); or

(ii) any other international organization that is designated by the President by Executive order for the purposes of this section, effective as of the date of publication of such order in the Federal Register.

(3)(A) A person's state of mind is "knowing" with respect to conduct, a circumstance, or a result if—

(i) such person is aware that such person is engaging in such conduct, that such circumstance exists, or that such result is substantially certain to occur; or

(ii) such person has a firm belief that such circumstance exists or that such result is substantially certain to occur.

(B) When knowledge of the existence of a particular circumstance is required for an offense, such knowledge is established if a person is aware of a high probability of the existence of such circumstance, unless the person actually believes that such circumstance does not exist.

(4)(A) The term "routine governmental action" means only an action which is ordinarily and commonly performed by a foreign official in—

(i) obtaining permits, licenses, or other official documents to qualify a person to do business in a foreign country;

(ii) processing governmental papers, such as visas and work orders;

(iii) providing police protection, mail pick-up and delivery, or scheduling inspections associated with contract performance or inspections related to transit of goods across country;

(iv) providing phone service, power and water supply, loading and unloading cargo, or protecting perishable products or commodities from deterioration; or

(v) actions of a similar nature.

(B) The term "routine governmental action" does not include any decision by a foreign official whether, or on what terms, to award new business to or to continue business with a particular party, or any action taken by a foreign official involved in the decision-making process to encourage a decision to award new business to or continue business with a particular party.

(5) The term "interstate commerce" means trade, commerce, transportation, or communication among the several States, or between any foreign

country and any State or between any State and any place or ship outside thereof, and such term includes the intrastate use of—

(A) a telephone or other interstate means of communication, or

(B) any other interstate instrumentality. (i) Alternative Jurisdiction

(1) It shall also be unlawful for any United States person to corruptly do any act outside the United States in furtherance of an offer, payment, promise to pay, or authorization of the payment of any money, or offer, gift, promise to give, or authorization of the giving of anything of value to any of the persons or entities set forth in paragraphs (1), (2), and (3) of subsection (a), for the purposes set forth therein, irrespective of whether such United States person makes use of the mails or any means or instrumentality of interstate commerce in furtherance of such offer, gift, payment, promise, or authorization.

(2) As used in this subsection, a "United States person" means a national of the United States (as defined in section 101 of the Immigration and Nationality Act (8 U.S.C. § 1101)) or any corporation, partnership, association, joint-stock company, business trust, unincorporated organization, or sole proprietorship organized under the laws of the United States or any State, territory, possession, or commonwealth of the United States, or any political subdivision thereof.

15 U.S.C. § 78dd-3 Prohibited foreign trade practices by persons other than issuers or domestic concerns

(a) Prohibition

It shall be unlawful for any person other than an issuer that is subject to section 78dd-1 [Section 30A of the Exchange Act] of this title or a domestic concern, or for any officer, director, employee, or agent of such person or any stockholder thereof acting on behalf of such person, while in the territory of the United States, corruptly to make use of the mails or any means or instrumentality of interstate commerce or to do any other act in furtherance of an offer, payment, promise to pay, or authorization of the payment of any money, or offer, gift, promise to give, or authorization of the giving of anything of value to—

(1) any foreign official for purposes of—

(i) influencing any act or decision of such foreign official in his official capacity, (ii) inducing such foreign official to do or omit to do any act in violation of the lawful duty of such official, or (iii) securing any improper advantage; or

inducing such foreign official to use his influence with a foreign government or instrumentality thereof to affect or influence any act or decision of such government or instrumentality, in order to assist such person in obtaining or retaining business for or with, or directing business to, any person;

(2) any foreign political party or official thereof or any candidate for foreign political office for purposes of—

(A) (i) influencing any act or decision of such party, official, or candidate in its or his official capacity, (ii) inducing such party, official, or candidate to do or omit to do an act in violation of the lawful duty of such party, official, or candidate, or (iii) securing any improper advantage; or

(B) inducing such party, official, or candidate to use its or his influence with a foreign government or instrumentality thereof to affect or influence any act or decision of such government or instrumentality, in order to assist such person in obtaining or retaining business for or with, or directing business to, any person; or

(3) any person, while knowing that all or a portion of such money or thing of value will be offered, given, or promised, directly or indirectly, to any foreign official, to any foreign political party or official thereof, or to any candidate for foreign political office, for purposes of—

(A) (i) influencing any act or decision of such foreign official, political party, party official, or candidate in his or its official capacity, (ii) inducing such foreign official, political party, party official, or candidate to do or omit to do any act in violation of the lawful duty of such foreign official, political party, party official, or candidate, or (iii) securing any improper advantage; or

(B) inducing such foreign official, political party, party official, or candidate to use his or its influence with a foreign government or instrumentality thereof to affect or influence any act or decision of such government or instrumentality, in order to assist such person in obtaining or retaining business for or with, or directing business to, any person.

(b) Exception for routine governmental action

Subsection (a) of this section shall not apply to any facilitating or expediting payment to a foreign official, political party, or party official the purpose of which is to expedite or to secure the performance of a routine governmental action by a foreign official, political party, or party official.

(c) Affirmative defenses

It shall be an affirmative defense to actions under subsection (a) of this section that—

(1) the payment, gift, offer, or promise of anything of value that was made, was lawful under the written laws and regulations of the foreign official's, political party's, party official's, or candidate's country; or

(2) the payment, gift, offer, or promise of anything of value that was made, was a reasonable and bona fide expenditure, such as travel and lodging expenses, incurred by or on behalf of a foreign official, party, party official, or candidate and was directly related to—

(A) the promotion, demonstration, or explanation of products or services; or

(B) the execution or performance of a contract with a foreign government or agency thereof.

(d) Injunctive relief

(1) When it appears to the Attorney General that any person to which this section applies, or officer, director, employee, agent, or stockholder thereof, is engaged, or about to engage, in any act or practice constituting a violation of subsection (a) of this section, the Attorney General may, in his discretion, bring a civil action in an appropriate district court of the United States to enjoin such act or practice, and upon a proper showing, a permanent injunction or a temporary restraining order shall be granted without bond.

(2) For the purpose of any civil investigation which, in the opinion of the Attorney General, is necessary and proper to enforce this section, the Attorney General or his designee are empowered to administer oaths and affirmations, subpoena witnesses, take evidence, and require the production of any books, papers, or other documents which the Attorney General deems relevant or material to such investigation. The attendance of witnesses and the production of documentary evidence may be required from any place in the United States, or any territory, possession, or commonwealth of the United States, at any designated place of hearing.

(3) In case of contumacy by, or refusal to obey a subpoena issued to, any person, the Attorney General may invoke the aid of any court of the United States within the jurisdiction of which such investigation or proceeding is carried on, or where such person resides or carries on business, in requiring the attendance and testimony of witnesses and the production of books, papers, or other documents. Any such court may issue an order requiring such person to appear before the Attorney General or his designee, there to produce records, if so ordered, or to give testimony touching the matter under investigation. Any failure to obey such order of the court may be punished by such court as a contempt thereof.

(4) All process in any such case may be served in the judicial district in which such person resides or may be found. The Attorney General may make such rules relating to civil investigations as may be necessary or appropriate to implement the provisions of this subsection.

(e) Penalties

(1)(A) Any juridical person that violates subsection (a) of this section shall be fined not more than $2,000,000.

(B) Any juridical person that violates subsection (a) of this section shall be subject to a civil penalty of not more than $10,000 imposed in an action brought by the Attorney General.

(2)(A) Any natural person who willfully violates subsection (a) of this section shall be fined not more than $100,000 or imprisoned not more than 5 years, or both.

(B) Any natural person who violates subsection (a) of this section shall be subject to a civil penalty of not more than $10,000 imposed in an action brought by the Attorney General.

(3) Whenever a fine is imposed under paragraph (2) upon any officer, director, employee, agent, or stockholder of a person, such fine may not be paid, directly or indirectly, by such person.

(f) Definitions

For purposes of this section:

(1) The term "person," when referring to an offender, means any natural person other than a national of the United States (as defined in 8 U.S.C. § 1101) or any corporation, partnership, association, joint-stock company, business trust, unincorporated organization, or sole proprietorship organized under the law of a foreign nation or a political subdivision thereof

(2)(A) The term "foreign official" means any officer or employee of a foreign government or any department, agency, or instrumentality thereof, or of a public international organization, or any person acting in an official capacity for or on behalf of any such government or department, agency, or instrumentality, or for or on behalf of any such public international organization.

For purposes of subparagraph (A), the term "public international organization" means—

(i) an organization that has been designated by Executive Order pursuant to Section 1 of the International Organizations Immunities Act (22 U.S.C. § 288); or

(ii) any other international organization that is designated by the President by Executive order for the purposes of this section, effective as of the date of publication of such order in the Federal Register.

(3)(A) A person's state of mind is "knowing" with respect to conduct, a circumstance, or a result if—

(i) such person is aware that such person is engaging in such conduct, that such circumstance exists, or that such result is substantially certain to occur; or

(ii) such person has a firm belief that such circumstance exists or that such result is substantially certain to occur.

(B) When knowledge of the existence of a particular circumstance is required for an offense, such knowledge is established if a person is aware of a high probability of the existence of such circumstance, unless the person actually believes that such circumstance does not exist.

(4)(A) The term "routine governmental action" means only an action which is ordinarily and commonly performed by a foreign official in—

(i) obtaining permits, licenses, or other official documents to qualify a person to do business in a foreign country;

(ii) processing governmental papers, such as visas and work orders;

(iii) providing police protection, mail pick-up and delivery, or scheduling inspections associated with contract performance or inspections related to transit of goods across country;

(iv) providing phone service, power and water supply, loading and unloading cargo, or protecting perishable products or commodities from deterioration; or

(v) actions of a similar nature.

(B) The term "routine governmental action" does not include any decision by a foreign official whether, or on what terms, to award new business to or to continue business with a particular party, or any action taken by a foreign official involved in the decision-making process to encourage a decision to award new business to or continue business with a particular party.

(5) The term "interstate commerce" means trade, commerce, transportation, or communication among the several States, or between any foreign country and any State or between any State and any place or ship outside thereof, and such term includes the intrastate use of—

(A) a telephone or other interstate means of communication, or

(B) any other interstate instrumentality.

* * *

15 U.S.C. § 78m [Section 13 of the Securities Exchange Act of 1934]

Periodical and other reports

(a) Reports by issuer of security; contents

Every issuer of a security registered pursuant to section 78l of this title shall file with the Commission, in accordance with such rules and regulations as the Commission may prescribe as necessary or appropriate for the proper protection of investors and to insure fair dealing in the security—

(1) such information and documents (and such copies thereof) as the Commission shall require to keep reasonably current the information and documents required to be included in or filed with an application or registration statement filed pursuant to section 78l of this title, except that the Commission may not require the filing of any material contract wholly executed before July 1, 1962.

(2) such annual reports (and such copies thereof), certified if required by the rules and regulations of the Commission by independent public accountants, and such quarterly reports (and such copies thereof), as the Commission may prescribe.

Every issuer of a security registered on a national securities exchange shall also file a duplicate original of such information, documents, and reports with the exchange. In any registration statement, periodic report, or other reports to be filed with the Commission, an emerging growth company need not present selected financial data in accordance with section 229.301 of title 17, Code of Federal Regulations, for any period prior to the earliest audited period presented in connection with its first registration statement that became effective under this chapter or the Securities Act of 1933 [15 U.S.C. §§ 77a, et seq.] and, with respect to any such statement or reports, an emerging growth company may not be required to comply with any new or revised financial accounting standard until such date that a company that is not an issuer (as defined under section 7201 of this title) is required to comply with such new or revised accounting standard, if such standard applies to companies that are not issuers.

(b) Form of report; books, records, and internal accounting; directives

(1) The Commission may prescribe, in regard to reports made pursuant to this chapter, the form or forms in which the required information shall be set forth, the items or details to be shown in the balance sheet and the earnings statement, and the methods to be followed in the preparation of reports, in the appraisal or valuation of assets and liabilities, in the determination of depreciation and depletion, in the differentiation of recurring and nonrecurring income, in the differentiation of investment and operating income, and in the preparation, where the Commission deems it necessary or desirable, of separate and/or consolidated balance sheets or income accounts of any person directly or indirectly controlling or controlled by the issuer, or any person under direct or indirect common control with the issuer; but in the case of the reports of any person whose methods of accounting are prescribed under the provisions of any law of the United States, or any rule or regulation thereunder, the rules and regulations of the Commission with respect to reports

shall not be inconsistent with the requirements imposed by such law or rule or regulation in respect of the same subject matter (except that such rules and regulations of the Commission may be inconsistent with such requirements to the extent that the Commission determines that the public interest or the protection of investors so requires).

Every issuer which has a class of securities registered pursuant to section 78l of this title and every issuer which is required to file reports pursuant to section 78o(d) of this title shall—

(A) make and keep books, records, and accounts, which, in reasonable detail, accurately and fairly reflect the transactions and dispositions of the assets of the issuer;

(B) devise and maintain a system of internal accounting controls sufficient to provide reasonable assurances that—

(i) transactions are executed in accordance with management's general or specific authorization;

(ii) transactions are recorded as necessary (I) to permit preparation of financial statements in conformity with generally accepted accounting principles or any other criteria applicable to such statements, and (II) to maintain accountability for assets;

(iii) access to assets is permitted only in accordance with management's general or specific authorization; and

(iv) the recorded accountability for assets is compared with the existing assets at reasonable intervals and appropriate action is taken with respect to any differences; and

(C) notwithstanding any other provision of law, pay the allocable share of such issuer of a reasonable annual accounting support fee or fees, determined in accordance with section 7219 of this title.

(3)(A) With respect to matters concerning the national security of the United States, no duty or liability under paragraph (2) of this subsection shall be imposed upon any person acting in cooperation with the head of any Federal department or agency responsible for such matters if such act in cooperation with such head of a department or agency was done upon the specific, written directive of the head of such department or agency pursuant to Presidential authority to issue such directives. Each directive issued under this paragraph shall set forth the specific facts and circumstances with respect to which the provisions of this paragraph are to be invoked. Each such directive shall, unless renewed in writing, expire one year after the date of issuance.

(B) Each head of a Federal department or agency of the United States who issues such a directive pursuant to this paragraph shall maintain a complete file of all such directives and shall, on October 1 of each year, transmit a summary of matters covered by such directives in force at any time during the previous year to the Permanent Select Committee on Intelligence of the House of Representatives and the Select Committee on Intelligence of the Senate.

(4) No criminal liability shall be imposed for failing to comply with the requirements of paragraph (2) of this subsection except as provided in paragraph (5) of this subsection.

(5) No person shall knowingly circumvent or knowingly fail to implement a system of internal accounting controls or knowingly falsify any book, record, or account described in paragraph (2).

Where an issuer which has a class of securities registered pursuant to section 78l of this title or an issuer which is required to file reports pursuant to section 78o(d) of this title holds 50 per centum or less of the voting power with respect to a domestic or foreign firm, the provisions of paragraph (2) require only that the issuer proceed in good faith to use its influence, to the extent reasonable under the issuer's circumstances, to cause such domestic or foreign firm to devise and maintain a system of internal accounting controls consistent with paragraph (2). Such circumstances include the relative degree of the issuer's ownership of the domestic or foreign firm and the laws and practices governing the business operations of the country in which such firm is located. An issuer which demonstrates good faith efforts to use such influence shall be conclusively presumed to have complied with the requirements of paragraph (2).

(6) For the purpose of paragraph (2) of this subsection, the terms "reasonable assurances" and "reasonable detail" mean such level of detail and degree of assurance as would satisfy prudent officials in the conduct of their own affairs.

* * *

15 U.S.C. § 78ff Penalties [Section 32 of the Securities Exchange Act of 1934]

(a) Willful violations; false and misleading statements

Any person who willfully violates any provision of this chapter (other than section 78dd-1 of this title [Section 30A of the Exchange Act]), or any rule or regulation thereunder the violation of which is made unlawful or the observance of which is required under the terms of this chapter, or any person who willfully and knowingly makes, or causes to be made, any statement in any application, report, or document required to be filed under this chapter or any rule or regulation thereunder or any undertaking contained in a registration statement as provided in subsection (d) of section 78o of this title, or by any self-regulatory organization in connection with an application for membership or participation therein or to become associated with a member thereof, which statement was false or misleading with respect to any material fact, shall upon conviction be fined not more than $5,000,000, or imprisoned not more than 20 years, or both, except that when such person is a person other than a natural person, a fine not exceeding $25,000,000 may be imposed; but no person shall be subject to imprisonment under this section for the violation of any rule or regulation if he proves that he had no knowledge of such rule or regulation.

(b) Failure to file information, documents, or reports

Any issuer which fails to file information, documents, or reports required to be filed under subsection (d) of section 78o of this title or any rule or regulation thereunder shall forfeit to the United States the sum of $100 for each and every day such failure to file shall continue. Such forfeiture, which shall be in lieu of any criminal penalty for such failure to file which might be deemed to arise under subsection (a) of this section, shall be payable into the Treasury of the United States and shall be recoverable in a civil suit in the name of the United States.

(c) Violations by issuers, officers, directors, stockholders, employees, or agents of issuers

(1)(A) Any issuer that violates subsection (a) or (g) of section 78dd-1 [Section 30A of the Exchange Act] of this title shall be fined not more than $2,000,000.

(B) Any issuer that violates subsection (a) or (g) of section 78dd-1

[Section 30A of the Exchange Act]of this title shall be subject to a civil penalty of not more than $10,000 imposed in an action brought by the Commission.

(2)(A) Any officer, director, employee, or agent of an issuer, or stockholder acting on behalf of such issuer, who willfully violates subsection (a) or (g) of section 78dd-1 [Section 30A of the Exchange Act] of this title shall be fined not more than $100,000, or imprisoned not more than 5 years, or both.

(B) Any officer, director, employee, or agent of an issuer, or stockholder acting on behalf of such issuer, who violates subsection (a) or (g) of section 78dd-1 [Section 30A of the Exchange Act] of this title shall be subject to a civil penalty of not more than $10,000 imposed in an action brought by the Commission.

(3) Whenever a fine is imposed under paragraph (2) upon any officer, director, employee, agent, or stockholder of an issuer, such fine may not be paid, directly or indirectly, by such issuer.

End Notes

[1] S. REP. No. 95-114, at 4 (1977) [hereinafter S. REP. No. 95-114], *available at* http://www.justice.gov/criminal/fraud/fcpa/history/1977/ senaterpt-95-114.pdf.

[2] *Id.*; H.R. REP. No. 95-640, at 4-5 (1977) [hereinafter H. R. REP. No. 95-640], *available at* http://www.justice.gov/criminal/fraud/fcpa/ history/1977/houseprt-95-640.pdf. The House Report made clear Congress's concerns:

The payment of bribes to influence the acts or decisions of foreign officials, foreign political parties or candidates for foreign political office is unethical. It is counter to the moral expectations and values of the American public. But not only is it unethical, it is bad business as well. It erodes public confidence in the integrity of the free market system. It short-circuits the marketplace by directing business to those companies too inefficient to compete in terms of price, quality or service, or too lazy to engage in honest salesmanship, or too intent upon unloading marginal products. In short, it rewards corruption instead of efficiency and puts pressure on ethical enterprises to lower their standards or risk losing business.

Id.

[3] *See, e.g.*, U.S. AGENCY FoR INT'L DEv., USAID ANTICoRRUPTIoN STRATEGY 5-6 (2005), *available at* http://transition.usaid.gov/policy/ ads/200/200mbo.pdf. The growing recognition that corruption poses a severe threat to domestic and international security has galvanized efforts to combat it in the United States and abroad. *See, e.g.*, Int'l Anti-Corruption and Good Governance Act of 2000, Pub. L. No. 106-309, § 202, 114 Stat. 1090 (codified as amended at 22 U.S.C. §§ 2151-2152 (2000)) (noting that "[w]idespread corruption endangers the stability and security of societies, undermines democracy, and jeopardizes the social, political, and economic development of a society. . . . [and that] [c]orruption facilitates criminal activities, such as money laundering, hinders economic development, inflates the costs of doing business, and undermines the legitimacy of the government and public trust").

[4] *See* Maryse Tremblay & Camille Karbassi, *Corruption and Human Trafficking* 4 (Transparency Int'l, Working Paper No. 3, 2011), *available at* http://issuu.com/transparencyinternational /docs/ti-working_paper_ human_trafficking_28_jun_2011; U.S. AGENCY FoR INT'L DEv., FoREIGN AID IN THE NATIoNAL INTEREST 40 (2002), *available at* http://pdf.usaid.gov/pdf_docs/PDABW900.pdf ("No problem does more to alienate citizens from their political leaders and institutions, and to undermine political stability and economic development, than endemic corruption among the government, political party leaders, judges, and bureaucrats. The more endemic the corruption is, the more likely it is to be accompanied by other serious deficiencies in the rule of law: smuggling, drug trafficking, criminal violence, human rights abuses, and personalization of power.").

[5] President George W. Bush observed in 2006 that "the culture of corruption has undercut development and good governance and . . . . impedes our efforts to promote freedom and democracy, end poverty, and combat international crime and terrorism." President's

Statement on Kleptocracy, 2 PUB. PAPERS 1504 (Aug. 10, 2006), *available at* http://georgewbush-whitehouse.archives.gov/news/ releases/2006/08/20060810.html. The administrations of former President George W. Bush and President Barack Obama both recognized the threats posed to security and stability by corruption. For instance, in issuing a proclamation restricting the entry of certain corrupt foreign public officials, former President George W. Bush recognized "the serious negative effects that corruption of public institutions has on the United States' efforts to promote security and to strengthen democratic institutions and free market systems. . . ." Proclamation No. 7750, 69 Fed. Reg. 2287 (Jan. 14, 2004). Similarly, President Barack Obama's National Security Strategy paper, released in May 2010, expressed the administration's efforts and commitment to promote the recognition that "pervasive corruption is a violation of basic human rights and a severe impediment to development and global security." THE WHITE HoUSE, NATIoNAL SECURITY STRATEGY 38 (2010), *available at* http://www.whitehouse.gov/sites/default/files/rss_viewer/national_security_ strategy.pdf.

[6] *See, e.g.*, INT'L CHAMBER oF CoMMERCE, ET AL., CLEAN BUSINESS IS GooD BUSINESS: THE BUSINESS CASE AGAINST CoRRUPTIoN (2008), *available at* http://www.unglobalcompact.org/docs/news_ events/8.1/clean_business_is_good_business.pdf; World Health Org., *Fact Sheet No. 335, Medicines: Corruption and Pharmaceuticals* (Dec. 2009), *available at* http://www.who.int/mediacentre/factsheets/fs335/ en/; Daniel Kaufmann, *Corruption: The Facts*, FoREIGN PoL'Y, Summer 1997, at 119-20; Paolo Mauro, *Corruption and Growth*, 110 Q. J. Econ. 681, 683, 705 (1995) (finding that "corruption lowers private investment . . . [and] reduc[es] economic growth . . ."); THE WoRLD BANK, THE DATA REvoLUTIoN: MEASURING GovERNANCE AND CoRRUPTIoN, (Apr. 8, 2004), *available at* http://go.worldbank.org/87JUY8GJH0.

[7] *See, e.g.*, *The Corruption Eruption*, ECoNoMIST (Apr. 29, 2010), *available at* http://www.economist.com/node/16005114 ("The hidden costs of corruption are almost always much higher than companies imagine. Corruption inevitably begets ever more corruption: bribe-takers keep returning to the trough and bribe-givers open themselves up to blackmail."); Daniel Kaufmann and Shang-Jin Wei, *Does "Grease Money" Speed Up the Wheels of Commerce?* 2 (Nat'l Bureau of Econ. Research, Working Paper No. 7093, 1999), *available at* http://www.nber.org/ papers/w7093.pdf ("Contrary to the 'efficient grease' theory, we find that firms that pay more bribes are also likely to spend more, not less, management time with bureaucrats negotiating regulations, and face higher, not lower, cost of capital.").

[8] For example, in a number of recent enforcement actions, the same employees who were directing or controlling the bribe payments were also enriching themselves at the expense of the company. *See, e.g.*, Complaint, SEC v. Peterson, No. 12-cv-2033 (E.D.N.Y. 2012), ECF No. 1, *available at* http://www.sec.gov/litigation/complaints/2012/ comp-pr2012-78.pdf; Criminal Information, United States v. Peterson, No. 12-cr-224 (E.D.N.Y. 2012), ECF No. 7 [hereinafter *United States v. Peterson*], *available at* http://www.justice.gov/criminal /fraud/fcpa/cases/ petersong/petersong-information.pdf; Plea Agreement, United States v. Stanley, No. 08-cr-597 (S.D. Tex. 2008), ECF No. 9 [hereinafter *United States v. Stanley*], *available at* http://www.justice.gov/criminal/fraud/ fcpa/cases/stanleya/09-03-08stanley-plea-agree.pdf; Plea Agreement, United States v. Sapsizian, No. 06-cr-20797 (S.D. Fla. 2007), ECF No. 42 [hereinafter *United States v. Sapsizian*], *available at* http://www.justice. gov/criminal/fraud/fcpa/cases/sapsizianc/06-06-07sapsizian-plea.pdf.

[9] *See, e.g.*, Complaint, SEC v. Tyco Int'l Ltd., 06-cv-2942 (S.D.N.Y. 2006), ECF No. 1 [hereinafter *SEC v. Tyco Int'l*], *available at* http://www.sec. gov/litigation/complaints/2006 /comp19657.pdf; Complaint, SEC v. Willbros Group, Inc., No. 08-cv-1494 (S.D. Tex. 2008), ECF No. 1 [hereinafter *SEC v. Willbros*], *available at* http://www.sec.gov/litigation/ complaints/2008/comp20571.pdf.

[10] *See* Plea Agreement, United States v. Bridgestone Corp., No. 11-cr651 (S.D. Tex. 2011), ECF No. 21, *available at* http://www.justice.gov/ criminal/fraud/fcpa/cases/bridgestone/10-05-11bridgestone-plea.pdf.

[11] *See* S. REp. No. 95-114, at 6; H.R. REp. 95-640, at 4*; see also* A. Carl Kotchian, *The Payoff: Lockheed's 70-Day Mission to Tokyo*, SATURDAY REv., Jul. 9, 1977, at 7.

[12] U.S. SEC. AND EXCHANGE CoMM., REpoRT oF THE SECURITIES AND EXCHANGE CoMMISSIoN oN QUESTIoNABLE AND ILLEGAL CoRpoRATE PAYMENTS AND PRACTICES 2-3 (1976).

[13] *See* H.R. REp. No. 95-640, at 4-5; S. REp. No. 95-114, at 3-4.

[14] H.R. REp. No. 95-640, at 4-5; S. REp. No. 95-114, at 4. The Senate Report observed, for instance, that "[m]anagements which resort to corporate bribery and the falsification of records to enhance their business reveal a lack of confidence about themselves," while citing the Secretary of the Treasury's testimony that "'[p]aying bribes—apart from being morally repugnant and illegal in most countries—is simply not necessary for the successful conduct of business here or overseas.'" *Id.*

[15] *See* S. REp. No. 100-85, at 46 (1987) (recounting FCPA's historical background and explaining that "a strong antibribery statute could help U.S. corporations resist corrupt demands . . . .") [hereinafter S. REp. No. 100-85].

[16] S. REp. No. 95-114, at 7.

[17] Omnibus Trade and Competitiveness Act of 1988, Pub. L. No. 100- 418, § 5003, 102 Stat. 1107, 1415-25 (1988); *see also* H.R. REp. No. 100-576, at 916-24 (1988) (discussing FCPA amendments, including changes to standard of liability for acts of third parties) [hereinafter H.R. REp. No. 100-576].

[18] *See* Omnibus Trade and Competitiveness Act of 1988, § 5003(d). The amended statute included the following directive:

It is the sense of the Congress that the President should pursue the negotiation of an international agreement, among the members of the Organization of Economic Cooperation and Development, to govern persons from those countries concerning acts prohibited with respect to issuers and domestic concerns by the amendments made by this section. Such international agreement should include a process by which problems and conflicts associated with such acts could be resolved.

Id.; *see also* S. REp. No. 105-277, at 2 (1998) (describing efforts by Executive Branch to encourage U.S. trading partners to enact legislation similar to FCPA following 1988 amendments) [hereinafter S. REp. No. 105-277].

[19] Convention on Combating Bribery of Foreign Public Officials in International Business Transactions art. 1.1, Dec. 18, 1997, 37 I.L.M. 1 [hereinafter Anti-Bribery Convention]. The Anti-Bribery Convention requires member countries to make it a criminal offense "for any person intentionally to offer, promise or give any undue pecuniary or other advantage, whether directly or through intermediaries, to a foreign public official, for that official or for a third party, in order that the official act or refrain from acting in relation to the performance of official duties, in order to obtain or retain business or other improper advantage in the conduct of international business." The Convention and its commentaries also call on all parties (a) to ensure that aiding and abetting and authorization of an act of

bribery are criminal offenses, (b) to assert territorial jurisdiction "broadly so that an extensive physical connection to the bribery act is not required," and (c) to assert nationality jurisdiction consistent with the general principles and conditions of each party's legal system. *Id.* at art. 1.2, cmts. 25, 26.

[20] *See* International Anti-Bribery and Fair Competition Act of 1998, Pub. L. 105-366, 112 Stat. 3302 (1998); *see also* S. REp. No. 105-277, at 2-3 (describing amendments to "the FCPA to conform it to the requirements of and to implement the OECD Convention").

[21] There is no private right of action under the FCPA. *See, e.g.*, Lamb v. Phillip Morris, Inc., 915 F.2d 1024, 1028-29 (6th Cir. 1990); McLean v. Int'l Harvester Co., 817 F.2d 1214, 1219 (5th Cir. 1987).

[22] U.S. DEpT. oF JUSTICE, U.S. ATToRNEYS' MANUAL § 9-47.110 (2008) [hereinafter USAM], *available at* http://www.justice.gov/usao/ eousa/foia_reading_room/usam/.

[23] Go to http://export.gov/worldwide_us/index.asp for more information.

[24] Additional information about publicly available market research and due diligence assistance is available online. *See* In'l Trade Admin., *Market Research and Due Diligence*, *available at* http://export.gov/ salesandmarketing/eg_main_018204.asp. The International Company Profile reports include a listing of the potential partner's key officers and senior management; banking relationships and other financial information about the company; and market information, including sales and profit figures and potential liabilities. They are not, however, intended to substitute for a company's own due diligence, and the Commercial Service does not offer ICP in countries where Dun & Bradstreet or other private sector vendors are already performing this service. *See* In'l Trade Admin., *International Company Profile*, *available at* http://export.gov/salesandmarketing/eg_main_018198.asp.

[25] The Commercial Services' domestic and foreign offices can also be found at http://export.gov/usoffices/index.asp and http://export.gov/ worldwide_us/index.asp.

[26] This form can be located at http://tcc.export.gov/Report_a_Barrier/ index.asp.

[27] *See* IN'L TRADE ADMIN., "DoING BUSINESS IN" GUIDES, *available at* http://export.gov/about/eg_main_016806.asp.

[28] The BUSINESS ETHICS MANUAL is available at http://www.ita.doc.gov/goodgovernance /business_ethics/manual.asp.

[29] Information about the Advocacy Center can be found at http://export. gov/advocacy.

[30] Reports on U.S. compliance with these treaties can be found at http:// www.justice.gov/criminal/fraud/fcpa/intlagree/.

[31] *See* Statement on Signing the International Anti-Bribery and Fair Competition Act of 1998, 34 WEEKLY CoMp. PRES. DoC. 2290, 2291 (Nov. 10, 1998) ("U.S. companies have had to compete on an uneven playing field . . . . The OECD Convention . . . is designed to change all that. Under the Convention, our major competitors will be obligated to criminalize the bribery of foreign public officials in international business transactions.").

[32] Colombia is also a member of the Working Group and is expected to accede to the Anti-Bribery Convention.

[33] OECD, *Country Monitoring of the OECD Anti-Bribery Convention*, *available at* http://www.oecd.org/document/12/0,3746, en_2649_34859_35692940_1_1_1_1,00.html.

[34] OECD, *Phase 3 Country Monitoring of the OECD Anti-Bribery Convention*, *available at* http://www.oecd.org/document/31/0,3746, en_2649_34859_44684959_1_1_1_1,00.html.

[35] OECD, *Country Reports on the Implementation of the OECD Anti-Bribery Convention*, *available at* http://www.oecd.org/document/24/0,3 746,en_2649_34859_1933144_1_1_1_1,00.html.

[36] The OECD Phase 1, 2, and 3 reports on the United States, as well as the U.S. responses to questionnaires, are available at http://www.justice. gov/criminal/fraud/fcpa/intlagree.

[37] *See* OECD Working Group on Bribery, *United States: Phase 3, Report on the Application of the Convention on Combating Bribery of Foreign Public Officials in International Business Transactions and the 2009 Revised Recommendation on Combating Bribery in International Business Transactions*, Oct. 2010, at 61-62 (recommending that the United States "[c]onsolidate and summarise publicly available information on the application of the FCPA in relevant sources"), *available at* http://www. oecd.org/dataoecd/10/49 /46213841.pdf.

[38] United Nations Convention Against Corruption, Oct. 31, 2003, S. TREATY Doc. No. 109-6, 2349 U.N.T.S. 41, *available at* http://www. unodc.org/documents/treaties/UNCAC /Publications/Convention/08- 50026_E.pdf [hereinafter UNCAC].

[39] For more information about the UNCAC review mechanism, see *Mechanism for the Review of Implementation of the United Nations Convention Against Corruption*, United Nations Office on Drugs and Crime, *available at* http://www.unodc.org/documents/treaties/ UNCAC/Publications/ReviewMechanism-BasicDocuments/ Mechanism_for_the_Review_ofjmplementation_-_Basic_ Documents_-_E.pdf.

[40] For information about the status of UNCAC, see United Nations Office on Drugs and Crime, *UNCAC Signature and Ratification Status as of 12 July 2012*, *available at* http://www.unodc.org/unodc/en/treaties/ CAC/signatories.html.

[41] Organization of American States, Inter-American Convention Against Corruption, Mar. 29, 1996, 35 I.L.M. 724, *available at* http://www.oas. org/juridico/english/treaties/b-58.html. For additional information about the status of the IACAC, see Organization of American States, Signatories and Ratifications, *available at* http://www.oas.org/juridico/ english/Sigs/b-58.html.

[42] Council of Europe, Criminal Law Convention on Corruption, Jan. 27, 1999, 38 I.L.M. 505, *available at* http://conventions.coe.int/Treaty/en/ Treaties/html/173.htm.

[43] For additional information about GRECO, see Council of Europe, *Group of States Against Corruption*, *available at* http://www.coe.int/t/ dghl/monitoring/greco/default_EN.asp. The United States has not yet ratified the GRECO convention.

[44] The text of the FCPA statute is set forth in the appendix. *See also* Jury Instructions at 21-27, United States v. Esquenazi, No. 09-cr-21010 (S.D. Fla. Aug. 5, 2011), ECF No. 520 [hereinafter *United States v. Esquenazi*] (FCPA jury instructions); Jury Instructions at 14-25, United States v. Kay, No. 01-cr-914 (S.D. Tex. Oct. 6, 2004), ECF No. 142 (same), *aff'd*, 513 F.3d 432, 446-52 (5th Cir. 2007), *reh'g denied*, 513 F.3d 461 (5th Cir. 2008) [hereinafter *United States v. Kay*]; Jury Instructions at 76-87, United States v. Jefferson, No. 07-cr-209 (E.D. Va. July 30, 2009), ECF No. 684 [hereinafter *United States v. Jefferson*] (same); Jury Instructions at 8-10, United States v. Green, No. 08-cr-59 (C.D. Cal. Sept. 11, 2009), ECF No. 288 [hereinafter *United States v. Green*] (same); Jury Instructions at 23-29, United States v. Bourke, No. 05-cr-518 (S.D.N.Y. July 2009) [hereinafter *United States v. Bourke*] (same, not docketed); Jury Instructions at 2-8, United States v. Mead, No. 98-cr-240 (D.N.J. Oct. 1998) [hereinafter *United States v. Mead*] (same).

[45] The provisions of the FCPA applying to issuers are part of the Securities Exchange Act of 1934 [hereinafter Exchange Act]. The anti-bribery provisions can be found at Section 30A of the Exchange Act, 15 U.S.C. § 78dd-1.

[46] 15 U.S.C. § 78*l*.

[47] 15 U.S.C. § 78*o*(d).

[48] SEC enforcement actions have involved a number of foreign issuers. *See*, *e.g.*, Complaint, SEC v. Magyar Telekom Plc., *et al.*, No. 11-cv-9646 (S.D.N.Y. Dec. 29, 2011), ECF No. 1 (German and Hungarian companies), *available at* http://www.sec.gov/litigation/complaints/2011/comp22213-co.pdf; Complaint, SEC v. Alcatel-Lucent, S.A., No. 10-cv-24620 (S.D. Fla. Dec. 27, 2010), ECF No. 1 [hereinafter *SEC v. Alcatel-Lucent*] (French company), *available at* http://www.sec.gov/litigation/complaints/2010/comp21795.pdf; Complaint, SEC v. ABB, Ltd., No. 10-cv-1648 (D.D.C. Sept. 29, 2010), ECF No. 1 [hereinafter *SEC v. ABB*] (Swiss company), *available at* http://www.sec.gov/litigation /complaints/2010/comp-pr2010-175. pdf; Complaint, SEC v. Daimler AG, No. 10-cv-473 (D.D.C. Apr. 1, 2010), ECF No. 1 [hereinafter *SEC v. Daimler AG*] (German company), *available at* http://sec.gov/litigation/complaints/2010/comppr2010-51.pdf; Complaint, SEC v. Siemens Aktiengesellschaft, No. 08- cv-2167 (D.D.C. Dec. 12, 2008), ECF No. 1 [hereinafter *SEC v. Siemens AG*] (Germany company), *available at* http://www.sec.gov/litigation/complaints/2008/comp20829.pdf. Certain DOJ enforcement actions have likewise involved foreign issuers. *See, e.g.*, Criminal Information, United States v. Magyar Telekom, Plc., No. 11-cr-597 (E.D. Va. Dec. 29, 2011), ECF No. 1, *available at* http://www.justice.gov/criminal/fraud/ fcpa/cases/magyar-telekom/2011-12-29-information-magyar-telekom. pdf; Non-Pros. Agreement, In re Deutsche Telekom AG (Dec. 29, 2011), *available at* http://www.justice.gov/criminal/fraud/fcpa/cases/deutsche-telekom/2011-12-29-deustche-telekom-npa.pdf; Criminal Information, United States v. Alcatel-Lucent, S.A., No. 10-cr-20907 (S.D. Fla. Dec. 27, 2010), ECF No. 1 [hereinafter *United States v. Alcatel-Lucent, S.A.*], *available at* http://www.justice.gov/criminal /fraud/fcpa/cases/alcateletal/12-27-10alcatel-et-al-info.pdf; Criminal Information, United States v. Daimler AG, No. 10-cr-63 (D.D.C. Mar. 22, 2010), ECF No. 1 [hereinafter *United States v. Daimler AG*], *available at* http://www. justice.gov/criminal/fraud/fcpa/cases /daimler/03-22-10daimlerag-info. pdf; Criminal Information, United States v. Siemens Aktiengesellschaft, No. 08-cr-367 (D.D.C. Dec. 12, 2008), ECF No. 1 [hereinafter *United States v. Siemens AG*], *available at* http://www.justice.gov/criminal/ fraud/fcpa/cases /siemens/12-12-08siemensakt-info.pdf.

[49] *See* http://www.sec.gov/divisions/corpfin/internatl/companies.shtml.

[50] *See, e.g.*, Complaint, SEC v. Turner, *et al.*, No. 10-cv-1309 (D.D.C. Aug. 4, 2010), ECF No. 1 [hereinafter, *SEC v. Turner*] (charging a Lebansese/Canadian agent of a UK company listed on U.S. exchange with violating the FCPA for bribes of Iraqi officials), *available at* http:// www.sec.gov/litigation/complaints/2010/comp21615.pdf; Indictment, United States v. Naaman, No. 08-cr-246 (D.D.C. Aug. 7, 2008), ECF No. 3 [hereinafter *United States v. Naaman*] (same), *available at* http:// www.justice.gov/criminal/fraud/fcpa/cases/naamano /08-07-08naamanindict.pdf; Complaint, SEC v. Elkin, *et al.*, No. 10-cv-661 (D.D.C. Apr. 28, 2010), ECF No. 1 [hereinafter *SEC v. Elkin*] (charging an employee of U.S. publicly traded company with violating FCPA for bribery of officials in Kyrgyzstan), *available at* http://www.sec.gov/ litigation/complaints/2010/comp21509.pdf; Criminal Information, United States v. Elkin, No. 10-cr-15 (W.D. Va. Aug. 3, 2010), ECF No. 8 [hereinafter *United States v. Elkin*] (same), *available at* http://www. justice.gov/criminal/fraud/fcpa/cases/elkin/08-03-10elkin-information. pdf; Indictment, United States v. Tesler, *et al.*, No. 09-cr-98 (S.D. Tex. Feb. 17, 2009), ECF No. 1 [hereinafter *United States v. Tesler*] (charging a British agent of U.S. publicly traded company with violating the FCPA for bribery of Nigerian officials), *available at* http://www.justice. gov/criminal/fraud/fcpa/cases/tesler/tesler-indict.pdf; Superseding

Indictment, *United States v. Sapsizian*, et al., *supra* note 8, ECF 32 (charging a French employee of French company traded on a U.S. exchange with violating the FCPA).

[51] 15 U.S.C. § 78dd-2.

[52] 15 U.S.C. § 78dd-2(h)(1).

[53] 15 U.S.C. § 78dd-2(a). *See, e.g.*, Superseding Indictment, United States v. Nexus Technologies, *et al.*, No. 08-cr-522 (E.D. Pa. Oct. 28, 2009), ECF No. 106 [hereinafter *United States v. Nexus Technologies*] (private U.S. company and corporate executives charged with violating FCPA for bribes paid in Vietnam), *available at* http://www.justice.gov/criminal/fraud/fcpa/cases/nguyenn/09-04-08nguyen-indict.pdf; Indictment, *United States v. Esquenazi*, *supra* note 44, (private U.S. company and corporate executives charged with FCPA violations for bribes paid in Haiti), *available at* http://www.justice.gov/criminal/fraud/fcpa/cases/ esquenazij/12-08-09esquenazi-indict.pdf.

[54] 15 U.S.C. § 78dd-3(a). As discussed above, foreign companies that have securities registered in the United States or that are required to file periodic reports with the SEC, including certain foreign companies with American Depository Receipts, are covered by the FCPA's anti-bribery provisions governing "issuers" under 15 U.S.C. § 78dd-1.

[55] *See* International Anti-Bribery and Fair Competition Act of 1998, Pub. L. 105-366, 112 Stat. 3302 (1998); 15 U.S.C. § 78dd-3(a); *see also* U.S. DEPT. oF JUSTICE, CRIMINAL RESoURCE MANUAL § 9-1018 (Nov. 2000) (the Department "interprets [Section 78dd-3(a)] as conferring jurisdiction whenever a foreign company or national *causes* an act to be done within the territory of the United States by any person acting as that company's or national's agent."). This interpretation is consistent with U.S. treaty obligations. *See* S. REP. No. 105-2177 (1998) (expressing Congress' intention that the 1998 amendments to the FCPA "conform it to the requirements of and to implement the OECD Convention."); Anti-Bribery Convention at art. 4.1, *supra* note 19 ("Each Party shall take such measures as may be necessary to establish its jurisdiction over the bribery of a foreign public official when the offence is committed in whole or in part in its territory.").

[56] 15 U.S.C. § 78dd-3(a); *see, e.g.*, Criminal Information, United States v. Alcatel-Lucent France, S.A., *et al.*, No. 10-cr-20906 (S.D. Fla. Dec. 27, 2010), ECF No. 1 [hereinafter *United States v. Alcatel-Lucent France*] (subsidiary of French publicly traded company convicted of conspiracy to violate FCPA), *available at* http://www.justice.gov/criminal/fraud/ fcpa/cases/alcatel-lucent-sa-etal/12-27-10alcatel-et-al-info.pdf; Criminal Information, United States v. DaimlerChrysler Automotive Russia SAO, No. 10-cr-64 (D.D.C. Mar. 22, 2010), ECF No. 1 (subsidiary of German publicly traded company convicted of violating FCPA), *available at* http://www.justice.gov/criminal/fraud/fcpa/cases/daimler/03-22-10daimlerrussia-info.pdf; Criminal Information, United States v. Siemens S.A. (Argentina), No. 08-cr-368 (D.D.C. Dec. 12, 2008), ECF No. 1 (subsidiary of German publicly traded company convicted of violating FCPA), *available at* http://www.justice.gov/criminal/fraud /fcpa/cases/ siemens/12-12-08siemensargen-info.pdf.

[57] *See* 15 U.S.C. §§ 78dd-2(h)(5) (defining "interstate commerce"), 78dd3(f)(5) (same); *see also* 15 U.S.C. §78c(a)(17).

[58] 15 U.S.C. §§ 78dd-2(h)(5), 78dd-3(f)(5).

[59] *See* 15 U.S.C. § 78dd-3.

[60] Criminal Information, United States v. JGC Corp., No. 11-cr-260 (S.D. Tex. Apr. 6, 2011), ECF No. 1 [hereinafter *United States v. JGC Corp.*], *available at* http://www.justice.gov /criminal/fraud/fcpa/cases/ jgc-corp/04-6-11jgc-corp-info.pdf; Criminal Information, United States v. Snamprogetti Netherlands B.V., No. 10-cr-460 (S.D. Tex. Jul. 7, 2010), ECF No. 1

[hereinafter *United States v. Snamprogetti*], *available at* http://www.justice.gov/criminal /fraud/fcpa/cases/snamprogetti/07-07- 10snamprogetti-info.pdf.

[61] *See* 15 U.S.C. §§ 78dd-1(g) ("irrespective of whether such issuer or such officer, director, employee, agent, or stockholder makes use of the mails or any means or instrumentality of interstate commerce in furtherance of such offer, gift, payment, promise, or authorization"), 78dd-2(i) (1) ("irrespective of whether such United States person makes use of the mails or any means or instrumentality of interstate commerce in furtherance of such offer, gift, payment, promise, or authorization").

[62] S. REP. No. 105-277 at 2 ("[T]he OECD Convention calls on parties to assert nationality jurisdiction when consistent with national legal and constitutional principles. Accordingly, the Act amends the FCPA to provide for jurisdiction over the acts of U.S. businesses and nationals in furtherance of unlawful payments that take place wholly outside the United States. This exercise of jurisdiction over U.S. businesses and nationals for unlawful conduct abroad is consistent with U.S. legal and constitutional principles and is essential to protect U.S. interests abroad.").

[63] *Id.* at 2-3.

[64] 15 U.S.C. §§ 78dd-1(a), 78dd-2(a), 78dd-3(a).

[65] *See* H.R. REP. No. 95-831, at 12 (referring to "business purpose" test).

[66] *See, e.g.*, Complaint, *SEC v. Siemens AG*, *supra* note 48; Criminal Information, *United States v. Siemens AG*, *supra* note 48.

[67] In amending the FCPA in 1988, Congress made clear that the business purpose element, and specifically the "retaining business" prong, was meant to be interpreted broadly:

The Conferees wish to make clear that the reference to corrupt payments for "retaining business" in present law is not limited to the renewal of contracts or other business, but also includes a prohibition against corrupt payments related to the execution or performance of contracts or the carrying out of existing business, such as a payment to a foreign official for the purpose of obtaining more favorable tax treatment. The term should not, however, be construed so broadly as to include lobbying or other normal representations to government officials. H.R. REP. No. 100-576, at 1951-52 (internal citations omitted).

[68] *See, e.g.*, Complaint, SEC v. Panalpina, Inc., No. 10-cv-4334 (S.D. Tex. Nov. 4, 2010), ECF No. 1 [hereinafter *SEC v. Panalpina, Inc.*], *available at* http://www.sec.gov/litigation /complaints/2010/comp21727.pdf; Criminal Information, United States v. Panalpina, Inc., No. 10-cr765 (S.D. Tex. Nov. 4, 2010), ECF No. 1 [hereinafter *United States v. Panalpina, Inc.*], *available at* http://www.justice.gov/criminal/fraud/ fcpa/cases/panalpina-inc/11-04-10panalpina-info.pdf; Criminal Information, United States v. Panalpina World Transport (Holding) Ltd., No. 10-cr-769 (S.D. Tex. Nov. 4, 2010), ECF No. 1, *available at* http://www.justice.gov/criminal/fraud/fcpa/cases/panalpinaworld/11-04-10panalpina-world-info.pdf; *see also* Press Release, U.S. Sec. and Exchange Comm., SEC Charges Seven Oil Services and Freight Forwarding Companies for Widespread Bribery of Customs Officials (Nov. 4, 2010) ("The SEC alleges that the companies bribed customs officials in more than 10 countries in exchange for such perks as avoiding applicable customs duties on imported goods, expediting the importation of goods and equipment, extending drilling contracts, and lowering tax assessments."), *available at* http://www.sec.gov/ news/press/2010/2010-214.htm; Press Release, U.S. Dept. of Justice, Oil Services Companies and a Freight Forwarding Company Agree to Resolve Foreign Bribery Investigations and to Pay More Than $156 Million in Criminal Penalties (Nov. 4, 2010) (logistics provider and its subsidiary engaged in scheme to pay thousands of bribes totaling at least $27 million to numerous foreign officials on behalf of customers in oil and gas industry "to circumvent

local rules and regulations relating to the import of goods and materials into numerous foreign jurisdictions"), *available at* http://www.justice.gov/opa/pr/2010/November/10- crm-1251.html.

[69] United States v. Kay, 359 F.3d 738, 755-56 (5th Cir. 2004).

[70] *Id.* at 749. Indeed, the *Kay* court found that Congress' explicit exclusion of facilitation payments from the scope of the FCPA was evidence that "Congress intended for the FCPA to prohibit *all other* illicit payments that are intended to influence non-trivial official foreign action in an effort to aid in obtaining or retaining business for some person." *Id.* at 749-50 (emphasis added).

[71] *Id.* at 750.

[72] *Id.* at 749-55.

[73] *Id.* at 756 ("It still must be shown that the bribery was intended to produce an effect—here, through tax savings—that would 'assist in obtaining or retaining business.'").

[74] The FCPA does not explicitly define "corruptly," but in drafting the statute Congress adopted the meaning ascribed to the same term in the domestic bribery statute, 18 U.S.C. § 201(b). *See* H.R. REP. No. 95-640, at 7.

[75] The House Report states in full:

The word "corruptly" is used in order to make clear that the offer, payment, promise, or gift, must be intended to induce the recipient to misuse his official position; for example, wrongfully to direct business to the payor or his client, to obtain preferential legislation or regulations, or to induce a foreign official to fail to perform an official function. The word "corruptly" connotes an evil motive or purpose such as that required under 18 U.S.C. 201(b) which prohibits domestic bribery. As in 18 U.S.C. 201(b), the word "corruptly" indicates an intent or desire wrongfully to influence the recipient. It does not require that the act [be] fully consummated or succeed in producing the desired outcome.

Id. The Senate Report provides a nearly identical explanation of the meaning of the term:

The word "corruptly" is used in order to make clear that the offer, payment, promise, or gift, must be intended to induce the recipient to misuse his official position in order to wrongfully direct business to the payor or his client, or to obtain preferential legislation or a favorable regulation. The word "corruptly" connotes an evil motive or purpose, an intent to wrongfully influence the recipient.

S. Rep. No. 95-114, at 10.

[76] *See* 15 U.S.C. §§ 78dd-1(a), 78dd-2(a), 78dd-3(a).

[77] *See, e.g.*, Complaint, SEC v. Monsanto Co., No. 05-cv-14 (D.D.C. Jan. 6, 2005) (among other things, the company paid a $50,000 bribe to influence an Indonesian official to repeal an unfavorable law, which was not repealed despite the bribe), *available at* http://www.sec.gov/ litigation/complaints/comp19023.pdf; Criminal Information, United States v. Monsanto Co., No. 05-cr-8 (D.D.C. Jan. 6, 2005), *available at* http://www.justice.gov/criminal/fraud/fcpa/cases/monsanto-co/01-06- 05monsanto-info.pdf.

[78] Jury instructions in FCPA cases have defined "corruptly" consistent with the definition found in the legislative history. *See, e.g.*, Jury Instructions at 22-23, *United States v. Esquenazi*, *supra* note 44; Jury Instructions at 10, *United States v. Green*, *supra* note 44; Jury Instructions at 35, *United States v. Jefferson*, *supra* note 44; Jury Instructions at 25, *United States v. Bourke*, *supra* note 44; Jury Instructions at 17, *United States v. Kay*, *supra* note 44; Jury Instructions at 5, *United States v. Mead*, *supra* note 44.

[79] *See* Complaint, SEC v. Innospec, Inc., No. 10-cv-448 (D.D.C. Mar. 18, 2010), ECF No. 1 [hereinafter *SEC v. Innospec*], *available at* http:// www.sec.gov/litigation/complaints/2010 /comp21454.pdf; Criminal Information at 8, United States v. Innospec Inc., No. 10-cr-61

(D.D.C. Mar. 17, 2010), ECF No. 1 [hereinafter *United States v. Innospec*], *available at* http://www.justice.gov/criminal/fraud/fcpa/cases/innospecinc/03-17-10innospec-info.pdf.

[80] *See* Complaint, *SEC v. Innospec*, *supra* note 79; Criminal Information, *United States v. Innospec*, *supra* note 79.

[81] *See* 15 U.S.C. §§ 78dd-1(c)(2)(A), 78dd-2(g)(2)(A), and 78dd-3(3)(2) (A).

[82] *Compare* 15 U.S.C. § 78ff(c)(1)(A) (corporate criminal liability under issuer provision) *with* § 78ff(c)(2)(A) (individual criminal liability under issuer provision); *compare* 15 U.S.C. § 78dd-2(g)(1)(A) (corporate criminal liability under domestic concern provision) *with* § 78dd-2(g) (2)(A) (individual criminal liability under issuer provision); *compare* 15 U.S.C. § 78dd-3(e)(1)(A) (corporate criminal liability for territorial provision) *with* § 78dd-3(e)(2)(A) (individual criminal liability for territorial provision). However, companies still must act corruptly. *See* Section 30A(a), 15 U.S.C. § 78dd-1(a); 15 U.S.C. §§ 78dd-2(a), 78dd-3(a).

[83] United States v. Kay, 513 F.3d 432, 448 (5th Cir. 2007); *see also* Jury Instructions at 38, *United States v. Esquenazi*, *supra* note 44; Jury Instructions at 10, *United States v. Green*, *supra* note 44; Jury Instructions at 35, *United States v. Jefferson*, *supra* note 44; Jury Instructions at 25, *United States v. Bourke*, *supra* note 44; Jury Instructions at 5, *United States v. Mead*, *supra* note 44.

[84] Bryan v. United States, 524 U.S. 184, 191-92 (1998) (construing "willfully" in the context of 18 U.S.C. § 924(a)(1)(A)) (quoting Ratzlaf v. United States, 510 U.S. 135, 137 (1994)); *see also Kay*, 513 F.3d at 446- 51 (discussing *Bryan* and term "willfully" under the FCPA).

[85] *Kay*, 513 F.3d at 447-48; Stichting Ter Behartiging Van de Belangen Van Oudaandeelhouders In Het Kapitaal Van Saybolt Int'l B.V. v. Schreiber, 327 F.3d 173, 181 (2d Cir. 2003).

[86] The phrase "anything of value" is not defined in the FCPA, but the identical phrase under the domestic bribery statute has been broadly construed to include both *tangible* and *intangible* benefits. *See, e.g.*, United States v. Moore, 525 F.3d 1033, 1048 (11th Cir. 2008) (rejecting defendant's objection to instruction defining sex as a "thing of value," which "unambiguously covers intangible considerations"); United States v. Gorman, 807 F.2d 1299, 1304-05 (6th Cir. 1986) (holding that loans and promises of future employment are "things of value"); United States v. Williams, 705 F.2d 603, 622-23 (2d Cir. 1983) (approving jury instruction that stock could be a "thing of value" if defendant believed it had value, even though the shares had no commercial value, and noting that "[t]he phrase 'anything of value' in bribery and related statutes has consistently been given a broad meaning").

[87] Section 30A(a), 15 U.S.C. § 78dd-1(a); 15 U.S.C. §§ 78dd-2(a), 78dd3(a) (emphasis added).

[88] Like the FCPA, the domestic bribery statute, 18 U.S.C. § 201, prohibits giving, offering, or promising "anything of value." Numerous domestic bribery cases under Section 201 have involved "small" dollar bribes. *See, e.g.*, United States v. Franco, 632 F.3d 880, 882-84 (5th Cir. 2011) (affirming bribery convictions of inmate for paying correctional officer $325 to obtain cell phone, food, and marijuana, and noting that 18 U.S.C. § 201 does not contain minimum monetary threshold); United States v. Williams, 216 F.3d 1099, 1103 (D.C. Cir. 2000) (affirming bribery conviction for $70 bribe to vehicle inspector); United States v. Traitz, 871 F.2d 368, 396 (3rd Cir. 1989) (affirming bribery conviction for $100 bribe paid to official of Occupational Health and Safety Administration); United States v. Hsieh Hui Mei Chen, 754 F.2d 817, 822 (9th Cir. 1985) (affirming bribery convictions including $100 bribe to immigration official); United States v. Bishton, 463 F.2d 887, 889 (D.C. Cir. 1972) (affirming bribery conviction for $100 bribe to division chief of District of Columbia Sewer Operations Division).

[89] Complaint, *SEC v. Daimler AG*, *supra* note 48; Criminal Information, *United States v. Daimler AG*, *supra* note 48.

[90] Complaint, SEC v. Halliburton Company and KBR, Inc., No. 09-cv399 (S.D. Tex. Feb. 11, 2009), ECF No 1 [hereinafter *SEC v. Halliburton and KBR*], *available at* http://www.sec.gov/litigation/complaints/2009/ comp20897.pdf; Criminal Information, United States v. Kellogg Brown & Root LLC, No. 09-cr-71, ECF No. 1 (S.D. Tex. Feb. 6, 2009) [hereinafter *United States v. KBR*], *available at* http://www.justice.gov/ criminal/fraud/fcpa/cases/kelloggb/02-06-09kbr-info.pdf.

[91] Complaint, *SEC v. Halliburton and KBR*, *supra* note 90; Criminal Information, *United States v. KBR*, *supra* note 90.

[92] *See, e.g.*, Complaint, SEC v. RAE Sys. Inc., No. 10-cv-2093 (D.D.C. Dec. 10, 2010), ECF No. 1 [hereinafter *SEC v. RAE Sys., Inc.*] (fur coat, among other extravagant gifts), *available at* http://www.sec.gov/ litigation/complaints/2010/comp21770.pdf; Non-Pros. Agreement, In re RAE Sys. Inc. (Dec. 10, 2010) [hereinafter *In re RAE Sys. Inc.*] (same), *available at* http://www.justice.gov/criminal/fraud/fcpa/cases/ rae-systems/12-10-10rae-systems.pdf; Complaint, *SEC v. Daimler AG*, *supra* note 48 (armored Mercedes Benz worth €300,000); Criminal Information, *United States v. Daimler AG*, *supra* note 48 (same).

[93] *See* Complaint, SEC v. ABB Ltd, No. 04-cv-1141 (D.D.C. July 6, 2004), ECF No. 1, *available at* http://www.sec.gov/litigation/ complaints/comp18775.pdf; Criminal Information, United States v. ABB Vetco Gray Inc., *et al.*, No. 04-cr-279 (S.D. Tex. June 22, 2004), ECF No. 1 [hereinafter *United States v. ABB Vetco Gray*], *available at* http://www.justice.gov /criminal/fraud/fcpa/cases/abb/06-22- 04abbvetco-info.pdf.

[94] Complaint, SEC v. UTStarcom, Inc., No. 09-cv-6094 (N.D. Cal. Dec. 31, 2009), ECF No. 1 [hereinafter *SEC v. UTStarcom*], *available at* http://www.sec.gov/litigation/complaints /2009/comp21357.pdf; Non-Pros. Agreement, In re UTStarcom Inc. (Dec. 31, 2009) [hereinafter *In re UTStarcom*], *available at* http://www.justice.gov/criminal/fraud/fcpa/ cases/utstarcom-inc/12-31-09utstarcom-agree.pdf.

[95] Complaint, *SEC v. UTStarcom*, *supra* note 94; Non-Pros. Agreement, *In re UTStarcom*, *supra* note 94.

[96] Complaint, *SEC v. UTStarcom*, *supra* note 94; Non-Pros. Agreement, *In re UTStarcom*, *supra* note 94.

[97] Complaint, SEC v. Lucent Technologies Inc., No. 07-cv-2301 (D.D.C. Dec. 21, 2007), ECF No.1 [hereinafter *SEC v. Lucent*], *available at* http://www.sec.gov/litigation /complaints/2007/comp20414.pdf; Non-Pros. Agreement, In re Lucent Technologies (Nov. 14, 2007) [hereinafter *In re Lucent*], *available at* http://www.justice.gov/criminal/ fraud/fcpa/ cases/lucent-tech/11-14-07lucent-agree.pdf.

[98] Complaint, *SEC v. Lucent*, *supra* note 97; Non-Pros. Agreement, *In re Lucent*, *supra* note 97.

[99] The company consented to the entry of a final judgment permanently enjoining it from future violations of the books and records and internal controls provisions and paid a civil penalty of $1,500,000. Complaint, *SEC v. Lucent*, *supra* note 97. Additionally, the company entered into a non-prosecution agreement with DOJ and paid a $1,000,000 monetary penalty. Non-Pros. Agreement, *In re Lucent*, *supra* note 97.

[100] United States v. Liebo, 923 F.2d 1308, 1311 (8th Cir. 1991).

[101] Judgment, United States v. Liebo, No. 89-cr-76 (D. Minn. Jan. 31, 1992), *available at* http://www.justice.gov/criminal/fraud/fcpa/cases/ liebor/1992-01-31-liebor-judgment.pdf.

[102] Complaint, SEC v. Schering-Plough Corp., No. 04-cv-945 (D.D.C. June 9, 2004), ECF No. 1, *available at* http://www.sec.gov/litigation/ complaints/comp18740.pdf; Admin. Proceeding Order, In the Matter of Schering-Plough Corp., Exchange Act Release No. 49838 (June 9,

2004) (finding that company violated FCPA accounting provisions and imposing $500,000 civil monetary penalty), *available at* http://www.sec. gov/litigation/admin/34-49838.htm.

[103] FCPA opinion procedure releases can be found at http://www. justice.gov/criminal/fraud /fcpa/. In the case of the company seeking to contribute the $1.42 million grant to a local MFI, DOJ noted that it had undertaken each of these due diligence steps and controls, in addition to others, that would minimize the likelihood that anything of value would be given to any officials of the Eurasian country. U.S. DEpT. oF JUSTICE, FCPA Op. RELEASE 10-02 (July 16, 2010), *available at* http://www. justice.gov/criminal/fraud/fcpa /opinion/2010/1002.pdf.

[104] U.S. DEpT. oF JUSTICE, FCPA Op. RELEASE 95-01 (Jan. 11, 1995), *available at* http://www.justice.gov/criminal/fraud/fcpa/ opinion/1995/9501.pdf.

[105] *Id.*

[106] *Id.*

[107] U.S. DEpT. oF JUSTICE, FCPA Op. RELEASE 97-02 (Nov. 5, 1997), *available at* http://www.justice.gov/criminal/fraud/fcpa/ opinion/1997/9702.pdf; U.S. DEpT. oF JUSTICE, FCPA Op. RELEASE 06-01 (Oct. 16, 2006), *available at* http://www.justice.gov /criminal/ fraud/fcpa/opinion/2006/0601.pdf.

[108] U.S. DEpT. oF JUSTICE, FCPA Op. RELEASE 06-01 (Oct. 16, 2006).

[109] *Id.*

[110] *Id.*

[111] *See* Section 30A(a)(1)-(3) of the Exchange Act, 15 U.S.C. § 78dd-1(a) (1)-(3); 15 U.S.C. §§ 78dd-2(a)(1)-(3), 78dd-3(a)(1)-(3).

[112] Section 30A(f)(1)(A) of the Exchange Act, 15 U.S.C. § 78dd-1(f)(1) (A); 15 U.S.C. §§ 78dd-2(h)(2)(A), 78dd-3(f)(2)(A).

[113] Under the FCPA, any person "acting in an official capacity for or on behalf of" a foreign government, a department, agency, or instrumentality thereof, or a public international organization, is a foreign official. Section 30A(f)(1)(A), 15 U.S.C. § 78dd-1(f)(1)(A); 15 U.S.C. §§ 78dd-2(h)(2)(A), 78dd-2(f)(2)(A). *See also* U.S. DEpT. oF JUSTICE, FCPA Op. RELEASE No. 10-03, at 2 (Sept. 1, 2010), *available at* http://www.justice.gov /criminal/fraud/fcpa/opinion/2010/1003.pdf (listing safeguards to ensure that consultant was not acting on behalf of foreign government).

[114] *But see* Sections 30A(b) and f(3)(A) of the Exchange Act, 15 U.S.C. § 78dd-1(b) & (f)(3); 15 U.S.C. §§ 78dd-2(b) & (h)(4), 78dd-3(b) & (f) (4) (facilitating payments exception).

[115] Even though payments to a foreign government may not violate the anti-bribery provisions of the FCPA, such payments may violate other U.S. laws, including wire fraud, money laundering, and the FCPA's accounting provisions. This was the case in a series of matters brought by DOJ and SEC involving kickbacks to the Iraqi government through the United Nations Oil-for-Food Programme. *See, e.g.*, Complaint, *SEC v. Innospec*, *supra* note 79; Criminal Information, *United States v. Innospec*, *supra* note 79; Complaint, SEC v. Novo Nordisk A/S, No. 09-cv-862 (D.D.C. May 11, 2009), ECF No. 1, *available at* http://www.sec.gov/ litigation/complaints/2009/comp21033.pdf; Criminal Information, United States v. Novo Nordisk A/S, No. 09-cr-126 (D.D.C. May 11, 2009), ECF No. 1, *available at* http://www.justice.gov/criminal/ fraud/fcpa/cases/nordiskn/05-11-09novo-info.pdf; Complaint, SEC v. Ingersoll-Rand Company Ltd., No. 07-cv-1955 (D.D.C. Oct. 31, 2007), ECF No. 1, *available at* http://www.sec.gov/litigation/ complaints /2007/comp20353.pdf; Criminal Information, United States v. Ingersoll-Rand Italiana SpA, No. 07-cr-294 (D.D.C. Oct. 31, 2007), ECF No. 1, *available at* http://www.justice.gov /criminal/fraud/fcpa/cases/ingerand-italiana/10-31-07ingersollrand-info.pdf; Complaint,

SEC v. York Int'l Corp., No. 07-cv-1750 (D.D.C. Oct. 1, 2007), ECF No. 1 [hereinafter *SEC v. York Int'l Corp.*], *available at* http://www.sec. gov/litigation/complaints/2007/comp20319.pdf; Criminal Information, United States v. York Int'l Corp., No. 07-cr-253 (D.D.C. Oct. 1, 2007), ECF No. 1 [hereinafter *United States v. York Int'l Corp.*], *available at* http://www.justice.gov/criminal/fraud/fcpa/cases/york/10-01-07yorkinfo.pdf; Complaint, SEC v. Textron Inc., No. 07-cv-1505 (D.D.C. Aug. 23, 2007), ECF No. 1 [hereinafter *SEC v. Textron*], *available at* http:// www.sec.gov/litigation/complaints /2007/comp20251.pdf; Non-Pros. Agreement, In re Textron Inc. (Aug. 23, 2007), *available at* http://www. justice.gov/criminal /fraud/fcpa/cases/textron-inc/08-21-07textronagree.pdf. DOJ has issued opinion procedure releases concerning payments (that were, in essence, donations) to government agencies or departments. *See* U.S. DEpT. oF JUSTICE, FCPA Op. RELEASE 09-01 (Aug. 3, 2009) (involving donation of 100 medical devices to foreign government), *available at* http://www.justice.gov/criminal/fraud/ fcpa/opinion/2009 /0901.pdf; U.S. DEpT. oF JUSTICE, FCPA Op. RELEASE 06-01 (Oct. 16, 2006) (involving contribution of $25,000 to regional customs department to pay incentive rewards to improve local enforcement of anti-counterfeiting laws), *available at* http://www.justice. gov/criminal/fraud/fcpa/opinion /2006/0601.pdf.

116 The United States has some state-owned entities, like the Tennessee Valley Authority, that are instrumentalities of the government. McCarthy v. Middle Tenn. Elec. Membership Corp., 466 F.3d 399, 411 n.18 (6th Cir. 2006) ("[T]here is no question that TVA is an agency and instrumentality of the United States.") (internal quotes omitted).

117 During the period surrounding the FCPA's adoption, state-owned entities held virtual monopolies and operated under state-controlled price-setting in many national industries around the world. *See generally* WoRLD BANK, BUREAUCRATS IN BUSINESS: THE ECoNoMICS AND PoLITICS oF GoVERNMENT OWNERSHIp, WoRLD BANK PoLICY RESEARCH Report at 78 (1995); SUNITA KIKERI AND AISHETU KoLo, STATE ENTERpRISES, THE WoRLD BANK GRoUp (Feb. 2006), *available at* http://rru.worldbank.org/documents/ publicpolicyjournal/304Kikeri_Kolo.pdf.

118 *Id.* at 1 ("[A]fter more than two decades of privatization, government ownership and control remains widespread in many regions—and in many parts of the world still dominates certain sectors.").

119 To date, consistent with the approach taken by DOJ and SEC, all district courts that have considered this issue have concluded that this is an issue of fact for a jury to decide. *See* Order, United States v. Carson, 2011 WL 5101701, No. 09-cr-77 (C.D. Cal. May 18, 2011), ECF No. 373 [hereinafter *United States v. Carson*]; United States v. Aguilar, 783 F. Supp. 2d 1108 (C.D. Cal. 2011); Order, *United States v. Esquenazi*, *supra* note 44, ECF No. 309; *see also* Order, United States v. O'Shea, No. 09-cr-629 (S.D. Tex. Jan. 3, 2012), ECF No. 142; Order, United States v. Nguyen, No. 08-cr-522 (E.D. Pa. Dec. 30, 2009), ECF No. 144. These district court decisions are consistent with the acceptance by district courts around the country of over 35 guilty pleas by individuals who admitted to violating the FCPA by bribing officials of state-owned or state-controlled entities. *See* Government's Opposition to Defendants' Amended Motion to Dismiss Counts One Through Ten of the Indictment at 18, *United States v. Carson*, *supra* note 119, ECF No. 332; Exhibit I, *United States v. Carson*, *supra* note 119, ECF No. 335 (list of examples of enforcement actions based on foreign officials of state-owned entities).

120 Jury Instructions, *United States v. Esquenazi*, *supra* note 44, ECF No. 520; Order at 5 and Jury Instructions, *United States* v. *Carson*, *supra* note 119, ECF No. 373 and ECF No. 549; *Aguilar*, 783 F. Supp. 2d at 1115.

121 Criminal Information, United States v. C.E. Millier Corp., *et al.*, No. 82-cr-788 (C.D. Cal. Sept. 17, 1982), *available at* http://www. justice.gov/criminal/fraud/fcpa/cases/ce-miller/1982-09-17-ce-millerinformation.pdf.

122 *See* Complaint, SEC v. Sam P. Wallace Co., Inc., *et al.*, No. 81-cv1915 (D.D.C. Aug. 31, 1982); Criminal Information, United States v. Sam P. Wallace Co., Inc., No. 83-cr-34 (D.P.R. Feb. 23, 1983), *available at* http://www.justice.gov/criminal/fraud/fcpa/cases/sam-wallacecompany/1983-02-23-sam-wallace-company-information.pdf; *see also* Criminal Information, United States v. Goodyear Int'l Corp., No. 89- cr-156 (D.D.C. May 11, 1989) (Iraqi Trading Company identified as "instrumentality of the Government of the Republic of Iraq"), *available at* http://www.justice.gov/criminal/fraud/fcpa/cases/goodyear/1989-05-11-goodyear-information.pdf.

123 *See* Complaint, *SEC v. ABB*, *supra* note 48; Criminal Information at 3, United States v. ABB Inc., No. 10-cr-664 (S.D. Tex. Sept. 29, 2010), ECF No. 1 [hereinafter *United States v. ABB*], *available at* http:// www.justice.gov/criminal/fraud/fcpa/cases/abb/09-20-10abbinc-info. pdf; Constitución Política de los Estados Unidos Mexicanos [C.P.], as amended, art. 27, Diario Oficial de la Federación [DO], 5 de Febrero de 1917 (Mex.); Ley Del Servicio Publico de Energia Electrica, as amended, art. 1-3, 10, Diario Oficial de la Federación [DO], 22 de Diciembre de 1975 (Mex.).

124 *See* Indictment at 2, *United States v. Esquenazi*, *supra* note 44, ECF No. 3; Affidavit of Mr. Louis Gary Lissade at 1-9, *id.*, ECF No. 417-2.

125 Criminal Information at 30-31, *United States v. Alcatel-Lucent France*, *supra* note 56, ECF No. 10.

126 *Id.*

127 *See* International Anti-Bribery and Fair Competition Act of 1998, Pub. L. 105-366 § 2, 112 Stat. 3302, 3303, 3305, 3308 (1998).

128 Section 30A(F)(1)(B) of the Exchange Act, 15 U.S.C. § 78dd-1(f)(1) (B); 15 U.S.C. §§ 78dd-2(h)(2)(B), 78dd-3(f)(2)(B).

129 Third parties and intermediaries themselves are also liable for FCPA violations. Section 30A(a) of the Exchange Act, 15 U.S.C. § 78dd-1(a); 15 U.S.C. §§ 78dd-2(a), and 78dd-3(a).

130 Section 30A(a)(3) of the Exchange Act, 15 U.S.C. § 78dd-1(a)(3); 15 U.S.C. §§ 78dd-2(a)(3), 78dd-3(a)(3).

131 *See, e.g.*, Complaint, SEC v. Johnson & Johnson, No. 11-cv-686 (D.D.C. Apr. 8, 2011) [hereinafter *SEC v. Johnson & Johnson*] (bribes paid through Greek and Romanian agents)), *available at* http://www.sec. gov/litigation/complaints/2011/comp21922.pdf; Criminal Information, United States v. DePuy, Inc., No. 11-cr-99 (D.D.C. Apr. 8, 2011), ECF No. 1 [hereinafter *United States v. DePuy*] (bribes paid through Greek agents), *available at* http://www.justice.gov/criminal/fraud/fcpa/cases/depuy-inc/04-08-11depuy-info.pdf;
Complaint, *SEC v. ABB, supra* note 48 (bribes paid through Mexican agents); Criminal Information, *United States v. ABB*, *supra* note 123 (same); Criminal Information, United States v. Int'l Harvester Co., No. 82-cr-244 (S.D. Tex. Nov. 17, 1982) (bribes paid through Mexican agent), *available at* http://www.justice. gov/criminal/fraud/fcpa/cases /international-harvester/1982-11-17- international-harvester-information.pdf.

132 *See* Criminal Information, United States v. Marubeni Corp., No. 12- cr-22 (S.D. Tex. Jan. 17, 2012), ECF No. 1 [hereinafter *United States v. Marubeni*], *available at* http://www.justice. gov/criminal/fraud/fcpa/cases/marubeni/2012-01-17-marubeni-information.pdf; Criminal Information, *United States v. JGC Corp.*, *supra* note 60, ECF No. 1; Criminal Information, *United States v. Snamprogetti*, *supra* note 60, ECF No. 1; Complaint, SEC v. ENI, S.p.A. and Snamprogetti Netherlands B.V., No. 10-cv-2414 (S.D. Tex. July 7, 2010), ECF No. 1,

available at http://www.sec.gov/litigation /complaints/2010/comp-pr2010-119.pdf; Criminal Information, United States v. Technip S.A., No. 10-cr-439 (S.D. Tex. June 28, 2010), ECF No. 1 [hereinafter *United States v. Technip*], *available at* http://www.justice.gov/criminal/fraud/fcpa/cases/technipsa/06-28-10-technip-%20information.pdf; Complaint, SEC v. Technip, No. 10-cv-2289 (S.D. Tex. June 28, 2010), ECF No. 1 [hereinafter *SEC v. Technip*], *available at* http://www.sec.gov /litigation/complaints/2010/ comp-pr2010-110.pdf; Indictment, *United States v. Tesler, supra* note 50; Complaint, *SEC v. Halliburton and KBR, supra* note 90; Criminal Information, *United States v. KBR, supra* note 90; Criminal Information, *United States v. Stanley*, No. 08-cr-597 (S.D. Tex. Sept. 3, 2008), ECF No. 1, *available at* http://justice.gov/criminal/fraud/fcpa/cases/stanleya/08- 29-08stanley-info.pdf.

[133] *See* Criminal Information, United States v. AGA Medical Corp., No. 08-cr-172, ECF No. 1 (D. Minn. June 3, 2008), *available at* http://www. justice.gov/criminal/fraud /fcpa/cases /agamedcorp/06-03-08aga-info. pdf.

[134] Complaint, *SEC v. Innospec, supra* note 79; Criminal Information, *United States v. Innospec, supra* note 79; Superseding Criminal Information, *United States v. Naaman, supra* note 50, ECF No. 15, *available at* http://www.justice.gov/criminal/fraud/fcpa/cases/ naamano/06-24-10naaman-supsersed-info.pdf; Complaint, *SEC v. Turner, supra* note 50.

[135] *See* sources cited *supra* note 68.

[136] *See* sources cited *supra* note 68.

[137] Section 30A(a)(3) of the Exchange Act, 15 U.S.C. § 78dd-1(a)(3); 15 U.S.C. §§ 78dd-2(a)(3), 78dd-3(a)(3).

[138] *See* Section 30A(f)(2)(A) of the Exchange Act, 15 U.S.C. § 78dd-1(f) (2)(A); 15 U.S.C. §§ 78dd-2(h)(3)(A), 78dd-3(f)(3)(A).

[139] *See* Section 30A(f)(2)(B) of the Exchange Act, 15 U.S.C. § 78dd-1(f) (2)(B); 15 U.S.C. §§ 78dd-2(h)(3)(B), 78dd-3(f)(3)(B). The "knowing" standard was intended to cover "both prohibited actions that are taken with 'actual knowledge' of intended results as well as other actions that, while falling short of what the law terms 'positive knowledge,' nevertheless evidence a conscious disregard or deliberate ignorance of known circumstances that should reasonably alert one to the high probability of violations of the Act." H.R. REp. No. 100-576, at 920; *see also* Omnibus Trade and Competitiveness Act of 1988, Pub. L. No. 100-418, § 5003, 102 Stat. 1107, 1423-24 (1988).

[140] H.R. REp. No. 100-576, at 920 (1988).

[141] Section 30A(c)(1) of the Exchange Act, 15 U.S.C. § 78dd-1(c)(1); 15 U.S.C. §§ 78dd-2(c)(1), 78dd-3(c)(1).

[142] H.R. REp. No. 100-576, at 922. The conferees also noted that "[i]n interpreting what is 'lawful under the written laws and regulations' . . . the normal rules of legal construction would apply." *Id.*

[143] *See* United States v. Kozeny, 582 F. Supp. 2d 535, 537-40 (S.D.N.Y. 2008). Likewise, the court found that a provision under Azeri law that relieved bribe payors of criminal liability if they were extorted did not make the bribe payments legal. Azeri extortion law precludes the prosecution of the payor of the bribes for the illegal payments, but it does not make the payments legal. *Id.* at 540-41.

[144] Section 30A(c)(2)(A), (B) of the Exchange Act, 15 U.S.C. § 78dd-1(c) (2); 15 U.S.C. §§ 78dd-2(c)(2), 78dd-3(c)(2).

[145] For example, the Eighth Circuit Court of Appeals found that providing airline tickets to a government official in order to corruptly influence that official may form the basis for a violation of the FCPA's anti-bribery provisions. *See Liebo*, 923 F. 2d at 1311-12.

[146] *See generally* U.S. DEpT. oF JUSTICE, FCPA Op. RELEASE 11-01 (June 30, 2011) (travel, lodging, and meal expenses of two foreign officials for two-day trip to United States to learn about services of U.S. adoption service provider), *available at* http://www.justice.gov/criminal/ fraud/fcpa/opinion/2011/11-01.pdf; U.S. DEpT. oF JUSTICE, FCPA Op. RELEASE 08-03 (July 11, 2008) (stipends to reimburse minimal travel expenses of local, government-affiliated journalists attending press conference in foreign country), *available at* http://www.justice.gov/ criminal/fraud/fcpa/opinion /2008/0803.pdf; U.S. DEpT. oF JUSTICE, FCPA Op. RELEASE 07-02 (Sept. 11, 2007) (domestic travel, lodging, and meal expenses of six foreign officials for six-week educational program), *available at* http://www.justice.gov/criminal/fraud/fcpa/ opinion/2007/0702.pdf; U.S. DEpT. oF JUSTICE, FCPA Op. RELEASE 07-01 (July 24, 2007) (domestic travel, lodging, and meal expenses of six foreign officials for four-day educational and promotional tour of U.S. company's operations sites), *available at* http://www.justice. gov/criminal/fraud/fcpa/opinion/2007/0701.pdf; U.S. DEpT. oF JUSTICE, FCPA Op. RELEASE 04-04 (Sept. 3, 2004) (travel, lodging, and modest per diem expenses of five foreign officials to participate in nine-day study tour of mutual insurance companies), *available at* http://www.justice.gov/criminal/fraud /fcpa /opinion/2004/0404. pdf; U.S. DEpT. oF JUSTICE, FCPA Op. RELEASE 04-03 (June 14, 2004) (travel, lodging, meal, and insurance expenses for twelve foreign officials and one translator on ten-day trip to three U.S. cities to meet with U.S. public sector officials), *available at* http://www.justice.gov/ criminal/fraud/fcpa/opinion/2004/0403.pdf; U.S. DEpT. oF JUSTICE, FCPA Op. RELEASE 04-01 (Jan. 6, 2004) (seminar expenses, including receptions, meals, transportation and lodging costs, for one-and-a-half day comparative law seminar on labor and employment law in foreign country), *available at* http://www.justice.gov/criminal/fraud/fcpa/opinion/2004/0401.pdf; U.S. DEpT. oF JUSTICE, FCPA Op. RELEASE 96-01 (Nov. 25, 1996) (travel, lodging, and meal expenses of regional government representatives to attend training courses in United States), *available at* http://www.justice.gov/criminal/fraud/fcpa/ opinion/1996/9601.pdf; U.S. DEpT. oF JUSTICE, FCPA Op. RELEASE 92-01 (Feb. 1992) (training expenses so that foreign officials could effectively perform duties related to execution and performance of joint-venture agreement, including seminar fees, airfare, lodging, meals, and ground transportation), *available at* http://www.justice.gov/criminal/ fraud/fcpa/review/1992 /r9201.pdf.

[147] U.S. DEpT. oF JUSTICE, FCPA Op. RELEASE 11-01 (June 30, 2011); U.S. DEpT. oF JUSTICE, FCPA Op. RELEASE 07-02 (Sept. 11, 2007); U.S. DEpT. oF JUSTICE, FCPA Op. RELEASE 07-01 (July 24, 2007); U.S. DEpT. oF JUSTICE, FCPA Op. RELEASE 04-04 (Sept. 3, 2004); U.S. DEpT. oF JUSTICE, FCPA Op. RELEASE 04-03 (June 14, 2004); U.S. DEpT. oF JUSTICE, FCPA Op. RELEASE 04-01 (Jan. 6, 2004).

[148] U.S. DEpT. oF JUSTICE, FCPA Op. RELEASE 96-01 (Nov. 25, 1996).

[149] U.S. DEpT. oF JUSTICE, FCPA Op. RELEASE 11-01 (June 30, 2011); U.S. DEpT. oF JUSTICE, FCPA Op. RELEASE 07-02 (Sept. 11, 2007); U.S. DEpT. oF JUSTICE, FCPA Op. RELEASE 07-01 (July 24, 2007); U.S. DEpT. oF JUSTICE, FCPA Op. RELEASE 04-04 (Sept. 3, 2004); U.S. DEpT. oF JUSTICE, FCPA Op. RELEASE 04-01 (Jan. 6, 2004) .

[150] U.S. DEpT. oF JUSTICE, FCPA Op. RELEASE 04-01 (Jan. 6, 2004).

[151] U.S. DEpT. oF JUSTICE, FCPA Op. RELEASE 08-03 (July 11, 2008).

[152] U.S. DEpT. oF JUSTICE, FCPA Op. RELEASE 11-01 (June 30, 2011); U.S. DEpT. oF JUSTICE, FCPA Op. RELEASE 92-01 (Feb. 1992).

[153] U.S. DEpT. oF JUSTICE, FCPA Op. RELEASE 08-03 (July 11, 2008).

[154] *Id.*

[155] *Id.*; U.S. DEpT. oF JUSTICE, FCPA Op. RELEASE 04-03 (June 14, 2004); U.S. DEpT. oF JUSTICE, FCPA Op. RELEASE 04-01 (Jan. 6, 2004); U.S. DEpT. oF JUSTICE, FCPA Op. RELEASE 07-01 (July 24, 2007).

[156] U.S. DEpT. oF JUSTICE, FCPA Op. RELEASE 11-01 (June 30, 2011); U.S. DEpT. oF JUSTICE, FCPA Op. RELEASE 07-02 (Sept. 11, 2007); U.S. DEpT. oF JUSTICE, FCPA Op. RELEASE 07-01 (July 24, 2007); U.S. DEpT. oF JUSTICE, FCPA Op. RELEASE 04-04 (Sept. 3, 2004); U.S. DEpT. oF JUSTICE, FCPA Op. RELEASE 04-03 (June 14, 2004); U.S. DEpT. oF JUSTICE, FCPA Op. RELEASE 04-01 (Jan. 6, 2004).

[157] U.S. DEpT. oF JUSTICE, FCPA Op. RELEASE 07-01 (July 24, 2007); U.S. DEpT. oF JUSTICE, FCPA Op. RELEASE 08-03 (July 11, 2008).

[158] For example, DOJ has previously approved expenditures on behalf of family members or for entertainment purposes under certain, limited circumstances. *See, e.g.*, U.S. DEpT. oF JUSTICE, FCPA REv. P. RELEASE 83-02 (July 26, 1983) (declining to take enforcement action against company seeking to provide promotional tour for foreign official and wife, where both had already planned a trip to the United States at their own expense and company proposed to pay only for all reasonable and necessary actual domestic expenses for the extension of their travel to allow the promotional tour, which would not exceed $5,000), *available at* http://www.justice.gov/criminal/fraud/fcpa/review/1983/r8302.pdf.

[159] Unlike the local law and bona fide expenditures defenses, the facilitating payments exception is not an affirmative defense to the FCPA. Rather, payments of this kind fall outside the scope of the FCPA's bribery prohibition. Prior to 1988, the "facilitating payments" exception was incorporated into the definition of "foreign official," which excluded from the statute's purview officials whose duties were primarily ministerial or clerical. *See* Foreign Corrupt Practices Act of 1977, Pub. L. No. 95-213, § 104(d)(2), 91 Stat. 1494, 1498 (1977) (providing that the term foreign official "does not include any employee of a foreign government or any department, agency, or instrumentality thereof whose duties are essentially ministerial or clerical"). The original exception thus focused on the duties of the recipient, rather than the purpose of the payment. In practice, however, it proved difficult to determine whether a foreign official's duties were "ministerial or clerical." S. REp. No. 100- 85, at 53. Responding to criticism that the statutory language "does not clearly reflect Congressional intent and the boundaries of the prohibited conduct," Congress revised the FCPA to define the exception in terms of the purpose of the payment. H. REp. No. 100-40, pt. 2, at 77. In doing so, Congress reiterated that while its policy to exclude facilitating payments reflected practical considerations of enforcement, "such payments should not be condoned." *Id.* The enacted language reflects this narrow purpose.

[160] In exempting facilitating payments, Congress sought to distinguish them as "payments which merely move a particular matter toward an eventual act or decision or which do not involve any discretionary action," giving the examples of "a gratuity paid to a customs official to speed the processing of a customs document" or "payments made to secure permits, licenses, or the expeditious performance of similar duties of an essentially ministerial or clerical nature which must of necessity be performed in any event." H.R. REp. No. 95-640, at 8.

[161] Section 30A(f)(3)(B) of the Exchange Act, 15 U.S.C. § 78dd-1(f)(3) (B); 15 U.S.C. §§ 78dd-2(h)(4)(B), 78dd-3(f)(4)(B).

[162] In a 2004 decision, the Fifth Circuit emphasized this precise point, commenting on the limited nature of the facilitating payments exception: A brief review of the types of routine governmental actions enumerated by Congress shows how limited Congress wanted to

make the grease exceptions. Routine governmental action, for instance, includes "obtaining permits, licenses, or other official documents to qualify a person to do business in a foreign country," and "scheduling inspections associated with contract performance or inspections related to transit of goods across country." Therefore, routine governmental action does not include the issuance of *every* official document or *every* inspection, but only (1) documentation that qualifies a party to do business and (2) scheduling an inspection—very narrow categories of largely non-discretionary, ministerial activities performed by mid- or low-level foreign functionaries. United States v. Kay; 359 F.3d 738, 750-51 (5th Cir. 2004) (internal footnote omitted) (emphasis in original).

[163] Non-Pros. Agreement, In re Helmerich & Payne, Inc. (July 29, 2009) [hereinafter *In re Helmerich & Payne*], *available at* http://www.justice. gov/criminal/fraud /fcpa/cases /helmerich-payne/06-29-09helmerichagree.pdf; Admin. Proceeding Order, In the Matter of Helmerich & Payne, Inc., Exchange Act Release No. 60400 (July 30, 2009) [hereinafter *In the Matter of Helmerich & Payne*], *available at* http://www.sec.gov/ litigation/admin /2009/34-60400.pdf.

[164] Criminal Information, Vetco Gray Controls Inc., *et al.*, No. 07- cr-4 No. (S.D. Tex. Jan. 5, 2007), ECF Nos. 1-2, *available at* http:// www.justice.gov/criminal/fraud/fcpa/cases/vetco-controls/02-06- 07vetcogray-info.pdf.

[165] Complaint, SEC v. Noble Corp., No. 10-cv-4336 (S.D. Tex. Nov. 4, 2010), ECF No. 1, *available at* http://www.sec.gov/litigation/ complaints/2010/comp21728.pdf; Non-Pros. Agreement, In re Noble Corp. (Nov. 4, 2010), *available at* http://www.justice.gov/criminal/ fraud/fcpa/cases/noble-corp/11-04-10noble-corp-npa.pdf; *see also sources cited supra* note 68.

[166] Working Group on Bribery, *2009 Recommendation of the Council for Further Combating Bribery of Foreign Public Officials in International Business Transactions*, at § VI (recommending countries should periodically review their policies and approach to facilitation payments and should encourage companies to prohibit or discourage facilitation payments "in view of the corrosive effect of small facilitation payments, particularly on sustainable economic development and the rule of law"); Working Group on Bribery, *United States: Phase 3*, at 24 (Oct. 15, 2010), *available at* http://www.oecd.org /dataoecd/10/49/46213841. pdf (commending United States for steps taken in line with 2009 recommendation to encourage companies to prohibit or discourage facilitation payments).

[167] Facilitating payments are illegal under the U.K. Bribery Act 2010, which came into force on July 1, 2011, and were also illegal under prior U.K. legislation. *See* Bribery Act 2010, c.23 (Eng.), *available at* http://www.legislation.gov.uk/ukpga/2010/23/contents; *see also* U.K. MINISTRY oF JUSTICE, *The Bribery Act 2010: Guidance About Procedures Which Relevant Commercial Organisations Can Put into Place to Prevent Persons Associated with Them from Bribing (Section 9 of the Bribery Act 2010)*, at 18 (2011), *available at* http://www.justice.gov.uk/ guidance/docs/bribery-act-2010-guidance.pdf.

[168] *See, e.g.*, Non-Pros. Agreement, *In re Helmerich & Payne*, *supra* note 163; Admin. Proceeding Order, *In the Matter of Helmerich & Payne*, *supra* note 163.

[169] In order to establish duress or coercion, a defendant must demonstrate that the defendant was under unlawful, present, immediate, and impending threat of death or serious bodily injury; that the defendant did not negligently or recklessly create a situation where he would be forced to engage in criminal conduct (e.g., had been making payments as part of an ongoing bribery scheme); that the defendant had no reasonable legal alternative to violating the law; and that there was a direct causal relationship between the criminal action and the avoidance

of the threatened harm. *See* Eleventh Circuit Pattern Jury Instr., Special Instr. No. 16 (2003); *see also* Fifth Circuit Pattern Jury Instr. No. 1.36 (2001); Sixth Circuit Pattern Jury Instr. No. 6.05 (2010); Seventh Circuit Pattern Jury Instr. No. 6.08 (1998); Ninth Circuit Pattern Jury Instr. No. 6.5 (2010); 1A Kevin F. O'Malley, Jay E. Grenig, Hon. William C. Lee, *Federal Jury Practice and Instructions* § 19.02 (6th ed. 2008 & Supp. 2012).

[170] S. REP. No. 95-114, at 11.

[171] *Id.* at 10.

[172] *Id.* at 11.

[173] United States v. Kozeny, 582 F. Supp. 2d 535, 540 n.31 (S.D.N.Y. 2008).

[174] *Kozeny*, 582 F. Supp. 2d at 540 (citing S. REP. No. 95-114, at 10-11).

[175] *Id.*

[176] These payments, however, must be accurately reflected in the company's books and records so that the company and its management are aware of the payments and can assure that the payments were properly made under the circumstances. For example, in one instance, a Kazakh immigration prosecutor threatened to fine, jail, or deport employees of a U.S. company's subsidiary. Believing the threats to be genuine, the employees in Kazakhstan sought guidance from senior management of the U.S. subsidiary and were authorized to make the payments. The employees then paid the government official a total of $45,000 using personal funds. The subsidiary reimbursed the employees, but it falsely recorded the reimbursements as "salary advances" or "visa fines." The parent company, which eventually discovered these payments, as well as other improperly booked cash payments made to a Kazakhstani consultant to obtain visas, was charged with civil violations of the accounting provisions. Admin. Proceeding Order, In the Matter of NATCO Group Inc., Exchange Act Release No. 61325 (Jan. 11, 2010), *available at* http://www.sec.gov /litigation/admin/2010/34-61325.pdf (imposing cease-and-desist order and $65,000 civil monetary penalty).

[177] *See* Jury Instructions at 21, United States v. Aguilar, No. 10-cr-1031 (C.D. Cal. May 16, 2011), ECF No. 511.

[178] *See, e.g.*, Pacific Can Co. v. Hewes, 95 F.2d 42, 46 (9th Cir. 1938) ("Where one corporation is controlled by another, the former acts not for itself but as directed by the latter, the same as an agent, and the principal is liable for the acts of its agent within the scope of the agent's authority."); United States v. NYNEX Corp., 788 F. Supp. 16, 18 n.3 (D.D.C. 1992) (holding that "[a] corporation can of course be held criminally liable for the acts of its agents," including "the conduct of its subsidiaries.").

[179] *Pacific Can Co.*, 95 F.2d at 46; *NYNEX Corp.*, 788 F. Supp. at 18 n.3.

[180] *See, e.g.*, Standard Oil Co. v. United States, 307 F.2d 120, 127 (5th Cir. 1962).

[181] Admin. Proceeding Order, In the Matter of United Industrial Corp., Exchange Act Release No. 60005 (May 29, 2009), *available at* http:// www.sec.gov/litigation/admin/2009/34-60005.pdf; *see also* Lit. Release No. 21063, *SEC v. Worzel* (May 29, 2009), *available at* http://www.sec. gov/litigation/litreleases/2009/lr21063.htm.

[182] *See, e.g.*, Philip Urofksy, *What You Don't Know Can Hurt You: Successor Liability Resulting From Inadequate FCPA Due Diligence in M&A Transactions*, 1763 PLI/CorP. 631, 637 (2009) ("As a legal matter, when one corporation acquires another, it assumes any existing liabilities of that corporation, including liability for unlawful payments, regardless of whether it knows of them."). Whether or not successor liability applies to a particular corporate transaction depends on the facts involved and state, federal, and, potentially, foreign law.

[183] *See, e.g.*, Carolyn Lindsey, *More Than You Bargained for: Successor Liability Under the U.S. Foreign Corrupt Practices Act*, 35 OHIo N.U. L. REv. 959, 966 (2009) ("Allowing a company to escape its debts and liabilities by merging with another entity is considered to lead to an unjust result.").

[184] *See, e.g.*, Melrose Distillers, Inc. v. United States, 359 U.S. 271, 274 (1959) (affirming criminal successor liability for antitrust violations); United States v. Alamo Bank of Texas, 880 F.2d 828, 830 (5th Cir. 1989) (affirming criminal successor liability for Bank Secrecy Act violations); United States v. Polizzi, 500 F.2d 856, 907 (9th Cir. 1974) (affirming criminal successor liability for conspiracy and Travel Act violations); United States v. Shields Rubber Corp., 732 F. Supp. 569, 571-72 (W.D. Pa. 1989) (permitting criminal successor liability for customs violations); *see also* United States v. Mobile Materials, Inc., 776 F.2d 1476, 1477 (10th Cir. 1985) (allowing criminal post-dissolution liability for antitrust, mail fraud, and false statement violations);.

[185] Complaint, SEC v. The Titan Corp., No. 05-cv-411 (D.D.C. Mar. 1, 2005) (discovery of FCPA violations during pre-acquisition due diligence protected potential acquiring company and led to termination of merger agreement), *available at* http://www.sec.gov/litigation/complaints/ comp19107.pdf; Criminal Information, United States v. Titan Corp., No. 05-cr-314 (S.D. Cal. Mar. 1, 2005) (same) [hereinafter *United States v. Titan Corp.*], *available at* http://www.justice.gov/criminal/fraud/fcpa/ cases/titan-corp/03-01-05titan-info.pdf.

[186] For a discussion of declinations, see Chapter 7.

[187] *See* Complaint, SEC v. El Paso Corp., No. 07-cv-899 (S.D.N.Y. Feb. 7, 2007), ECF No. 1 [hereinafter *SEC v. El Paso Corp.*] (charging company with books and records and internal controls charges for improper payments to Iraq under U.N. Oil-for-Food Programme), *available at* http://www.sec.gov/litigation/complaints/2007/comp19991.pdf.

[188] Complaint, SEC v. Alliance One Int'l, Inc., No. 10-cv-1319 (D.D.C. Aug. 6, 2010), ECF No. 1, *available at* http://www.sec.gov/litigation/ complaints/2010/comp21618-alliance-one.pdf; Non-Pros. Agreement, In re Alliance One Int'l, Inc. (Aug. 6, 2010), *available at* http://www. justice.gov/criminal/fraud/fcpa/cases/alliance-one/08-06-10allianceone-npa.pdf; Criminal Information, United States v. Alliance One Int'l AG, No. 10-cr-17 (W.D. Va. Aug. 6, 2010), ECF No. 3, *available at* http://www.justice.gov/criminal /fraud/fcpa/cases/alliance-one/08-06- 10alliance-one-info.pdf; Criminal Information, United States v. Alliance One Tobacco Osh, LLC, No. 10-cr-16 (W.D. Va. Aug. 6, 2010), ECF No. 3, *available at* http://www.justice.gov/criminal/fraud/fcpa/cases/ alliance-one/08-06-10alliance-one-tobaccoinfo.pdf.

[189] *See* Criminal Information, United States v. Syncor Taiwan, Inc., No. 02-cr-1244 (C.D. Cal. Dec. 5, 2002), ECF No. 1, *available at* http:// www.justice.gov/criminal/fraud /fcpa/cases/syncor-taiwan/12-05- 02syncor-taiwan-info.pdf; Plea Agreement, United States v. Syncor Taiwan, Inc., No. 02-cr-1244 (C.D. Cal. Dec. 9, 2002), ECF No. 14, *available at* http://www.justice.gov/criminal/fraud/fcpa/cases/syncortaiwan/12-03-02syncor-taiwan-plea-agree.pdf.

[190] *See* Complaint, SEC v. Syncor Int'l Corp., No. 02-cv-2421 (D.D.C. Dec. 10, 2002), ECF No. 1, *available at* http://www.sec.gov/litigation/ complaints/comp17887.htm; SEC v. Syncor International Corp., SEC Lit. Rel. 17997, (Dec. 10, 2002), *available at* http://www.sec.gov/ litigation/litreleases/lr17887.htm.

[191] *See* Complaint, *SEC v. York Int'l Corp.*, *supra* note 115; Criminal Information, *United States v. York Int'l Corp.*, *supra* note 115.

[192] *See* Criminal Information, United States v. Latin Node, Inc., No. 09-cr-20239 (S.D. Fla. Mar. 23, 2009), ECF No. 1, *available at* http:// www.justice.gov/criminal/fraud/fcpa/cases/litton-applied/03-23- 09latinnode-info.pdf; eLandia Int'l Inc., Annual Report (Form 10-K), at 20 (Apr. 2, 2009), *available at* http://www.sec.gov/Archives/edgar/ data/1352819 /000119312509070961/d10k.htm.

[193] *See* Criminal Information, United States v. Salvoch, No. 10-cr-20893 (S.D. Fla. Dec. 17, 2010), ECF No. 3, *available at* http://www.justice. gov/criminal/fraud/fcpa/cases /salvoch/12-17-10salvoch-info.pdf; Criminal Information, United States v. Vasquez, No. 10-cr-20894 (S.D. Fla. Dec. 17, 2010), ECF No. 3, *available at* http://www.justice.gov/ criminal/fraud/fcpa/cases/vasquezjp/12-17-10vasquez-juan-info.pdf; Indictment, United States v. Granados, *et al.*, No. 10-cr-20881, (S.D. Fla. Dec. 14, 2010), ECF No. 3, *available at* http://www.justice.gov/ criminal/fraud/fcpa/cases/granados-jorge/12-21-10granados-indict.pdf.

[194] *See* Deferred Pros. Agreement, *United States v. Snamprogetti*, *supra* note 60, ECF No. 3, *available at* http://www.justice.gov/criminal/fraud/ fcpa/cases/snamprogetti/07-07-10snamprogetti-dpa.pdf.

[195] *Compare* Criminal Information, *United States v. Snamprogetti*, *supra* note 60, *with* Deferred Pros. Agreement, *United States v. Snamprogetti*, *supra* note 60, ECF No. 3.

[196] *See* Press Release, General Electric Co., General Electric Agrees to Acquire InVision (Mar. 15, 2004), *available at* http://www.ge.com/files/ usa/company/investor/downloads /sharpeye_press_release.pdf; Press Release, U.S. Dept. of Justice, InVision Tech. Inc. Enters into Agreement with the United States (Dec. 6, 2004), *available at* http://www.justice. gov/opa/pr/2004/December/04_crm_780.htm; Company News*; G.E. Gets InVision, a Maker of Bomb Detectors*, N.Y. TIMES, Dec. 7, 2004, at C4.

[197] Non-Pros. Agreement, In re InVision (Dec. 3, 2004), *available at* http://www.justice.gov /criminal/fraud/fcpa/cases/invision-tech/12-03- 04invisiontech-agree.pdf; Non-Pros. Agreement, In re General Elec. Co., (Dec. 3, 2004), *available at* http://www.justice.gov /criminal/fraud/fcpa/ cases/invision-tech/12-03-04invisiontech-agree-ge.pdf; Complaint, SEC v. GE InVision, Inc., f/k/a InVision Technologies, Inc., No. 05-cv-660, (N.D. Cal. Feb. 14, 2005), ECF No. 1, *available at* http://www.sec.gov/ litigation/complaints/comp 19078.pdf.

[198] *See* U.S. DEpT. oF JUSTICE, FCPA Op. RELEASE 08-02 (June 13, 2008), *available at* http://www.justice.gov/criminal/fraud/fcpa/ opinion/2008/0802.pdf*; see also* Press Release, U.S. Dept. of Justice, Pfizer H.C.P. Corp. Agrees to Pay $15 Million Penalty to Resolve Foreign Bribery Investigation (Aug. 7, 2012) ("In the 18 months following its acquisition of Wyeth, Pfizer Inc., in consultation with the department, conducted a due diligence and investigative review of the Wyeth business operations and integrated Pfizer Inc.'s internal controls system into the former Wyeth business entities. The department considered these extensive efforts and the SEC resolution in its determination not to pursue a criminal resolution for the pre-acquisition improper conduct of Wyeth subsidiaries."), *available at* http://www.justice.gov/opa/pr/2012/ August/12-crm-980.html.

[199] 18 U.S.C. § 2.

[200] In enacting the FCPA in 1977, Congress explicitly noted that "[t]he concepts of aiding and abetting and joint participation would apply to a violation under this bill in the same manner in which those concepts have always applied in both SEC civil actions and in implied private actions brought under the securities laws generally." H.R. REp. No. 95-640, at 8.

[201] *Pinkerton* held that a conspirator may be found guilty of a substantive offense committed by a co-conspirator in furtherance of the conspiracy if the co-conspirator's acts were reasonably foreseeable. *See* Pinkerton v. United States, 328 U.S. 640, 647-48 (1946).

[202] *See* United States v. MacAllister, 160 F.3d 1304, 1307 (11th Cir. 1998); United States v. Winter, 509 F.2d 975, 982 (5th Cir. 1975).

[203] *See* Criminal Information, *United States v. Marubeni*, *supra* note 132; Criminal Information, *United States v. JGC Corp.*, *supra* note 60; Criminal Information, *United States v. Snamprogetti*, *supra* note 60; *see also* Criminal Information, *United States v. Technip*, *supra* note 132.

[204] Section 20(e) of the Exchange Act, "Prosecution of Persons Who Aid and Abet Violations," explicitly provides that, for purposes of a civil action seeking injunctive relief or a civil penalty, "any person that knowingly or recklessly provides substantial assistance to another person in violation of a provision of this chapter, or of any rule or regulation issued under this chapter, shall be deemed to be in violation of such provision to the same extent as the person to whom such assistance is provided." Section 20(e) of the Exchange Act, 15 U.S.C. § 78t(e).

[205] Under Section 21C(a) of the Exchange Act, the SEC may impose a cease-and-desist order through the SEC's administrative proceedings upon any person who is violating, has violated, or is about to violate any provision of the Exchange Act or any rule or regulation thereunder, and upon any other person that is, was, or would be a cause of the violation, due to an act or omission the person knew or should have known would contribute to such violation. Section 21C(a) of the Exchange Act,15 U.S.C. § 78u-3(a).

[206] *See* Complaint, *SEC v. Panalpina, Inc.*, *supra* note 68.

[207] 18 U.S.C. § 3282(a) provides: "Except as otherwise expressly provided by law, no person shall be prosecuted, tried, or punished for any offense, not capital, unless the indictment is found or the information is instituted within five years next after such offense shall have been committed."

[208] *See* Grunewald v. United States, 353 U.S. 391, 396-97 (1957) (holding government must prove conspiracy still existed and at least one overt act was committed within the statute of limitations); Fiswick v. United States, 329 U.S. 211, 216 (1946) ("The statute of limitations, unless suspended, runs from the last overt act during the existence of the conspiracy. The overt acts averred and proved may thus mark the duration, as well as the scope, of the conspiracy.") (citation omitted); *see generally* Julie N. Sarnoff, *Federal Criminal Conspiracy*, 48 AM. CrIM. L. REV. 663, 676 (Spring 2011).

[209] 18 U.S.C. § 3292.

[210] 28 U.S.C. § 2462.

[211] S. REp. No. 95-114, at 3 (noting that, in the past, "corporate bribery has been concealed by the falsification of corporate books and records," that the accounting provisions "remove [] this avenue of coverup," and that "[t]aken together, the accounting requirements and criminal [anti-bribery] prohibitions . . . should effectively deter corporate bribery of foreign government officials").

[212] S. REp. No. 95-114, at 7.

[213] Section 13(b)(2)(A) of the Exchange Act, 15 U.S.C. § 78m(b)(2)(A).

[214] Section 13(b)(2)(B) of the Exchange Act, 15 U.S.C. § 78m(b)(2)(B).

[215] The accounting provisions contain a narrow exemption related to national security and the protection of classified information. Under this "national security" provision, "no duty or liability [under Section 13(b)(2) of the Exchange Act] shall be imposed upon any person acting in cooperation with the head of any federal department or agency responsible for

such matters if such act in cooperation with such head of a department or agency was done upon the specific, written directive of the head of such department or agency pursuant to Presidential authority to issue such directives." Section 13(b)(3) of the Exchange Act, 15 U.S.C. § 78m(b)(3). As Congress made clear, however, the exception is narrowly tailored and intended to prevent the disclosure of classified information. H.R. REp. 94-831, at 11, *available at* http://www.justice.gov/criminal/ fraud/fcpa/history/1977/corruptrpt-94-831.pdf.

[216] Section 13(b)(2)(A) of the Exchange Act, 15 U.S.C. § 78m(b)(2)(A).

[217] H.R. REp. No. 94-831, at 10.

[218] *Id.*

[219] Section 13(b)(7) of the Exchange Act, 15 U.S.C. § 78m(b)(7).

[220] H.R. REp. No. 100-576, at 917 (1988), *available athttp://www.justice.gov/criminal/fraud/fcpa/history/1988/tradeact-100-418.pdf.* Congress rejected the addition of proposed cost-benefit language to the definition "in response to concerns that such a statutory provision might be abused and weaken the accounting provisions at a time of increasing concern about audit failures and financial fraud and resultant recommendations by experts for stronger accounting practices and audit standards." *Id.*

[221] *See, e.g.*, Complaint, SEC v. Biomet, Inc., No. 12-cv-454 (D.D.C. Mar. 26, 2012), ECF No. 1 [hereinafter *SEC v. Biomet*], *available at* http:// www.sec.gov/litigation /comp22306.pdf; Criminal Information, United States v. Biomet, Inc., No. 12-cr-80 (D.D.C. Mar. 26, 2012) [hereinafter *United States v. Biomet*], *available at* http://www. justice.gov/criminal/fraud/fcpa/cases/biomet/2012-03-26-biometinformation. pdf; Complaint, SEC v. Smith & Nephew Inc., No. 12-cv187 (D.D.C. Feb. 6, 2012), ECF No. 1, *available at* http://www.sec.gov/ litigation/complaints /2012/comp22252.pdf; Criminal Information, United States v. Smith & Nephew plc., No. 12-cr-30 (D.D.C. Feb. 6, 2012), ECF No. 1, *available at* http://www.justice.gov/criminal/fraud/ fcpa/cases/smith-nephew/2012-02-06-s-n-information.pdf; Complaint, *SEC v. Johnson & Johnson, supra* note 131; Criminal Information, *United States v. DePuy, supra* note 131; Complaint, SEC v. Maxwell Technologies Inc., No. 11-cv-258 (D.D.C. Jan. 31, 2011), ECF No. 1 [hereinafter *SEC v. Maxwell Technologies*], *available at* http://www.sec. gov/litigation /complaints/2011 /comp21832.pdf; Criminal Information, United States v. Maxwell Technologies Inc., No. 11-cr-329 (S.D. Cal. Jan. 31, 2011), ECF No. 1, *available at* http://www.justice.gov /criminal/ fraud/fcpa/cases/maxwell/01-31-11maxwell-tech-info.pdf; Complaint, SEC v. Transocean, Inc., No. 10-cv-1891 (D.D.C. Nov. 4, 2010), ECF No. 1, *available at* http://www.sec.gov/litigation/complaints/2010/ comp21725.pdf; Criminal Information, United States v. Transocean, Inc., No. 10-cr-768 (S.D. Tex. Nov. 4, 2010), ECF No. 1, *available at* http://www.justice.gov/criminal/fraud/fcpa/cases/transocean-inc/11- 04-10 transocean-info.pdf.

[222] S. REP. No. 95-114, at 7.

[223] Section 13(b)(2)(B) of the Exchange Act, 15 U.S.C. § 78m(b)(2)(B).

[224] Section 13(b)(7) of the Exchange Act, 15 U.S.C. § 78m(b)(7).

[225] *See* Complaint, *SEC v. Siemens AG, supra* note 48; Criminal Information, *United States v. Siemens AG, supra* note 48.

[226] Complaint, *SEC v. Siemens AG, supra* note 48; Criminal Information, *United States v. Siemens AG, supra* note 48; Press Release, U.S. Dept. of Justice, Siemens AG and Three Subsidiaries Plead Guilty to Foreign Corrupt Practices Act Violations and Agree to Pay $450 Million in Combined Criminal Fines (Dec. 15, 2008), *available at* http://www. justice.gov/opa/pr/2008/December/08-crm-1105.html.

[227] *See, e.g.*, Complaint, *SEC v. Biomet, supra* note 221 (bribes paid to government healthcare providers in which phony invoices were used to justify payments and bribes were falsely recorded as "consulting fees" or "commissions" in company's books and records); Criminal Information, *United States v. Biomet, supra* note 221 (same); *SEC v. Alcatel-Lucent, supra* note 48 (bribes paid to foreign officials to secure telecommunications contracts where company lacked proper internal controls and permitted books and records to falsified); *United States v. Alcatel-Lucent, S.A., supra* note 48 (same).

[228] Complaint, *SEC v. Daimler AG, supra* note 48; Criminal Information, *United States v. Daimler AG, supra* note 48.

[229] *Id.*

[230] *Id.*

[231] *Id.*

[232] *Id.*

[233] *Id.*

[234] *See, e.g.*, Complaint, *SEC v. Tyco Int'l, supra* note 9; Complaint, SEC v. Willbros, No. 08-cv-1494 (S.D. Tex. May 14, 2008), ECF No. 1, *available at* http://www.sec.gov/litigation /complaints/2008/comp20571.pdf.

[235] *See, e.g.*, Complaint, *SEC v. Siemens AG, supra* note 48; Complaint, *SEC v. York Int'l Corp., supra* note 115; Complaint, *SEC v. Textron, supra* note 115; Criminal Information, United States v. Control Components, Inc., No. 09-cr-162 (C.D. Cal. July 22, 2009), ECF No. 1 [hereinafter *United States v. Control Components*], *available at* http://www.justice. gov/criminal/fraud/fcpa/cases/control-inc/07-22-09cci-info.pdf; Criminal Information, United States v. SSI Int'l Far East, Ltd., No. 06-cr398, ECF No. 1 (D. Or. Oct. 10, 2006) [hereinafter *United States v. SSI Int'l*], *available at* http://www.justice.gov/criminal /fraud/fcpa/cases/ ssi-intl/10-10-06ssi-information.pdf.

[236] *See, e.g.*, Complaint, *SEC v. El Paso Corp., supra* note 187; Complaint, *SEC v. Innospec, supra* note 79; Complaint, SEC v. Chevron Corp., 07- cv-10299 (S.D.N.Y. Nov. 14, 2007), ECF No. 1, *available at* http://www. sec.gov/litigation/complaints/2007/comp20363.pdf.

[237] Plea Agreement, *United States v. Stanley, supra* note 8; Plea Agreement, *United States v. Sapsizian, supra* note 8.

[238] *See* Complaint, *SEC v. Maxwell Technologies, supra* note 221.

[239] *See* Complaint, *SEC v. Willbros Group, supra* note 9.

[240] 15 U.S.C. § 7201, *et seq.*

[241] Exchange Act Rule 13a-15, 17 C.F.R. § 240.13a-15; Exchange Act Rule 15d-15, 17 C.F.R. § 240.15d-15; Item 308 of Regulation S-K, 17 C.F.R. § 229.308; Item 15, Form 20-F, *available at* http://www.sec.gov/ about/forms/form20-f.pdf; General Instruction (B), Form 40-F (for foreign private issuers), *available at* http://www.sec.gov/about/forms/ form40-f.pdf.

[242] *See* U.S. SEC. AND EXCHANGE CoMM., CoMMISSIoN GUIDANCE REGARDING MANAGEMENT'S REPoRT oN INTERNAL CoNTRoL oVER FINANCIAL REPoRTING UNDER SECTIoN 13(A) oR 15(D) oF THE SECURITIES EXCHANGE ACT oF 1934, Release No. 33-8810 (June 27, 2007), *available at* http://www.sec.gov /rules/interp/2007/33-8810. pdf.

[243] *Id.*

[244] Foreign Corrupt Practices Act of 1977, Pub. L. No. 95-213, § 102, 91 Stat. 1494 (1977).

[245] *See supra* note 48; *SEC v. Technip, supra* note 132, (French company); *United States v. Technip, supra* note 132, (same); *see also* Admin. Proceeding Order, In re Diageo plc, Exchange Act Release No. 64978 (SEC July 27, 2011) (UK company), *available at*

http://www.sec.gov/ litigation/admin/2011/34-64978.pdf; Admin. Proceeding Order, In re Statoil, ASA, Exchange Act Release No. 54599 (SEC May 29, 2009) (Norwegian company), *available at* http://www.sec.gov/litigation/ admin/2006/34-54599.pdf; Criminal Information, United States v. Statoil, ASA, No. 06-cr-960 (S.D.N.Y. Oct. 13, 2006) (same), *available at* http://www.justice.gov/criminal/fraud/fcpa/cases/statoil-asa-inc/10-13-09statoil-information.pdf.

[246] Although private companies are not covered by the books and records and internal controls provisions of the FCPA and do not fall within SEC's jurisdiction, such companies generally are required by federal and state tax laws and state corporation laws to maintain accurate books and records sufficient to properly calculate taxes owed. Further, most large private companies maintain their books and records to facilitate the preparation of financial statements in conformity with GAAP to comply with financial institutions' lending requirements.

[247] *See SEC v. RAE Sys. Inc., supra* note 92; *In re RAE Sys. Inc., supra* note 92.

[248] *See* Section 13(b)(6) of the Exchange Act, 15 U.S.C. § 78m(b) (6), which provides that where an issuer "holds 50 per centum or less of the voting power with respect to a domestic or foreign firm," the issuer must "proceed in good faith to use its influence, to the extent reasonable under the issuer's circumstances, to cause such domestic or foreign firm to devise and maintain a system of internal accounting controls consistent with [Section 13(b)(2)]."

[249] *See* 15 U.S.C. § 78m(b)(6). Congress added the language in subsection 78m(b)(6) to the FCPA in 1988, recognizing that "it is unrealistic to expect a minority owner to exert a disproportionate degree of influence over the accounting practices of a subsidiary." H.R. REP. No. 100-576, at 917. The Conference Report noted that, with respect to minority owners, "the amount of influence which an issuer may exercise necessarily varies from case to case. While the relative degree of ownership is obviously one factor, other factors may also be important in determining whether an issuer has demonstrated good-faith efforts to use its influence." *Id.*; *see also* S. REP. No. 100-85, at 50.

[250] Section 20(e) of the Exchange Act, titled "Prosecution of Persons Who Aid and Abet Violations," explicitly provides that for purposes of a civil action seeking injunctive relief or a civil penalty, "any person that knowingly or recklessly provides substantial assistance to another person in violation of a provision of this title, or of any rule or regulation issued under this title, shall be deemed to be in violation of such provision to the same extent as the person to whom such assistance is provided." *See* Section 20(e) of the Exchange Act, 15 U.S.C. § 78t(e).

[251] *See* Complaint at 11-12, *SEC v. Elkin, supra* note 50, ECF 1.

[252] *SEC v. Elkin, supra* note 50, ECF 6-9 (final judgments).

[253] *See, e.g.*, Complaint, SEC v. Nature's Sunshine Products, Inc., *et al.*, No. 09-cv-672 (D. Utah, July 31, 2009), ECF No. 2, *available at* http://www. sec.gov/litigation /litreleases/2009 /lr21162.htm.

[254] *See* Admin. Proceeding Order, In re Watts Water Technologies, Inc. and Leesen Chang, Exchange Act Release No. 65555 (SEC Oct. 13, 2011), *available at* http://www.sec.gov /litigation/admin/2011/34-65555.pdf.

[255] *Id.* at 2, 4, 6-7.

[256] Exchange Act Rule 13b2-1, 17 C.F.R. § 240.13b2-1.

[257] 15 U.S.C. § 78m(b)(5).

[258] Section 3(a)(9) of the Exchange Act, 15 U.S.C. § 78c(a)(9).

[259] Exchange Act Rule 13b2-2, 17 C.F.R. § 240.13b2-2

[260] Complaint, SEC v. Jennings, No. 11-cv-1444 (D.D.C. Jan. 24, 2011), ECF No. 1, *available at* http://www.sec.gov/litigation/ complaints/2011/comp21822.pdf.

[261] Complaint, *id.*, ECF No. 1; Final Judgment, *id.*, ECF No. 3.

[262] Serious Fraud Office, Innospec Ltd: Former CEO admits bribery to falsify product tests (July 30, 2012), *available at* http://www.sfo.gov. uk/press-room/latest-press-releases/press-releases-2012/innospec-ltd-- former-ceo-admits-bribery-to-falsify-product-tests.aspx.

[263] 15 U.S.C. § 78m(b)(4)-(5). Congress adopted this language in 1988 in order to make clear that, consistent with enforcement policy at the time, criminal penalties would not be imposed "for inadvertent or insignificant errors in books and records, or inadvertent violations of accounting controls." *See* S. REP. No. 100-85, at 49; H.R. REP. No. 100-576, at 916 ("The Conferees intend to codify current Securities and Exchange Commission (SEC) enforcement policy that penalties not be imposed for insignificant or technical infractions or inadvertent conduct.").

[264] 15 U.S.C. § 78ff(a).

[265] *See United States v. Alcatel-Lucent, S.A.*, *supra* note 48; *see also United States v. Alcatel-Lucent France*, *supra* note 56.

[266] *See* Deferred Prosecution Agreement, *United States v. Alcatel-Lucent, S.A.*, *supra* note 48, ECF No. 10, *available at* http://www.justice.gov/ criminal/fraud/fcpa/cases/alcatel-etal/02-22-11alcatel-dpa.pdf.

[267] *See* Plea Agreement, *United States v. Siemens AG*, *supra* note 48, ECF No. 14, *available at* http://www.justice.gov/criminal/fraud/fcpa/cases/ siemens/12-15-08siemensakt-plea.pdf.

[268] *See* Minute Entry of Guilty Plea, *United States v. Peterson*, *supra* note 8, ECF 13; *see also* Press Release, U.S. Dept. of Justice, Former Morgan Stanley Managing Director Pleads Guilty for Role in Evading Internal Controls Required by FCPA (Apr. 23, 2012), *available at* http://www. justice.gov/opa/pr/2012/April/12-crm-534.html.

[269] *See* Criminal Information, United States v. Baker Hughes Svcs. Int'l, No. 07-cr-129 (S.D. Tex. Apr. 11, 2007), ECF No. 1, *available at* http://www.justice.gov/criminal/fraud/fcpa /cases/baker-hughs/04-11- 07bakerhughesintl-info.pdf.

[270] *See United States v. Panalpina, Inc.*, *supra* note 68.

[271] *Id.*

[272] *See* FASB Statement of Financial Accounting Concepts No. 2, ¶¶ 63-80.

[273] PCAOB Auditing Standard No. 12 and PCAOB AU Section 325.

[274] *See* Section 10A of the Exchange Act, 15U.S.C. § 78j-1.

[275] 18 U.S.C. § 1952.

[276] *See, e.g.*, *United States v. Nexus Technologies*, *supra* note 53; Criminal Information, United States v. Robert Richard King, *et al.*, No. 01-cr-190 (W.D. Mo. June 27, 2001), *available at* http://www.justice.gov/criminal/ fraud/fcpa/cases/kingr-etal/05-03-02king-robert-indict.pdf; Superseding Indictment, *United States v. Mead*, *supra* note 44; Criminal Information, United States v. Saybolt North America Inc., *et al.*, No. 98-cr-10266 (D. Mass. Aug. 18, 1998), *available at* http://www.justice.gov/criminal/ fraud/fcpa/cases/saybolt/08-10-98saybolt-info.pdf.

[277] *See* Second Superseding Indictment, United States v. Kozeny, No. 05- cr-518 (S.D.N.Y. May 26, 2009), ECF No. 203, *available at* http://www. justice.gov/criminal/fraud/fcpa /cases/kozenyv/05-26-09bourke2ndsupersed-indict.pdfjudgment, United States v. Bourke, No. 05-cr-518 (S.D.N.Y. Nov. 12, 2009), ECF No. 253, *available at* http://www.justice. gov/criminal/fraud/fcpa/cases/kozenyv/11-12-09bourke-judgment.pdf.

[278] Plea Agreement, *United States v. Control Components*, *supra* note 235, ECF No. 7; *see also* Order, *United States v. Carson*, *supra* note 119, ECF No. 440 (denying motion to dismiss

counts alleging Travel Act violations), *available at* http://www.justice.gov/criminal/fraud/fcpa/ cases/carsons/2011-09-20-carson-minutes-denying-motion-to-dismiss. pdf.

[279] *See, e.g.*, Criminal Information, *United States v. Esquenazi*, *supra* note 44; Criminal Information, *United States v. Green*, *supra* note 44; Criminal Information, United States v. General Elec. Co., No. 92-cr-87 (S.D. Ohio July 22, 1992), *available at* http://www.justice.gov/criminal/fraud/fcpa/ cases/general-electric/1992-07-22-general-electric-information.pdf.

[280] Foreign officials may "not be charged with violating the FCPA itself, since the [FCPA] does not criminalize the receipt of a bribe by a foreign official." United States v. Blondek, 741 F.Supp. 116, 117 (N.D. Tex. 1990), *aff'd* United States v. Castle, 925 F.2d 831 (5th Cir. 1991) ("We hold that foreign officials may not be prosecuted under 18 U.S.C. § 371 for conspiring to violate the FCPA."). Foreign officials, however, can be charged with violating the FCPA when the foreign official acts as an intermediary of a bribe payment. *See, e.g.*, Information, United States v. Basu, No. 02-cr-475 (D.D.C. Nov. 26, 2002) (World Bank employee charged with wire fraud and FCPA violations for facilitating bribe payments to another World Bank official and Kenyan government official), *available at* http://www.justice.gov/criminal/fraud/fcpa/cases/ basu/11-26-02basu-info.pdf; Information, United States v. Sengupta, No. 02-cr-40 (D.D.C. Jan. 30, 2002), *available at* http://www.justice.gov/ criminal/fraud/fcpa/cases/sengupta/01-30-02sengupta-info.pdf.

[281] *See, e.g.*, Judgments, *United States v. Esquenazi*, *supra* note 44, ECF Nos. 182, 816, 824 (judgments against foreign official defendants).

[282] Criminal Information, *United States v. SSI Int'l*, *supra* note 235 (alleging violations of 18 U.S.C. §§ 1343, 1346); Plea Agreement, *United States v. SSI Int'l*, *supra* note 235, (Oct. 10, 2006), *available at* http:// www.justice.gov/criminal/fraud/fcpa/cases/control-inc/07-24-09cciplea-agree.pdf.

[283] *See* Ex-Im Bank, Form of Exporter's Certificate, EBD-M-56 (Jan. 2007), *available at* http://www.exim.gov/pub/ins/pdf/ebd-m-56.pdf.

[284] *See* 18 U.S.C. § 1001.

[285] 22 C.F.R. §§ 130.2, 130.9.

[286] For example, in *United States v. BAE Systems plc*, BAE pleaded guilty to conspiring to defraud the United States by impairing and impeding its lawful functions, to making false statements about its FCPA compliance program, and to violating the AECA and ITAR. BAE paid a $400 million fine and agreed to an independent corporate monitor to ensure compliance with applicable anti-corruption and export control laws. Criminal Information and Plea Agreement, United States v. BAE Sys. plc, No. 10-cr-35 (D.D.C. Mar. 1, 2010), ECF Nos.1, 8, *available at* http://www.justice.gov/criminal/fraud/fcpa/cases/bae-system/02-01- 10baesystems-info.pdf and http://www.justice.gov/criminal/fraud/fcpa/ cases/bae-system/03-01-10baesystems-plea-agree.pdf. In an action based on the same underlying facts as the criminal guilty plea, BAE entered a civil settlement with the Directorate of Defense Trade Controls for violations of AECA and ITAR, including over 2500 ITAR violations that included a failure to report the payment of fees or commissions associated with defense transactions and failure to maintain records involving ITAR-controlled transactions. BAE paid $79 million in penalties, and the State Department imposed a "policy of denial" for export licenses on three BAE subsidiaries involved in the wrongful conduct. Consent Agreement between BAE Sys. plc and Defense Trade Controls at 17-20, Bureau of Political-Military Affairs, U.S. Dept. of State (May 16, 2011), *available at* http://www.pmddtc.state.gov/compliance/consent_agreements/pdf/BAES_CA.pdf; Proposed Charging Letter, In re Investigation of BAE Systems plc Regarding Violations of

the Arms Export Control Act and the International Traffic in Arms Regulations, U.S. Dept. of State (May 2011), *available at* http://www.pmddtc.state. gov/compliance /consent_agreements/pdf/BAES_PCL.pdf.

[287] 26 U.S.C. § 162(c)(1); *see also* Plea Agreement, United States v. Smith, No. 07-cr-69 (C.D. Cal. Sept. 3, 2009), ECF No. 89, *available at* http:// www.justice.gov/criminal/fraud /fcpa/cases/smithl/09-03-09smithl-pleaagree.pdf; Criminal Information, *United States v. Titan Corp., supra* note 185.

[288] *See* USAM § 9-27.000.

[289] *See* USAM § 9-27.420 (setting forth considerations to be weighed when determining whether it would be appropriate to enter into plea agreement).

[290] *See* USAM § 9-28.000 *et seq.*

[291] *See* USAM § 9-28.710 (discussing attorney-client and work product protections).

[292] *See* http://www.sec.gov/divisions/enforce/enforcementmanual.pdf.

[293] *See* USAM§ 9-28.300.A; *see also* USAM § 9-28.700.B (explaining benefits of cooperation for both government and corporation).

[294] *See* USAM § 9-28.900 (discussing restitution and remediation). The commentary further provides that prosecutors should consider and weigh whether the corporation appropriately disciplined wrongdoers and a corporation's efforts to reform, including its quick recognition of the flaws in the program and its efforts to improve the program. *Id.*

[295] *See* USAM §§ 9-27.230, 9-27.420.

[296] U.S. SENTENCING GUIDELINES § 8B2.1(b)(7) (2011).

[297] *Id.* § 8C2.5(f)(2) (2011).

[298] U.S. SEC. AND EXCHANGE CoMM., REPoRT oF INVESTIGATIoN PURSUANT To SECTIoN 21(A) oF THE SECURITIES EXCHANGE ACT oF 1934 AND CoMMISSIoN STATEMENT oN THE RELATIoNSHIP oF CooPERATIoN To AGENCY ENFoRCEMENT DECISIoNS, SEC Rel. Nos. 34-44969 and AAER-1470 (Oct. 23, 2001) [hereinafter *Seaboard* Report] *available at* http://www.sec.gov/litigation/ investreport/34-44969.htm.

[299] U.S. SEC. AND EXCHANGE CoMM., PoLICY STATEMENT CoNCERNING CooPERATIoN BY INDIVIDUALS IN ITS INVESTIGATIoNS AND RELATED ENFoRCEMENTS ACTIoNS, 17 C.F.R. § 202.12 (Jan. 10, 2010), *available at* http://www.sec.gov/rules/policy/2010/34-61340.pdf.

[300] *See* U.S. SENTENCING GUIDELINES at § 8B2.1(a)(2).

[301] U.S. SENTENCING GUIDELINES § 8B2.1(b).

[302] *See generally* DEBBIE TRoKLUS, *ET AL.*, CoMPLIANCE 101: How To BUILD AND MAINTAIN AN EFFECTIVE CoMPLIANCE AND ETHICS PRoGRAM, SoCIETY oF CoRP. CoMPLIANCE AND ETHICS (2008) 3-9 [hereinafter CoMPLIANCE 101] (listing reasons to implement compliance program, including protecting company's reputation, creating trust between management and employees, preventing false statements to customers, creating efficiencies and streamlining processes, detecting employee and contractor fraud and abuse, ensuring high-quality products and services, and providing "early warning" system of inappropriate actions); TRANSPARENCY INT'L, BUSINESS PRINCIPLES FoR CoUNTERING BRIBERY: SMALL AND MEDIUM ENTERPRISE (SME) EDITIoN 5 (2008) (citing benefits of anti-bribery program like protecting reputation, creating record of integrity enhances opportunities to acquire government business, protecting company assets otherwise squandered on bribes); MARK PIETH, HARMoNISING ANTI-CoRRUPTIoN CoMPLIANCE: THE OECD GooD PRACTICE GUIDANCE 45-46 (2011) [hereinafter HARMoNISING ANTICoRRUPTIoN

COMPLIANCE] (citing need for compliance program to prevent and detect in-house risks, such as workplace security or conflicts of interest, and external risks, like anti-trust violations, embargo circumvention, environmental hazards, and money laundering).

303 Debarment authorities, such as the Department of Defense or the General Services Administration, may also consider a company's compliance program when deciding whether to debar or suspend a contractor. Specifically, the relevant regulations provide that the debarment authority should consider "[w]hether the contractor had effective standards of conduct and internal control systems in place at the time of the activity which constitutes cause for debarment or had adopted such procedures prior to any Government investigation of the activity cited as a cause for debarment," and "[w]hether the contractor has instituted or agreed to institute new or revised review and control procedures and ethics training programs." 48 C.F.R. § 9.406-1(a).

304 *Seaboard* Report, *supra* note 298; U.S. SEC. AND EXCHANGE COMM., REPORT OF INVESTIGATION PURSUANT TO SECTION 21(A) OF THE SECURITIES EXCHANGE ACT OF 1934 AND COMMISSION STATEMENT ON THE RELATIONSHIP OF COOPERATION TO AGENCY ENFORCEMENT DECISIONS, SEC Rel. No. 44969 (Oct. 23, 2001), *available at* http://www.sec.gov/litigation/investreport/34-44969.htm.

305 USAM § 9-28.300. When evaluating the pervasiveness of wrongdoing within the corporation, prosecutors are advised that while it may be appropriate to charge a corporation for minor misconduct where the wrongdoing was pervasive, "it may not be appropriate to impose liability upon a corporation, *particularly one with a robust compliance program in place*, under a strict *respondeat superior* theory for the single isolated act of a rogue employee." *Id.* § 9-28.500.A (emphasis added). Prosecutors should also consider a company's compliance program when examining any remedial actions taken, including efforts to implement an effective compliance program or to improve an existing one. As the commentary explains, "although the inadequacy of a corporate compliance program is a factor to consider when deciding whether to charge a corporation, that corporation's quick recognition of the flaws in the program and its efforts to improve the program are also factors to consider as to appropriate disposition of a case." *Id.* § 9-28.900.B. Finally, the Principles of Federal Prosecution of Business Organizations provides that prosecutors should consider the existence and effectiveness of the corporation's pre-existing compliance program in determining how to treat a corporate target. *Id.* § 9-28.800.

306 *See* USAM § 9-28.800.B; *see also* U.S. SENTENCING GUIDELINES § 8B2.1(a) (2011) ("The failure to prevent or detect the instant offense does not necessarily mean that the program is not generally effective in preventing and detecting criminal conduct.").

307 *See* Press Release, U.S. Dept. of Justice, Former Morgan Stanley Managing Director Pleads Guilty for Role in Evading Internal Controls Required by FCPA (Apr. 25, 2012) (declining to bring criminal case against corporate employer that "had constructed and maintained a system of internal controls, which provided reasonable assurances that its employees were not bribing government officials"), *available at* http:// www.justice.gov/opa /pr/2012/April/12-crm-534.html; Press Release, U.S. Sec. and Exchange Comm., SEC Charges Former Morgan Stanley Executive with FCPA Violations and Investment Adviser Fraud, No. 2012-78 (Apr. 25, 2012) (indicating corporate employer was not charged in the matter and had "cooperated with the SEC's inquiry and conducted a thorough internal investigation to determine the scope of the improper payments and other misconduct involved"), *available at* http://www.sec. gov/news/press/2012/2012-78.htm.

308 *See* USAM § 9-28.800.B.

[309] *See, e.g.*, INT'L CHAMBER oF CoMMERCE, ICC RULES oN CoMBATING CoRRUPTIoN (2011) [hereinafter ICC RULES oN CoMBATING CoRRUPTIoN], *available at* http://www.iccwbo. org/uploadedFiles/ICC/policy/business_in_society /Statements/ ICC_Rules_on_Combating_Corruption_2011edition.pdf; TRANSPARENCY INT'L, BUSINESS PRINCIPLES FoR CoUNTERING BRIBERY (2d ed. 2009) [hereinafter BUSINESS PRINCIPLES FoR CoUNTERING BRIBERY], *available at* http://www.transparency. org/global_priorities/private_sector/business_principles/; UNITED KINGDoM MINISTRY oF JUSTICE, THE BRIBERY ACT oF 2010, GUIDANCE ABoUT PRoCEDURES wHICH RELEVANT CoMMERCIAL oRGANISATIoNS CAN PUT INTo PLACE To PREVENT PERSoNS ASSoCIATED wITH THEM FRoM BRIBING (2010), *available at* http:// www.justice.gov.uk/downloads/legislation/bribery-act-2010-guidance. pdf; WoRLD BANK GRoUP, INTEGRITY CoMPLIANCE GUIDELINES (2011) [hereinafter INTEGRITY CoMPLIANCE GUIDELINES], *available at* http://siteresources.worldbank. org/INTDOII /Resources/Integrity_Compliance_Guidelines.pdf;ASIA-PACIFICECoNoMIC CooPERATIoN, APEC ANTI-CoRRUPTIoN CoDE oF CoNDUCT FoR BUSINESS (2007) [hereinafter APEC ANTI-CoRRUPTIoN CoDE], *available at* http://www.apec.org /Groups/SOM-Steering-Committeeon-Economic-and-Technical-Cooperation/Task-Groups/~/media/ Files/Groups/ACT/07_act_codebrochure.ashx; INT'L CHAMBER oF CoMMERCE, TRANSPARENCY INT'L, UNITED NATIoNS GLoBAL CoMPACT, and WoRLD ECoNoMIC FoRUM, RESISTING EXToRTIoN AND SoLICITATIoN IN INTERNATIoNAL TRANSACTIoNS: A CoMPANY TooL FoR EMPLoYEE TRAINING (2011), *available at* http://www3.weforum.org /docs/WEF_PACI_RESIST_Report_2011. pdf; INT'L CHAMBER oF CoMMERCE, ET AL., CLEAN BUSINESS IS GooD BUSINESS, *available at* http://www3.weforum.org/docs/ WEF_PACI_BusinessCase Fighting Corruption_2011.pdf; WoRLD ECoNoMIC FoRUM, PARTNERING AGAINST CoRRUPTIoN – PRINCIPLES FoR CoUNTERING BRIBERY (2009) [hereinafter PARTNERING AGAINST CoRRUPTIoN], *available at* http://www3. weforum.org/docs /WEF_PACI_Principles_ 2009.pdf; WoRKING GRoUP oN BRIBERY, OECD, GooD PRACTICE GUIDANCE oN INTERNAL CoNTRoLS, ETHICS, AND CoMPLIANCE 2010, [hereinafter OECD GooD PRACTICE GUIDANCE] a*vailable at* http://www.oecd. org/dataoecd/5/51/44884389.pdf; U.N. GLoBAL CoMPACT, THE TEN PRINCIPLES [hereinafter THE TEN PRINCIPLES] *available at* http:// www.unglobalcompact.org/about TheGC/TheTenPrinciples/index.html.

[310] This is also reflected in the *Sentencing Guidelines*, which recognizes that no single, formulaic set of requirements should be imposed, but instead focuses on a number of factors like applicable industry practice or the standards called for by any applicable governmental regulation, the size of the organization, and whether the organization has engaged in similar misconduct in the past. *See* U.S. SENTENCING GUIDELINES § 8B2.1 & app. note 2 (2011).

[311] This was underscored by then-SEC Commissioner Cynthia Glassman in 2003 in a speech on the SEC's implementation of the Sarbanes-Oxley Act: "[T]he ultimate effectiveness of the new corporate governance rules will be determined by the 'tone at the top.' Adopting a code of ethics means little if the company's chief executive officer or its directors make clear, by conduct or otherwise, that the code's provisions do not apply to them. . . . Corporate officers and directors hold the ultimate power and responsibility for restoring public trust by conducting themselves in a manner that is worthy of the trust that is placed in them." Cynthia Glassman, SEC Implementation of Sarbanes-Oxley: The New Corporate

Governance, Remarks at National Economists Club (April 7, 2003), *available at* http://www.sec.gov/news/speech/spch040703cag.htm .

[312] Indeed, research has found that "[e]thical culture is the single biggest factor determining the amount of misconduct that will take place in a business." ETHICS RESoURCE CENTER, 2009 NATIoNAL BUSINESS ETHICS SURVEY: ETHICS IN THE RECESSIoN (2009), at 41. Metrics of ethical culture include ethical leadership (tone at the top), supervisor reinforcement of ethical behavior (middle management reinforcement), and peer commitment (supporting one another in doing the right thing). ETHICS RESoURCE CENTER, 2011 NATIoNAL BUSINESS ETHICS SURVEY: WoRKpLACE ETHICS IN TRANSITIoN (2012) at 19. Strong ethical cultures and strong ethics and compliance programs are related, as data show that a well-implemented program helps lead to a strong ethical culture. *Id.* at 34. "Understanding the nature of any gap between the desired culture and the actual culture is a critical first step in determining the nature of any ethics-based risks inside the organization." David Gebler, *The Role of Culture* at 1.7, *in* SoCIETY oF CoRpoRATE CoMpLIANCE AND ETHICS, THE CoMpLETE CoMpLIANCE AND ETHICS MANUAL (2011). To create an ethical culture, attention must be paid to norms at all levels of an organization, including the "tone at the top," "mood in the middle," and "buzz at the bottom." *Id.* 1.9-1.10.

[313] *See, e.g.*, U.S. SENTENCING GUIDELINES § 8B2.1(2)(B)-(C) (2011).

[314] *Id.*

[315] *Id.*

[316] *Id.*

[317] *See, e.g.*, ETHICS AND CoMpLIANCE OFFICER ASSoCIATIoN FoUNDATIoN, THE ETHICS AND CoMpLIANCE HANDBooK: A PRACTICAL GUIDE FRoM LEADING ORGANIZATIoNS (2008) at 13-26 [hereinafter THE ETHICS AND CoMpLIANCE HANDBooK].

[318] *See* U.S. SENTENCING GUIDELINES § 8B2.1(b)(4) (2011).

[319] *See* U.S. SENTENCING GUIDELINES § 8B2.1(b)(6) (2011) ("The organization's compliance and ethics program shall be promoted and enforced consistently throughout the organization through (A) appropriate incentives to perform in accordance with the compliance and ethics program; and (B) appropriate disciplinary measures for engaging in criminal conduct and for failing to take reasonable steps to prevent or detect criminal conduct.").

[320] *See, e.g.*, JoSEpH E. MURpHY, SoCIETY oF CoRp. CoMpLIANCE AND ETHICS, USING INCENTIVES IN YoUR CoMpLIANCE AND ETHICS PRoGRAM (2011) at 1; THE ETHICS AND CoMpLIANCE HANDBooK, *supra* note 317, at 111-23.

[321] Stephen M. Cutler, Director, Division of Enforcement, SEC, *Tone at the Top: Getting It Right*, Second Annual General Counsel Roundtable (Dec. 3, 2004), *available at* http://www.sec.gov/news/speech/ spch120304smc.htm.

[322] *See, e.g.*, ICC RULES oN CoMBATING CoRRUpTIoN, *supra* note 309, at 8.

[323] *See, e.g.* U.S. SENTENCING GUIDELINES § 8B2.1(b)(5)(C); CoMpLIANCE 101, *supra* note 302, at 30-33.

[324] Corporate Board Member/FTI Consulting 2009 Legal Study, *Buckle Up. Boards and General Counsel May Face a Bumpy Ride in 2009*, at 5 ("Interestingly, while 67% of general counsel say their company is subject to compliance under the FCPA, 64% of those say there is room for improvement in their FCPA training and compliance programs.").

[325] *See* U.S. SENTENCING GUIDELINES § 8B2.1(b)(5)(B) ("The organization shall take reasonable steps . . . to evaluate periodically the effectiveness of the organization's compliance and ethics program.").

[326] *See, e.g.*, CoMpLIANCE 101, *supra* note 302, at 60-61; THE ETHICS AND CoMpLIANCE HANDBooK, *supra* note 317, at 155-60; BUSINESS PRINCIpLES FoR CoUNTERING BRIBERY, *supra* note 309, at 14.

[327] *See, e.g.*, Michael M. Mannix and David S. Black., *Compliance Issues in M&A: Performing Diligence on the Target's Ethics and Compliance Program* at 5.71-5.81, *in* SoCIETY oF CoRpoRATE CoMpLIANCE AND ETHICS, THE CoMpLETE CoMpLIANCE AND ETHICS MANUAL (2011).

[328] Complaint, SEC v. Syncor International Corp., *supra* note 190; Criminal Information, United States v. Syncor Taiwan, Inc., *supra* note 189.

[329] U.S. DEpT. oF JUSTICE, FCPA Op. RELEASE 08-02 (June 13, 2008), *available at* http://justice.gov/criminal/fraud/fcpa/opinion/2008/0802. pdf.

[330] Complaint, *SEC v. Rae Sys., Inc.*, *supra* note 92; Non-Pros. Agreement, *In re Rae Sys. Inc.*, *supra* note 92.

[331] U.S. DEpT. oF CoMMERCE, BUSINESS ETHICS: A MANUAL FoR MANAGING A RESpoNSIBLE BUSINESS ENTERpRISE IN EMERGING MARKET ECoNoMIES (2004), *available at* http://www.ita.doc.gov/ goodgovernance/adobe/bem_manual.pdf.

[332] U.S. DEpT. oF STATE, FIGHTING GLoBAL CoRRUpTIoN: BUSINESS RISK MANAGEMENT (2d ed. 2001), *available at* http://www.ogc.doc. gov/pdfs /Fighting_ Global_Corruption.pdf.

[333] *See* HARMoNISING ANTI-CoRRUpTIoN CoMpLIANCE, *supra* note 302, at 46 ("Anti-corruption compliance is becoming more and more harmonised worldwide.").

[334] OECD GooD PRACTICE GUIDANCE, *supra* note 309.

[335] APEC ANTI-CoRRUpTIoN CoDE, *supra* note 309.

[336] ICC RULES oN CoMBATING CoRRUpTIoN, *supra* note 309.

[337] BUSINESS PRINCIpLES FoR CoUNTERING BRIBERY, *supra* note 309.

[338] THE TEN PRINCIpLES, *supra* note 309.

[339] INTEGRITY CoMpLIANCE GUIDELINES, *supra* note 309.

[340] PARTNERING AGAINST CoRRUpTIoN, *supra* note 309.

[341] 15 U.S.C. §§ 78dd-2(g)(1)(A), 78dd-3(e)(1)(A), 78ff(c)(1)(A).

[342] 15 U.S.C. §§ 78dd-2(g)(2)(A), 78dd-3(e)(2)(A), 78ff(c)(2)(A).

[343] 15 U.S.C. § 78ff(a).

[344] 15 U.S.C. § 78ff(a).

[345] 18 U.S.C. § 3571(d); *see Southern Union v. United States*, 132 S. Ct. 2344, 2350-51 & n.4 (2012).

[346] 15 U.S.C. §§ 78dd-2(g)(3), 78dd-3(e)(3), 78ff(c)(3).

[347] The U.S. Sentencing Guidelines are promulgated by the U.S. Sentencing Commission:

> The United States Sentencing Commission ("Commission") is an independent agency in the judicial branch composed of seven voting and two non-voting *ex-officio* members. Its principal purpose is to establish sentencing policies and practices for the federal criminal justice system that will assure the ends of justice by promulgating detailed guidelines prescribing the appropriate sentences for offenders convicted of federal crimes. The Guidelines and policy statements promulgated by the Commission are issued pursuant to Section 994(a) of Title 28, United States Code.

U.S. SENTENCING GUIDELINES § 1A1.1 (2011).

[348] *Id.* at ch. 3-5.

[349] *Id.* § 2C1.1.

[350] *Id.* § 2C1.1(b).

[351] *Id.* § 3B1.1.

[352] *Id.* at ch. 4, § 5A.

[353] *Id.* § 2B1.1(b)(10)(B), 2B1.1(b)(18)(A).

[354] *Id.* § 8C2.4 (a).

[355] *Id.* § 8C2.5.

[356] *Id.* § 8C2.5(f), 8C2.5(g).

[357] DOJ has exercised this civil authority in limited circumstances in the last thirty years. *See, e.g.*, United States & SEC v. KPMG Siddharta Siddharta & Harsono, *et al.*, No. 01-cv-3105 (S.D. Tex. 2001) (entry of injunction barring company from future FCPA violations based on allegations that company paid bribes to Indonesian tax official in order to reduce the company's tax assessment); United States v. Metcalf & Eddy, Inc., No. 99-cv-12566 (D. Mass. 1999) (entry of injunction barring company from future FCPA violations and requiring maintenance of compliance program based on allegations that it paid excessive marketing and promotional expenses such as airfare, travel expenses, and per diem to an Egyptian official and his family); United States v. American Totalisator Co. Inc., No. 93-cv-161 (D. Md. 1993) (entry of injunction barring company from future FCPA violations based on allegations that it paid money to its Greek agent with knowledge that all or some of the money paid would be offered, given, or promised to Greek foreign officials in connection with sale of company's system and spare parts); United States v. Eagle Bus Manufacturing, Inc., No. 91-cv-171 (S.D. Tex. 1991) (entry of injunction barring company from future FCPA violations based on allegations that employees of the company participated in bribery scheme to pay foreign officials of Saskatchewan's state-owned transportation company $50,000 CAD in connection with sale of buses); United States v. Carver, *et al.*, No. 79-cv-1768 (S.D. Fla. 1979) (entry of injunction barring company from future FCPA violations based on allegations that Carver and Holley, officers and shareholders of Holcar Oil Corp., paid $1.5 million to Qatar foreign official to secure an oil drilling concession agreement); United States v. Kenny, *et al.*, No. 79-cv2038 (D.D.C. 1979) (in conjunction with criminal proceeding, entry of injunction barring company from future FCPA violations for providing illegal financial assistance to political party to secure renewal of stamp distribution agreement).

[358] 15 U.S.C. §§ 78dd-2(g)(1)(B), 78dd-3(e)(1)(B), 78ff(c)(1)(B); *see also* 17 C.F.R. § 201.1004 (providing adjustments for inflation).

[359] 15 U.S.C. §§ 78dd-2(g)(2)(B), 78dd-3(e)(2)(B), 78ff(c)(2)(B); *see also* 17 C.F.R. § 201.1004 (providing adjustments for inflation).

[360] 15 U.S.C. §§ 78dd-2(g)(3), 78dd-3(e)(3), 78ff(c)(3); *see also* 17 C.F.R. § 201.1004 (providing adjustments for inflation).

[361] Section 21(B)(b) of the Exchange Act, 15 U.S.C. § 78u(d)(3); *see also* 17 C.F.R. § 201.1004 (providing adjustments for inflation).

[362] *See* Securities Enforcement Remedies and Penny Stock Reform Act of 1990, Pub. L. No. 101-429, 104 Stat. 931 §§ 202, 301, 401, and 402 (codified in scattered sections of Title 15 of the United States Code).

[363] 48 C.F.R. §§ 9.406-2, 9.407-2.

[364] 48 C.F.R. § 9.402(b).

[365] *See* 48 C.F.R. §§ 9.406-1, 9.407-1(b)(2). Section 9.406-1 sets forth the following non-exhaustive list of factors:

1. Whether the contractor had effective standards of conduct and internal control systems in place at the time of the activity which constitutes cause for debarment or had adopted such procedures prior to any Government investigation of the activity cited as a cause for debarment.
2. Whether the contractor brought the activity cited as a cause for debarment to the attention of the appropriate Government agency in a timely manner.
3. Whether the contractor has fully investigated the circumstances surrounding the cause for debarment and, if so, made the result of the investigation available to the debarring official.
4. Whether the contractor cooperated fully with Government agencies during the investigation and any court or administrative action.
5. Whether the contractor has paid or has agreed to pay all criminal, civil, and administrative liability for the improper activity, including any investigative or administrative costs incurred by the Government, and has made or agreed to make full restitution.
6. Whether the contractor has taken appropriate disciplinary action against the individuals responsible for the activity which constitutes cause for debarment.
7. Whether the contractor has implemented or agreed to implement remedial measures, including any identified by the Government.
8. Whether the contractor has instituted or agreed to institute new or revised review and control procedures and ethics training programs.
9. Whether the contractor has had adequate time to eliminate the circumstances within the contractor's organization that led to the cause for debarment.
10. Whether the contractor's management recognizes and understands the seriousness of the misconduct giving rise to the cause for debarment and has implemented programs to prevent recurrence.

[366] 48 C.F.R. § 9.406-1(a).

[367] Exec. Order No. 12,549, 51 Fed. Reg. 6,370 (Feb. 18, 1986); Exec. Order No. 12,689, 54 Fed. Reg. 34131 (Aug. 18, 1989).

[368] 48 C.F.R. § 9.407-2(b).

[369] USAM § 9-28.1300 (2008).

[370] *See, e.g.*, AFRICAN DEVELOPMENT BANK GROUP, INTEGRITY AND ANTI-CORRUPTION PROGRESS REPORT 2009-2010 7, 14 ("As the premier financial development institution in Africa, the AfDB is determined to root out misconduct, fraud and corruption within its own ranks as well as in the implementation of the projects it finances. In order to do so, the Bank created an anti-corruption and fraud investigation division in November 2005 as its sole investigative body. The unit became operational in June 2006 and commenced investigations in January 2007. . . . Investigations conducted by the IACD [Integrity and Anti-Corruption Department] are not criminal proceedings; they are administrative in nature. Sanctions range from personnel disciplinary actions, such as separation, to loan cancellation and debarment for contractors, which can be temporary or permanent."), *available at* http://www.afdb.org/fileadmin/uploads/afdb/Documents/ Publications/Integrity%20and%20Anti-Corruption.pdf; The World Bank Group, *Procurement: Sanctions Committee* ("The World Bank's debarment process was first formulated in July, 1996, and the Sanctions Committee was established in November 1998 to review allegations and recommend sanctions to the President. Written procedures were issued in August 2001 and are posted on the Bank's website, along with the sanction actions."), *available at* http://web.worldbank.org/WBSITE/ EXTERNAL/PROJECTS

/PROCUREMENT/0,,contentMDK:5000 2288~pagePK:84271~piPK:84287~theSitePK:84266,00.html.

[371] *See* African Development Bank Group, Asian Development Bank, European Bank for Reconstruction and Development, Inter-American Development Bank Group and World Bank Group, *Agreement for Mutual Enforcement of Debarment Decisions* (Apr. 9, 2010), *available at* http://siteresources.worldbank.org/NEWS/Resources/ AgreementForMutual EnforcementofDebarmentDecisions.pdf.

[372] *Id.*; *see also* The World Bank Group, *Cross-Debarment Accord Steps Up Fight Against Corruption* (Apr. 9, 2010) ("'With today's cross-debarment agreement among development banks, a clear message on anticorruption is being delivered: Steal and cheat from one, get punished by all,' said World Bank Group President Robert B. Zoellick."), *available at* http:// web.worldbank.org/WBSITE/EXTERNAL/NEWS/0,,contentMDK:2 2535805~page PK:64257043~piPK:437376~theSitePK:4607,00.html.

[373] 22 C.F.R. §§ 126.7(a)(3)-(4), 120.27(a)(6).

[374] Authority under the AECA is delegated to the DDTC. *See* 22 C.F.R. § 120.1(a).

[375] 22 U.S.C. § 2778(g)(1)(A)(vi), (g)(3)(B).

[376] 22 C.F.R. § 127.7(c).

[377] *See supra* note 286.

[378] *See* Gary G. Grindler, Acting Dep. Att'y Gen., U.S. Dept. of Justice, Mem. to the Heads of Department Components and United States Attorneys on Additional Guidance on the Use of Monitors in Deferred Prosecution Agreements and Non-Prosecution (May 25, 2010), *available at* http://www.justice.gov/dag/dag-memo-guidancemonitors.pdf; Lanny A. Breuer, Assist. Att'y Gen., Dep't of Justice, Mem. to All Criminal Division Personnel on Selection of Monitors in Criminal Division Matters (June 24, 2009), *available at* http://www. justice.gov/criminal/fraud/fcpa/docs/response3-supp-appx-3.pdf; *see also* Craig S. Morford, Acting Dep. Att'y Gen., U.S. Dept. of Justice, Mem. to the Heads of Department Components and United States Attorneys on Selection and Use of Monitors in Deferred Prosecution Agreements and Non-Prosecution Agreements with Corporations (Mar. 7, 2008), *available at* http://www.justice.gov/dag/morforduseofmonitorsmemo-03072008.pdf.

[379] Historically, DOJ had, on occasion, agreed to DPAs with companies that were not filed with the court. That is no longer the practice of DOJ.

[380] USAM § 9-27.230.

[381] USAM § 9-27.230.B.

[382] DOJ has recently declined matters where some or all of the following circumstances were present: (1) a corporation voluntarily and fully disclosed the potential misconduct; (2) corporate principles voluntarily engaged in interviews with DOJ and provided truthful and complete information about their conduct; (3) a parent company conducted extensive pre-acquisition due diligence of potentially liable subsidiaries and engaged in significant remediation efforts post-acquisition; (4) a company provided information about its extensive compliance policies, procedures, and internal controls; (5) a company agreed to a civil resolution with the Securities and Exchange Commission while also demonstrating that criminal declination was appropriate; (6) only a single employee was involved in the improper payments; and (7) the improper payments involved minimal funds compared to overall business revenues.

[383] *See* Criminal Information, *United States v. Peterson*, *supra* note 8, Press Release, U.S. Dept. of Justice, Former Morgan Stanley Managing Director Pleads Guilty for Role in Evading Internal Controls Required by FCPA (Apr. 25, 2012), *available at*

http://www.justice.gov/opa/ pr/2012/April/12-crm-534.html ("After considering all the available facts and circumstances, including that Morgan Stanley constructed and maintained a system of internal controls, which provided reasonable assurances that its employees were not bribing government officials, the Department of Justice declined to bring any enforcement action against Morgan Stanley related to Peterson's conduct. The company voluntarily disclosed this matter and has cooperated throughout the department's investigation."); *see also* Press Release, U.S. Sec. and Exchange Comm., SEC Charges Former Morgan Stanley Executive with FCPA Violations and Investment Adviser Fraud (Apr. 25, 2012), *available at* http://www. sec.gov/news/press/2012/2012-78.htm ("Morgan Stanley, which is not charged in the matter, cooperated with the SEC's inquiry and conducted a thorough internal investigation to determine the scope of the improper payments and other misconduct involved.").

[384] SEC Rules of Practice, 17 C.F.R. § 201.102(e).

[385] Deferred Pros. Agreement, In the Matter of Tenaris, S.A. (May 17, 2011), *available at* http://www.sec.gov/news/press/2011/2011-112-dpa. pdf; *see also* Press Release, U.S. Sec. and Exchange Comm., Tenaris to Pay $5.4 Million in SEC's First-Ever Deferred Prosecution Agreement (May 17, 2011), *available at* http://www.sec.gov/news /press/2011/2011-112. htm.

[386] *See* Non-Pros. Agreement, In re Tenaris, S.A. (May 17, 2011), *available at* http://www.justice.gov/criminal/fraud/fcpa/cases/tenaris-sa/2011- 03-14-tenaris.pdf.

[387] *See* U.S. SEC. AND EXCHANGE COMM., ENFORCEMENT MANUAL § 6.2.3. (March 9, 2012), *available at* http://www.sec-gov/divisions/ enforce/enforcementmanual.pdf.

[388] *See id.* § 6.2.4.

[389] *See id.* § 2.6.

[390] 18 U.S.C. § 1514A(c).

[391] 18 U.S.C. § 1513(e).

[392] 15 U.S.C. § 78u-6(a)(3). The new provision defines "original information" to mean information that:

(A) is derived from the independent knowledge or analysis of a whistleblower; (B) is not known to the Commission from any other source, unless the whistleblower is the original source of the information; and (C) is not exclusively derived from an allegation made in a judicial or administrative hearing, in a governmental report, hearing, audit, or investigation, or from the news media, unless the whistleblower is a source of the information.

[393] 15 U.S.C. § 78u-6; *see also* Dodd-Frank Wall Street Reform and Consumer Protection Act, Pub. L. No. 111-203, § 922, 124 Stat. 1376, 1841-49 (2010).

[394] For detailed information about the program, including eligibility requirements and certain limitations that apply, see Section 922 of the Dodd-Frank Wall Street Reform and Consumer Protection Act, *available at* http://www.sec.gov/about/offices/owb/dodd-frank-sec-922.pdf, and the final rules on eligibility, Exchange Act Rule 21F-8, 17 C.F.R. § 240.21F-8.

[395] For example, the rules: (1) make a whistleblower eligible for an award if the whistleblower reports original information internally, and the company informs the SEC about the violations; (2) give whistleblowers 120 days to report information to the SEC after first reporting internally and still be treated as if he or she had reported to the SEC at the earlier reporting date , thus preserving their "place in line" for a possible whistleblower award from the SEC; and (3) provide that a whistleblower's voluntary participation in an entity's internal compliance and reporting systems is a factor that can increase the amount of an award, and that a whistleblower's interference with internal compliance and reporting

system is a factor that can decrease the amount of an award. *See* Exchange Act Rule 21F, 17 C.F.R. § 240.21F.

[396] *See* Exchange Act Rule 21F-7(b), 17 C.F.R. § 240.21F-7(b).

[397] For example, SEC staff will not disclose a whistleblower's identity in response to requests under the Freedom of Information Act. However, there are limits on SEC's ability to shield a whistleblower's identity, and in certain circumstances SEC must disclose it to outside entities. For example, in an administrative or court proceeding, SEC may be required to produce documents or other information that would reveal the whistleblower's identity. In addition, as part of ongoing SEC investigatory responsibilities, SEC staff may use information provided by a whistleblower during the course of the investigation. In appropriate circumstances, SEC may also provide information, subject to confidentiality requirements, to other governmental or regulatory entities. Exchange Act Rule 21F-7(a), 17 C.F.R. 240.21F-7(a).

[398] Although SEC does not have an opinion procedure release process, it has declared its decision to follow the guidance announced through DOJ's FCPA Opinion Release Procedure. U.S. Sec. and Exchange Comm., SEC Release No. 34-17099 (Aug. 29, 1980), *available at* http://www.sec.gov/news/digest/1980/dig082980.pdf. SEC Release No. 34 17099 stated that, to encourage issuers to take advantage of the DOJ's FCPA Review Procedure, as a matter of prosecutorial discretion, SEC would "not take enforcement action alleging violations of Section 30A in any case where an issuer has sought and obtained an FCPA Review letter from the Department, prior to May 31, 1981, stating that the Department will not take enforcement action under Section 30A with respect to the transaction involved." *Id.* The release further noted that it would revisit this policy once the DOJ had evaluated the results of the FCPA Review Procedure after its first year of operation. A second release stated that the SEC would continue to adhere to the policy announced in Release No. 34-17099. U.S. Sec. and Exchange Comm., SEC Release No. 34-18255 (Nov. 13, 1981), *available at* http://www.sec.gov/news/ digest/1981/dig111381.pdf.

[399] Both DOJ's opinion procedure releases (from 1993 to present) and review procedure releases (from 1980-1992) are available at http://www. justice.gov/criminal/fraud/fcpa/opinion.

[400] The full regulations relating to DOJ's opinion procedure are available at http://www.justice.gov/criminal/fraud/fcpa/docs/frgncrpt.pdf.

[401] 28 C.F.R. § 80.1.

[402] 28 C.F.R. § 80.3.

[403] 28 C.F.R. § 80.12 ("Neither the submission of a request for an FCPA Opinion, its pendency, nor the issuance of an FCPA Opinion, shall in any way alter the responsibility of an issuer to comply with the accounting requirements of 15 U.S.C. 78m(b)(2) and (3).").

[404] 28 C.F.R. § 80.4.

[405] 28 C.F.R. § 80.5.

[406] 28 C.F.R. § 80.6.

[407] 28 C.F.R. § 80.14(a). This non-disclosure policy applies regardless of whether DOJ responds to the request or the party withdraws the request before receiving a response. *Id.*

[408] 28 C.F.R. § 80.6.

[409] 28 C.F.R. § 80.2.

[410] In connection with any request for an FCPA opinion, DOJ may conduct whatever independent investigation it believes appropriate. 28 C.F.R. § 80.7.

[411] 28 C.F.R. § 80.15. Once a request is withdrawn, it has no effect. However, DOJ reserves the right to retain a copy of any FCPA opinion request, documents, and information submitted

during the opinion release procedure for any governmental purpose, subject to the restrictions on disclosures in 28 C.F.R. § 80.14.

[412] 28 C.F.R. § 80.8.

[413] 28 C.F.R. § 80.7. "Such additional information, if furnished orally, must be confirmed in writing promptly. The same person who signed the initial request must sign the written, supplemental information and must again certify it to be a true, correct and complete disclosure of the requested information." *Id.*

[414] 28 C.F.R. § 80.9 ("No oral clearance, release or other statement purporting to limit the enforcement discretion of the Department of Justice may be given. The requesting issuer or domestic concern may rely only upon a written FCPA opinion letter signed by the Attorney General or his designee.").

[415] 28 C.F.R. § 80.8. FCPA opinions do not bind or obligate any agency other than DOJ. They also do not affect the requesting party's obligations to any other agency or under any statutory or regulatory provision other than those specifically cited in the particular FCPA opinion. 28 C.F.R. § 80.11. If the conduct for which an FCPA opinion is requested is subject to approval by any other agency, such FCPA opinion may not be taken to indicate DOJ's views on any legal or factual issues before that other agency. 28 C.F.R. § 80.13.

[416] 28 C.F.R. § 80.10. DOJ can rebut this presumption by a preponderance of the evidence. A court determining whether the presumption has been rebutted weighs all relevant factors, including whether the submitted information was accurate and complete and the activity was within the scope of conduct specified in the request. *Id.* As of September 2012, DOJ has never pursued an enforcement action against a party for conduct that formed the basis of an FCPA opinion stating that the prospective conduct would violate DOJ's present enforcement policy.

[417] As a general matter, DOJ normally anonymizes much of the information in its publicly released opinions and includes the general nature and circumstances of the proposed conduct. DOJ does not release the identity of any foreign sales agents or other types of identifying information. 28 C.F.R. § 80.14(b). However, DOJ may release the identity of the requesting party, the foreign country in which the proposed conduct is to take place, and any actions DOJ took in response to the FCPA opinion request. *Id.* If a party believes that an opinion contains proprietary information, it may request that DOJ remove or anonymize those portions of the opinion before it is publicly released. 28 C.F.R. § 80.14(c).

[418] 28 C.F.R. § 80.16.

In: The Foreign Corrupt Practices Act
Editor: Randell Houpt
ISBN: 978-1-62417-845-0

Chapter 2

FOREIGN CORRUPT PRACTICES ACT (FCPA): CONGRESSIONAL INTEREST AND EXECUTIVE ENFORCEMENT*

Michael V. Seitzinger

SUMMARY

The Foreign Corrupt Practices Act of 1977 (FCPA) was enacted principally to prevent corporate bribery of foreign officials. This act had three major parts: (1) it required the keeping by corporations of accurate books, records, and accounts; (2) it required issuers registered with the Securities and Exchange Commission to maintain a responsible internal accounting control system; and (3) it prohibited bribery by American corporations of foreign officials.

For a number of years after passage of the act, Congress debated amending it in response to numerous criticisms. On August 23, 1988, the President signed into law the Omnibus Trade and Competitiveness Act of 1988, of which Title V is known as the Foreign Corrupt Practices Act Amendments of 1988.

The amendments maintained the three major parts of the 1977 Act, but significant changes were made. One of these changes enacted a "knowing"

---

* This is an edited, reformatted and augmented version of the Congressional Research Service Publication, CRS Report for Congress R41466, dated February 7, 2012.

standard in order to find violations of the act. This standard was intended to encompass "conscious disregard" and "willful blindness." The amendments provided certain defenses against finding violations of the act, such as that the gift is lawful under the laws of the foreign country and that the gift is a bona fide and reasonable expenditure or for the performance or execution of a contract with the foreign government.

In 1998 the act was further amended in order to implement the Organization of Economic Cooperation and Development Convention on Combating Bribery of Foreign Public Officials in International Business Transactions. These amendments expanded the scope of coverage to include some foreign persons and extended jurisdiction beyond the borders of the United States.

Criticisms of the act have continued. Especially prominent recently have been suggestions that businesses convicted of violating the Foreign Corrupt Practices Act should be debarred from receiving federal government contracts. Bills were introduced in the 111th Congress to address this issue.

In addition to congressional scrutiny of the act, the executive branch appears to have increased oversight of suspected American businesses for alleged violations. There have been a number of settlements and indictments concerning violations of the act. In early 2012 the federal government had both successes and losses resulting from its FCPA charges.

INTRODUCTION

During the mid-1970s investigations and administrative and legal actions against numerous domestic corporations revealed that the practice of making questionable or illegal payments by United States corporations to foreign government officials existed to some extent within the American business community. The legal and regulatory mechanisms for dealing with these payments had involved actions by the Securities and Exchange Commission (SEC) against public corporations for concealing from required public disclosure substantial payments made by the firm and the potential for an antitrust action for restraints of trade or fraud prosecutions by the Department of Justice.

Government officials and administrators contended that more direct prohibitions on foreign bribery and more detailed requirements concerning corporate recordkeeping and accountability were needed to deal effectively with the problem. The revelations of slush funds and secret payments by

American corporations were stated to have affected adversely American foreign policy, damaged abroad the image of American democracy, and impaired public confidence in the financial integrity of American corporations.[1]

FOREIGN CORRUPT PRACTICES ACT OF 1977

Congress responded with the passage of the Foreign Corrupt Practices Act (FCPA) of 1977.[2] The principal purpose of the 1977 Act was to prevent corporate bribery of foreign officials. It has three major provisions to attempt to accomplish this purpose.

The first major provision amended Section 13(b)[3] of the Securities Exchange Act of 1934[4] to require issuers which must register their securities with the SEC to keep detailed books, records, and accounts which accurately record corporate payments and transactions.

The second major provision required SEC registered issuers to institute and maintain an internal accounting control system to assure management's control, authority, and responsibility over the firm's assets.[5]

The third major provision of the original 1977 Foreign Corrupt Practices Act prohibited domestic corporations, whether or not registered with the SEC, from corruptly bribing a foreign official, a foreign political party, party official, or candidate for the purpose of obtaining or maintaining business. Two provisions of the 1977 Act[6] made it a crime for any American business to use the mails or interstate commerce to offer or pay money or anything of value to a foreign official or to a foreign political party, party official, or candidate for foreign political office in order to influence the person in his decision making or to use his influence to assist the firm in obtaining or retaining business.

The 1977 Act also prohibited the payment of money to any person by a business if the business knew or had reason to know that the payment was to be used to bribe a foreign official for his influence in obtaining or retaining business. Congressional intent appeared to place an affirmative responsibility on the corporation to exercise control over its officers, directors, and employees, and to take steps to assure that its foreign agents did not use corporate assets or payments made to them to bribe foreign officials.[7]

Under the 1977 Act not all payments to employees of foreign governments were intended by Congress to be considered illegal bribes. For example, the definition of "foreign official" excluded employees of a foreign government "whose duties are essentially ministerial or clerical." Also, the legislative history of the act specifically stated that it was not intended to cover "grease payments" to foreign officials, explained as payments for expediting shipments through customs or placing a transatlantic telephone call, securing required permits, or obtaining adequate police protection, transactions which may involve even the proper performance of duties.[8] The legislative history also suggested that extortions of money by foreign officials might be used as a defense against bribery charges by a business if its property or lives of its employees were threatened. An example used to illustrate acceptable payments was the payment to a foreign official to prevent the dynamiting of an oil rig.[9]

CRITICISMS OF THE FOREIGN CORRUPT PRACTICES ACT OF 1977

Almost since passage of the 1977 Act, frequent criticism of the operation of the act occurred. Opponents argued that the act had a chilling effect upon United States export trade and that many companies ceased foreign operations rather than face the uncertainties and the burdens of the act.

Critics of the 1977 Act also argued for removal of the "reason to know" standard concerning liability for actions of a firm's agent in a foreign country. This would eliminate the legal responsibility of the management of a domestic firm over the unauthorized and undirected actions of an agent without the necessity of management's also showing that it had no "reason to know" that the agent was using corporate funds, payments, or commissions to bribe foreign officials. These critics argued that American firms should not have to bear the responsibility of playing detective concerning the independent actions of persons that they retained as agents in foreign countries.

Critics also contended that the internal accounting controls required by the 1977 Act were too costly and burdensome upon domestic firms, especially when potential criminal penalties within the act for failure to institute adequate controls arguably made officials of firms overly and unnecessarily cautious in implementing costly accounting controls. The public recordkeeping requirements were also criticized as unduly burdensome. Critics of the act argued for a materiality standard for public recordkeeping in which a firm would be required to report only expenditures and outlays deemed material to the profits and revenues of the firm.

Another frequent criticism of the 1977 Act was that the United States was more interested in exporting its cultural biases than its products. It was argued that, in nations in which acceptance of a fee or payment by a government official from one doing business with the government is customary and not unlawful under the laws of that nation, no violation of a United States law should occur. Critics also argued that an international agreement among the world's industrialized nations prohibiting businesses of all those countries from bribing foreign officials was necessary to prevent businesses of other countries from gaining an unfair and harmful competitive advantage over American businesses.

FOREIGN CORRUPT PRACTICES ACT AMENDMENTS OF 1988

In response to these criticisms, Congress for a number of years considered amending the 1977 Foreign Corrupt Practices Act. After considerable debate through at least three Congresses, the Foreign Corrupt Practices Act Amendments of 1988 were signed into law as Title V of the Omnibus Trade and Competitiveness Act of 1988[10] on August 23, 1988. Although the amendments maintained the three major parts of the 1977 Act discussed above—the accounting standards, the requirements of SEC registered issuers, and the anti-bribery provisions—the 1988 amendments made some significant changes to the 1977 Act.

Section 5002 of the Trade Act amended Section 13(b) of the Securities Exchange Act to provide that no criminal liability shall be imposed for violation of the accounting standards unless a person knowingly circumvents or knowingly fails to implement a system of accurate and reasonable accounting controls. According to the legislative history, this provision was intended to ensure that criminal penalties would be imposed where acts of commission or omission in keeping books or records or administering accounting controls have the purpose of falsifying books, records, or accounts or of circumventing accounting controls. This was also intended to include the deliberate falsification of books and records and other conduct calculated to evade the internal accounting controls requirement.[11]

Section 5002 of the Trade Act also added to Section 13(b) of the Securities Exchange Act a provision that an issuer holding 50% or less of the voting power of a domestic or foreign firm is required to use its influence only in good faith to cause the domestic or foreign firm to devise and maintain a system of acceptable accounting controls. The House Report stated that this amendment was intended to recognize that it was unrealistic to expect a minority owner to exert a disproportionate degree of influence over the accounting practices of a subsidiary.[12]

For purposes of the accounting standards, "reasonable assurances" and "reasonable detail" mean such level of detail and degree of assurance as would satisfy prudent officials in the conduct of their own affairs. Thus, the prudent man qualification was adopted to clarify that the current standard does not require an unrealistic degree of exactitude or precision.

Section 5003 of the Trade Act amended the provisions of the Foreign Corrupt Practices Act concerning the anti-bribery prohibitions by issuers and domestic concerns. The Foreign Corrupt Practices Act continued to prohibit any issuer having a class of securities registered with the SEC or any officer, director, employee, or agent of the issuer or any stockholder acting on behalf of the issuer or any United States concern to offer, pay, promise to give, or authorize the giving of anything of value to a foreign official, a foreign political party, party official, candidate, or any person for the purpose of obtaining or maintaining business. Section 5003 amended the 1977 Act to prohibit payments to any foreign official for the purpose of "influencing any act or decision of such foreign official in his official capacity, or inducing such foreign official to do or omit to do any act in violation of the lawful duty of such official." This language was inserted so that the foreign bribery standard would conform to the domestic bribery standard found in 18 U.S.C. Section 201.[13]

The "knowing" requirement was retained, and the "recklessly disregarding" standard was abandoned in conference. However, the "knowing" requirement was intended to encompass the "conscious disregard" and "willful blindness" standards, including a conscious purpose to avoid learning the truth.

> [T]he Conferees agreed that "simple negligence" or "mere foolishness" should not be the basis for liability. However, the Conferees also agreed that the so-called "head-in-the-sand" problem—variously described in the pertinent authorities as "conscious disregard," "willful blindness" or "deliberate ignorance"—should be covered so that management officials could not take refuge from the act's prohibitions by their unwarranted obliviousness to any action (or inaction), language or

other "signalling device" that should reasonably alert them of the "high probability" of an FCPA violation.[14]

The major changes which Section 5003 of the Trade Act made in the 1977 Foreign Corrupt Practices Act had to do with when the bribery provisions apply to an American business or person acting on behalf of an American business. For example, the anti-bribery provisions under the 1988 Amendments did not apply to any facilitating or expediting payment to a foreign official, political party, or party official.

Further, an American business or individual may use one of the "affirmative defenses" in urging that no violation of the FCPA occurred. The first of these enumerated affirmative defenses is that the payment, gift, offer, or promise of anything of value that was made was lawful under the written laws and regulations of the foreign official's, political party's, party official's, or candidate's country. Another affirmative defense is that the payment, gift, offer, or promise of anything of value that was made was a reasonable and bona fide expenditure, such as travel and lodging expenses which were incurred by or on behalf of a foreign official, party, party official, or candidate, and was directly related to the promotion, demonstration, or explanation of products or services or the execution or performance of a contract with a foreign government or agency. This defense does not apply, however, if a payment or gift is corruptly made in return for an official act or omission because it is then not considered a bona fide, good faith payment.

In the definitional sections of the 1988 Amendments, the terms "knowing" and "routine governmental action" are especially important. A person's state of mind is "knowing" with respect to conduct, a circumstance, or a result if the person is aware of engaging in the conduct, that the circumstance exists, or that the result is substantially certain to occur or if the person has a firm belief that the circumstance exists or that the result is substantially certain to occur. When knowledge of the existence of a particular circumstance is required for an offense, the knowledge is established if a person is aware of a high probability of the existence of the circumstance, unless the person actually believes that the circumstance does not exist.

"Routine governmental action" is only ordinarily and commonly performed by a foreign official in obtaining permits, licenses, or other official documents to qualify a person to do business in a foreign country; processing governmental papers, providing police protection, mail pickup and delivery, or scheduling inspections associated with contract performance or inspections related to transit of goods across country; or providing phone service, power and water supply, loading and unloading cargo, or protecting perishable commodities or products from deterioration. The term does not include any decision by a foreign official whether or on what terms to award new business to or to continue business with a particular firm.

Criminal penalties for violations of the Foreign Corrupt Practices Act were increased. The anti-bribery fine for a firm or domestic concern was raised from $1 million to $2 million and for individuals from $10,000 to $100,000. The maximum imprisonment for bribery for an individual remained five years.[15] For willful violations of the accounting provisions the fine for a corporation may not exceed $25 million and for an individual not more than $5 million and/or imprisonment of up to 20 years.[16] The act also provides for civil penalties of up to $10,000 for violations of the bribery provisions.[17]

Foreign Corrupt Practices Act Amendments of 1998

In 1998 the Foreign Corrupt Practices Act was again amended in order to implement the Organization of Economic Cooperation and Development (OECD) Convention on Combating Bribery of Foreign Officials in International Business Transactions.[18] The 1998 Amendments expanded the scope of persons covered to include certain foreign nationals, such as any officer of a public international organization.[19] The 1998 Amendments also extended the act's jurisdiction beyond the borders of the United States.[20]

Continuing Congressional Concerns

Criticisms of the Foreign Corrupt Practices Act have continued over the years, ranging from its putting American businesses at a competitive disadvantage in the global marketplace to its permitting unethical forms of payment tantamount to bribery. Especially prominent recently has been a call that businesses convicted of violating the act should be barred from or strictly limited in receiving government contracts. Bills in the 111th Congress were introduced to address this issue. For example, H.R. 5366 would, unless waived by the head of a federal agency, permit any person found to have violated the Foreign Corrupt Practices Act to be proposed for debarment from any contract or grant awarded by the federal government. This bill was introduced on May

20, 2010, and reported by the Committee on Oversight and Government Reform on September 14, 2010, accompanied by H.Rept. 111-588. On September 15, 2010, the House passed the bill. On September 16, 2010, it was referred to the Senate Committee on Homeland Security and Governmental Affairs. The House report states the following need for the legislation: "Federal government contractors have used bribes in the past to influence the actions of foreign governments. The source of these bribes in part is American tax dollars paid by the federal government to contractors. This bill seeks to root out companies which tarnish the image of the United States of America by engaging in illegal activities."[21]

H.R. 5837 would prohibit an executive agency from entering into a contract for goods or services unless that person or entity has certified that it and each of its officers, employees, and agents have not violated the Foreign Corrupt Practices Act or any comparable law of any other country. A contractor awarded a contract by a federal agency would be prohibited from entering into any subcontract at any tier with any person or entity which has not made this certification.

Another bill would address the criticism that the act does not allow a private right of action. H.R. 2152 would amend the Foreign Corrupt Practices Act to authorize a private right of action against a company for violation of the act. Lawsuits have been brought to urge allowing a private right of action, but the Sixth Circuit in 1990 found that the act does not allow a private right of action.[22]

EXECUTIVE BRANCH OVERSIGHT

In addition to congressional scrutiny of the act, the executive branch appears to have increased oversight of suspected American businesses for alleged violations of the act. On January 19, 2010, the U.S. Department of Justice (DOJ) announced that it had indicted 22 executives and employees in the military and law enforcement products industry for engaging in schemes to bribe foreign government officials to obtain and retain business.[23] According to Assistant Attorney General Lanny A. Breuer, "This ongoing investigation is the first large-scale use of undercover law enforcement techniques to uncover FCPA violations and the largest action ever undertaken by the Justice Department against individuals for FCPA violations."[24]

Several other events indicate executive branch concerns with Foreign Corrupt Practices Act violations. On August 6, 2010, Mercator Corporation pled guilty to charges that it had made an illegal payment to a senior government official in Kazakhstan in violation of the act.[25] It has been reported that the Department of Justice and the Securities and Exchange Commission are looking into whether Merck has violated the act in multiple foreign countries.[26]

On July 27, 2010, General Electric agreed to pay $23.4 million to settle a complaint brought by the Securities and Exchange Commission that it had bribed Iraqi government officials to win contracts for supplying medical and water purification equipment under the United Nations oil-for-food program. It has been reported that the General Electric case is the fourth biggest such anti-bribery case brought in the oil-for-food program, after the cases filed against Siemens, Chevron, and Innospec.[27]

There have been reports that federal investigators have been looking into the possibility that Blackwater (renamed Xe) may have violated the Foreign Corrupt Practices Act. An indictment in April 2010 by a federal grand jury in North Carolina contained the following allegation:

> Another means [of circumventing the possession and disposition of arms] consisted of Blackwater/Xe's efforts to gain favor with the Government of the Kingdom of Jordan. When the King of Jordan came to examine Blackwater/Xe's training facility at Moyock, North Carolina, the defendants arranged to present the King and/or his entourage with several firearms as gifts. When the defendants subsequently realized they were unable to account for the disposition of the firearms, they falsified four separate Alcohol, Tobacco, and Firearms (ATF) Form 4473s for submission to federal authorities. The defendants falsely completed the forms to give the appearance that the weapons had been purchased by them as individuals.[28]

In October 2010 Assistant Attorney General Breuer emphasized that the United States takes seriously the enforcement of the Foreign Corrupt Practices Act. He is reported as stating that companies and individuals can expect to see "more and more prosecutions [under the 1977 Foreign Corrupt Practices Act] by the United States and more and more [joint] prosecutions with members of the OECD and throughout the world."[29]

In early 2012 the federal government had both successes and losses resulting from FCPA charges. For example, it was reported that the Justice Department's Criminal Division announced on January 17, 2012, that Marubeni Corporation had agreed to pay a $54.6 million criminal penalty to resolve charges for violating the FCPA during a 10-year-long scheme of bribing the Nigerian government for engineering, procurement, and construction contracts.[30] On January 30, 2012, however, a jury acquitted two businessmen charged by the Department of Justice with violating the FCPA involving a fake deal for the sale of goods to Gabon.[31] On January 31, 2012, a judge declared a mistrial involving three other businessmen in the same FBI sting case involving a military equipment contract for Gabon.[32]

End Notes

[1] S. REPT. 95-114, at 3 (1977).
[2] P.L. 95-213, Title I; 91 Stat. 1494 (1977).
[3] 15 U.S.C. §78m(b).
[4] 15 U.S.C. §§78a *et seq.*
[5] 15 U.S.C. §78m(b)(2)(B).
[6] 15 U.S.C. §§78dd-1 and 78dd-2.
[7] S. REPT. 95-114, at 1 (1977).
[8] S. REPT. 95-114, at 10 (1977).
[9] S. REPT. 95-114, at 10-11 (1977).
[10] P.L. 100-418, Title V; 102 Stat. 1107 (1988).
[11] H. REPT. 100-576, at 916-917 (1988).
[12] H. REPT. 100-576, at 917 (1988).
[13] H. REPT. 100-576, at 918 (1988).
[14] H. REPT. 100-576, at 920.
[15] 15 U.S.C. §78dd-2(g).
[16] 15 U.S.C. §78ff(a).
[17] 15 U.S.C. §78dd-2(g).
[18] P.L. 105-366; 112 Stat. 3302 (1998).
[19] 15 U.S.C. §78dd-1(f).
[20] 15 U.S.C. §§78dd-1(g) and 78dd-2(i). United States businesses and persons are prohibited from acting corruptly outside the United States "in furtherance of" a bribe whether or not using the "mails or any means or instrumentality of interstate commerce."
[21] H.REPT. 111-588, at 2 (2010).
[22] *Lamb v. Phillip Morris, Inc.*, 915 F.2d 1024, 1029-1030 (6th Cir. 1990).
[23] http://www.justice.gov/opa/pr/2010/January/10-crm-048.html.
[24] *Id.*
[25] *United States v. Mercator Corporation*, S3-03-CR (S.D.N.Y. Aug. 6, 2010).
[26] Linda A. Johnson, *Merck Being Probed for Possibly Violating Anti-Bribery Laws*, WASHINGTON POST, August 10, 2010, at A14.
[27] Zachary A. Goldfarb, *GE Agrees to Settle with SEC on Charges of Foreign Bribery*, WASHINGTON POST, July 28, 2010, at A11.
[28] http://www.fcpablog.com/blog/2010/4/19/blackwater-and-bribery.html.
[29] Breuer Says U.S. Expects High Marks for Foreign Corruption, Bribery Efforts, DAILY REPORT FOR EXECUTIVES, 197 DER EE-18 (BNA October 14, 2010).
[30] http://online.wsj.com/article/BT-CO-20120117-713964.html.
[31] http://legaltimes.typepad.com/blt/2012/01/jury-acquits-two-businessmen-in-fcpa-sting-case-.html.
[32] http://blogs.wsj.com/law/2012/01/31/judge-declares-mistrial-in-sting-bribery-case/.

INDEX

C

D

E

F

G

H

I

J

T